SMASHING HITLER'S PANZERS

*The Defeat of the Hitler Youth Panzer Division
in the Battle of the Bulge*

STEVEN ZALOGA

STACKPOLE
BOOKS

Guilford, Connecticut

Published by Stackpole Books
An imprint of The Rowman & Littlefield Publishing Group, Inc.
4501 Forbes Blvd., Ste. 200
Lanham, MD 20706
www.rowman.com

Distributed by NATIONAL BOOK NETWORK
800-462-6420

British Library Cataloguing in Publication Information available

Library of Congress Cataloging-in-Publication Data available

ISBN 978-0-8117-3777-7 (hardcover)
ISBN 978-0-8117-6762-0 (e-book)

♾️™ The paper used in this publication meets the minimum requirements of American
National Standard for Information Sciences—Permanence of Paper for Printed Library
Materials, ANSI/NISO Z39.48-1992.

Printed in the United States of America

Contents

INTRODUCTION

WHY DID HITLER'S 1944 ARDENNES OFFENSIVE FAIL?

In his classic account of the Battle of the Bulge, John S. D. Eisenhower wrote that "the action of the 2nd and 99th Divisions on the northern shoulder [of the Bulge] could well be considered the most decisive of the Ardennes campaign."[1] This assessment may seem obscure for most military history readers.

Indeed, the battles fought by the 2nd Infantry Division and the 99th Infantry Division during the first week of the Battle of the Bulge does not even have a commonly accepted name. It is sometimes called the Battle of the Twin Villages, although this is too narrow since the engagement encompassed fighting both before and after the struggle for the "Twin Villages" of Krinkelt-Rocherath. A better name might be the Battles for Elsenborn Ridge. Even though most of the fighting took place on the approaches to Elsenborn, and not actually on the ridge, it was this geographic feature that was key to the German Ardennes plan. Elsenborn Ridge controlled the most direct and viable route for the *Wehrmacht* to accomplish its operational goals in the Ardennes offensive. Stopping the *Wehrmacht* before the Elsenborn Ridge crushed any hope of success for Hitler's 1944 winter offensive.

The Battles for Elsenborn Ridge has been overlooked because most American accounts tend to assess the battle from the American perspective. To better appreciate the importance of the Battles for Elsenborn Ridge, it is essential to examine the offensive from the German perspective as well as the American.

The central focus of this book is the combat performance of the *12.SS-Panzer-Division "Hitlerjugend"* and its American opponents in the first week of the campaign. This subject was chosen for several reasons. To begin with, the *Hitlerjugend* division was one of the two panzer divisions that formed the spearhead of the attack in the area that Hitler considered the *Schwerpunkt*, that is, the focal point of the Ardennes attack. The success or failure of these two units largely determined the eventual outcome of the campaign. It was the *Hitlerjugend* that was assigned the mission of overrunning the American defenses on the Elsenborn Ridge.

Another reason this subject was chosen is that the performance of the *Hitlerjugend* division has not received as much attention as its partner in the attack, the *1. SS-Panzer-Division "Leibstandarte Adolf Hitler."* The *Leibstandarte* has received more coverage in English-language accounts because of its involvement in the Malmedy massacre, as well as combat actions of its most famous element, *Kampfgruppe Peiper*.

The defeat of the *12. SS-Panzer-Division "Hitlerjugend"* near Elsenborn Ridge is essential to understanding the failure of Hitler's Ardennes offensive.

Technical Notes

For readers unfamiliar with military jargon, I have used the traditional conventions when referring to military units. The US Army has traditionally used Arabic numerals for divisions and smaller independent formations (2nd Division, 741st Tank Battalion); Roman numerals for corps (V Corps); and spelled-out numbers for field armies (First US Army).

Infantry battalions are sometimes abbreviated in the fashion "2/38th Infantry," referring to the 2nd Battalion, 38th Infantry Regiment. Within a US Army infantry regiment, the three battalions had their companies lettered sequentially. So 1st Battalion consisted of A, B, and C Companies; D Company was the battalion's heavy weapons (machine gun and mortar) company. The 2nd Battalion included E, F, G, and H Companies. The 3rd Battalion included I, K, L, and M Companies. "J Company" was not used to avoid confusion with "I Company." The company designations were used in two fashions, "A Company" or "Company A." The rifle platoons within an infantry company were numbered 1st, 2nd, and 3rd Platoons.

I have left most of the German unit designations in the standard German form. I did this to make it easier for the reader to distinguish German from American units. In a few cases where the meaning of the German designation was not obvious, I have used English for clarity; for example, Army Group B rather than *Heeresgruppe B*. German unit designations generally place the unit number in front of the unit type for units a division or larger but place the number at the end of the unit type for units smaller than a division, so *2.Panzer-Division* but *Panzer-Regiment.2*. Subunits within a small formation precede the unit designation, followed by a slash. In the case of German small-unit designations, Arabic numerals indicate company while Roman numerals indicate battalion. So *2./GR.990* refers to the 2nd Company of

Grenadier-Regiment.990, and *II./GR.990* indicates the 2nd Battalion of *Grenadier-Regiment.990*.

German corps were designated with Roman numerals such as *LXVII.Armee-Korps*, but the alternate version *67.Armee-Korps* is used here for clarity. Field armies were designated in the fashion *7.Armee* but sometimes abbreviated *AOK.7*; the former style is used here.

The *Waffen-SS* followed normal German unit designation practices, but usually appended the unit designation with an honorific such as *12.SS-Panzer-Division "Hitlerjugend."* Perhaps the most confusing aspect of *Waffen-SS* designations was their new system of ranks. I have appended a chart showing the various *Waffen-SS* officer ranks and the *Heer* (German Army) and US Army equivalents on page 47.

The *Wehrmacht* in World War II tended to use centimeter measurements for the gun calibers of larger weapons and millimeters for small arms. I have used the contemporary practice of millimeters for all types, so 75mm instead of 7.5cm.

The maps presented here follow the usual World War II style of tactical unit symbols used by the US Army. Since the convention of blue and red coloration for the opposing sides cannot be used here, German units are colored in black, American units in white.

Regarding the times used in the text, the Allies began using British summer time on September 17, 1944, and the Germans went back to central European time on October 2, 1944, so both sides were using the same clock time during the Ardennes fighting. Since much of the fighting took place in the dark, it is worth remembering that first light in Belgium in mid-December was around 0720 hours (7:20 AM) and sunrise around 0800 (8:00 PM). Sunset was around 1640 hours (4:40 PM), with dusk lasting until 1720 (5:20 PM).

This book uses the German terminology for the chronology of the attack. The first day of the attack, Saturday, December 16, 1944, was called "X-Day" (*X-Tag*) and then the subsequent days in the pattern X+1, X+2, etc. This chronology has been kept since the timetable was essential to the success or failure of the German offensive. For convenience, the chronology is listed on the following page.

X-Day	Saturday, December 16
X+1	Sunday, December 17
X+2	Monday, December 18
X+3	Tuesday, December 19
X+4	Wednesday, December 20
X+5	Thursday, December 21
X+6	Friday, December 22

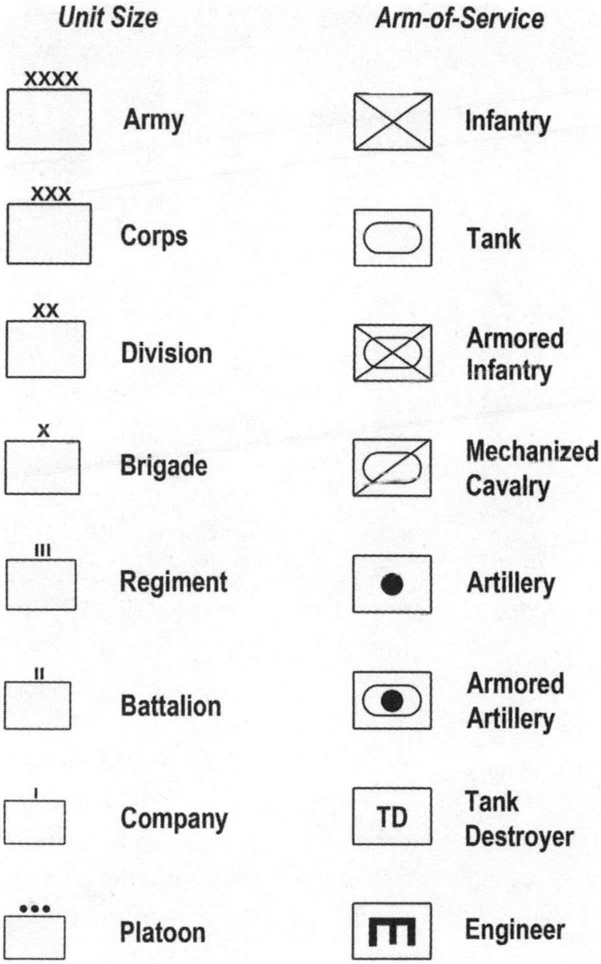

Unit Size

Army (XXXX)

Corps (XXX)

Division (XX)

Brigade (X)

Regiment (III)

Battalion (II)

Company (I)

Platoon (•••)

Arm-of-Service

Infantry

Tank

Armored Infantry

Mechanized Cavalry

Artillery

Armored Artillery

Tank Destroyer (TD)

Engineer

Acknowledgments

As with any project of this length and complexity, the author would like to thank many colleagues for their generous assistance. Danny S. Parker was kind enough to provide numerous documents located during his own research on the Ardennes campaign. Andrew E. Woods of the Colonel Robert McCormick Research Center of the First Division Museum at Cantigny Park provided a number of rare photos from the 1st Division collection. Darren Neely provided several photos from his own archival research. Stephen Andrew provided a number of photos of the Krinkelterwald taken during a battlefield tour in 2017. Marc Romanych from Digital History Archive provided assistance with the Westwall maps. Unless otherwise noted, the photos here are from official US sources including the National Archives and Records Administration in College Park, MD; the US Military History Institute at Carlisle, PA; the Patton Museum formerly at Fort Knox, KY; the Ordnance Museum at Aberdeen Proving Ground, MD; and the Library of Congress in Washington, DC.

Part 1

PLANS AND PREPARATIONS

Hitler's Plan

THE STRATEGIC SETTING

Hitler's plan for a surprise offensive in the Ardennes was prompted by Germany's desperate circumstances in the autumn of 1944. The *Wehrmacht* was on a death spiral to defeat. The summer campaigns had been a string of costly disasters. On the Russian Front, the Red Army had launched its Operation Bagration offensive that destroyed Army Group Center, then pushed beyond the Soviet borders into Poland. This was followed by offensives in other sectors. The most consequential of these was the drive into the Balkans. The Romanian army switched sides, and Germany's main source of oil, the Romanian oil fields, fell into Soviet hands in August 1944. Germany was quickly running out of fuel to power its war machines.

Following the D-Day invasion of Normandy in June 1944, the Anglo-American forces had finally broken out of Normandy and in August 1944 trapped much of Army Group B in the Falaise pocket. To make matters worse, a second amphibious assault, Operation Dragoon on August 15, 1944, created a second Allied front which quickly overwhelmed Army Group G in southern and central France. The defeated *Wehrmacht* stumbled its way back to the German frontier in the last week of August and first weeks of September in such confusion and disarray that it was later dubbed "the Void" by German commanders.

The scale of the disaster can be seen from German army casualty figures. Casualties in 1944 were about double those of 1943: 2.9 million versus 1.5 million. Casualties in 1944 alone amounted to 40 percent of total German casualties since the start of the war. German equipment losses present much the same picture. German armored vehicle losses on the Russian Front from 1941 to the end of 1943 had totaled 18,800; losses in 1944 were 14,537 on the Russian Front plus a further 4,513 in northwest Europe for a total of 19,050. In other words, German armored vehicle losses in 1944 alone exceeded the entire previous four years of war.

In the air, the Allied "Combined Bomber Offensive" was destroying German cities and industries. The US Eighth Air Force had waged its Operation Pointblank bomber offensive against the *Luftwaffe* in the first half of 1944, sweeping the skies of its once dangerous foe. In the late spring and early summer, the target shifted to the German synthetic fuel industry. In combination with the loss of the Romanian oil fields, the *Wehrmacht* was grinding to a halt from the lack of fuel.

On July 20, 1944, a faction within the army attempted to assassinate Hitler at his Wolf's Lair headquarters in Prussia. Many of the army commanders had lost faith in Hitler and his war. Hitler survived, but he no longer trusted most of the senior army commanders. In the wake of the assassination attempt, Hitler took complete control of war planning and stripped German field commanders of their tactical flexibility. *General* Hasso von Manteuffel, commander in the Ardennes, described the consequences:

> The previous style of flexible and self-reliant German military leadership was paralyzed, shifting more and more to mechanical and perfunctory execution of orders issued as Führer Directives, concocted in a map room far away from the battlefield. That spelled death for the traditional German "Art of Command" in mobile warfare. Even the most outstanding senior commanders, raised under the traditional training regime, were compelled to follow these orders to the letter, and were not permitted to independently make decisions, even in small tactical matters involving single divisions.[1]

The *Wehrmacht* was given a brief reprieve in the early autumn of 1944. The Allies had been too successful. The advance in both the east and west had been so rapid and so deep that the Allies had outrun their supply lines and had to pause before resuming major offensives.

The *Wehrmacht* received a last major infusion of blood. The declining supplies of fuel forced the *Luftwaffe* to ground many of its squadrons except the fighter units engaged in defending the Reich. Likewise, the *Kriegsmarine* was forced to abandon most naval activity except for its U-boats. This freed up a large number of air force and navy personnel who were transferred to the army to help rebuild the shattered infantry and panzer divisions.

In spite of Allied bomber attacks, German industry increased the production of some key weapons, including tanks and fighter planes. Yet this was something of a magician's trick. Tank production did increase, but at the cost of spare tank parts and trucks. Now, when panzers broke down, they were lost because there were no spare parts to repair them. More fighter planes were delivered to the *Luftwaffe*, but in many cases, the quality was so poor that crashes outside the combat zone rose to alarming levels.

In the face of these escalating disasters, Hitler reflexively chose to stage a surprise offensive in the desperate hope that a decisive victory could reverse Nazi Germany's impending slide to defeat. An offensive against the Red Army seemed pointless. It had suffered numerous crushing defeats, costing millions of soldiers, yet persevered time and time again in spite of the horrific casualties. Even if a German offensive in the East overwhelmed dozens of Red Army divisions, there seemed to be an unending supply of divisions to replace them.

Hitler considered the Anglo-American forces in the West to be a more vulnerable victim for his scheme. Coalitions are inevitably more vulnerable to battlefield defeats, since defeat can breed political mistrust and dissension. Hitler convinced himself that a stunning defeat of Anglo-American forces could break the bonds between London and Washington, as had the miraculous victory in 1940 that had shattered the British and French alliance. And where better to stage the attack than in the Ardennes, the turning point of the 1940 campaign! A second Dunkirk was the alluring prize.

The Plan Takes Shape

Hitler first outlined his concept of a surprise offensive in the Ardennes on September 16, 1944, at a conference of senior commanders. He intended to punch through Allied lines through the Ardennes and then cross the Meuse river to Antwerp, thereby cutting off the British 21st Army Group from the American 12th Army Group, creating "a new Dunkirk."[2] Hitler was convinced by Clausewitz's view that the offensive was the only decisive form of war; a continued reliance on a defensive strategy would ultimately end in Germany's defeat.

From a tactical perspective, Hitler's scheme was strongly shaped by two previous counteroffensives in the West: Operation Lüttich in August 1944 and the Vosges panzer offensive in September 1944. Operation Lüttich was a panzer attack intended to cut off the spearheads of Patton's Third US Army by a drive to the sea at Avranches. The attack petered out almost immediately after reaching only as far as Mortain, and local German commanders blamed Allied airpower for the defeat. Hitler took these observations seriously and planned to conduct the Ardennes operation in the late autumn of 1944, when the overcast skies would minimize the threat of Allied airpower.

The Vosges panzer offensive was another attempt to cut off the spearheads of the Third US Army, but this time when Patton's forces were on the verge of linking up with the Seventh US Army's blitzkrieg from southern France. Instead of a massed panzer attack as envisioned by Hitler, the panzer units were committed haphazardly over the course of more than a week, diluting their combat power and dooming the offensive.[3] From this experience, Hitler concluded that the key divisions earmarked for the Ardennes offensive must be kept in an untouchable reserve that could not be pilfered by local commanders to deal with short-term battlefield problems.

On October 9, 1944, Hitler instructed *Generaloberst* Alfred Jodl, the chief of operations of the Armed Forces High Command (*Oberkommando der Wehrmacht*, or OKW), to produce an outline plan.[4] The first draft was ready three days later. The OKW offered five options. From north to south these operations were the Netherlands, Liège-Aachen, Luxembourg, Lorraine, and Alsace.[5] None of these operations offered any real operational dividends except for Operation Liège-Aachen, essentially Hitler's Ardennes scheme. As a result, further planning focused on this sector.

Jodl's elaboration of Operation Liège-Aachen suggested two main variations usually dubbed the Big Solution and the Small Solution.[6] The Big Solution, Hitler's scheme to push from the Ardennes to Antwerp and destroy the twenty to thirty Allied divisions north of the penetration, would require a strategic shift to add considerable forces in the West. Other theaters would have to be deprived of replacements and supplies in favor of the Ardennes attack force. This could include the transfer of divisions from secondary theaters such as Italy, Norway, or Greece, as well as starving the Russian Front of reinforcements.

Without a strategic shift in resources to the West, Jodl argued that only the Small Solution had any hope of success. For the Small Solution, he proposed a less elaborate two-pronged offensive that would envelop and destroy most of the First US Army in the Aachen area. Jodl would later admit that he never had any confidence in Hitler's Big Solution and that the OKW never prepared any detailed studies of the conduct of the offensive once it had reached the Meuse river.[7]

Hitler refused to accept Jodl's premise that the Big Solution would require such a major shift in resources to succeed. He argued that the surprise element of the plan would magnify the power of the attack and that the forces could be provided by concentrating those already on the Western Front. Hitler ridiculed Jodl's Small Solution as a "half-measure" which could not decisively influence the outcome of the war. A postwar US Army assessment highlighted the inherent contradictions of the Big Solution:

> The result was a triple compromise. While Hitler had continually stressed the vast import of the [Ardennes] offensive for the continuation of the war, he failed to draw the only possible conclusion and

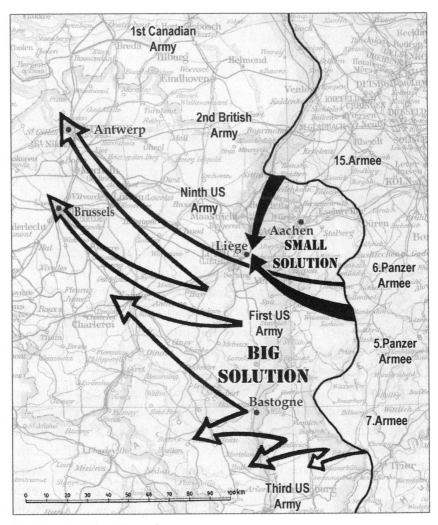

Watch on the Rhine: Alternatives

This map shows the two main options for the early Watch on the Rhine plan: the Small Solution, preferred by Jodl and most senior commanders, and the Big Solution, preferred by Hitler and the eventual choice.

revise the overall strategy accordingly. Consequently, the essential number of units for the "Big Solution" could not be accumulated, but despite this glaring incongruity between forces and objectives, Hitler stubbornly clung to the "Big Solution." Hitler's decision thus, in Jodl's words was "an act of desperation."[8]

German commanders later complained that Hitler wanted his Big Solution but was unwilling to pay for it with sufficient units and supplies. Jodl estimated that the Big Solution would take a minimum of forty divisions; Hitler at first proposed twenty-two divisions, but gradually conceded that at least twenty-nine would be needed. The total gradually increased as the demands of the mission were more fully appreciated.

The initial OKW plan prepared under Jodl's direction was code-named *Wacht am Rhein* (Watch on the Rhine). The code name was deliberately deceptive. Since the Allies were likely to notice the accumulation of German divisions west of the Rhine prior to the attack, a deception scheme was included in the plan. This deception scheme was intended to create the impression that the divisions were deployed there as a defensive measure to respond to the eventual Allied offensive toward the Rhine river.

The two principal headquarters in the West were not informed of Watch on the Rhine until October 22, 1944. That day, the chiefs of staff for *Generalfeldmarschall* Gerd von Rundstedt's *Oberbefehlshaber West* (OB West; High Command West) and *Generalfeldmarschall* Walter Model's Army Group B appeared at Hitler's Wolf's Lair command post in Prussia to be given a briefing on the goals of the offensive.[9] Their immediate task was to take Jodl's basic concept and begin to prepare a detailed battle plan for the first phase of the operation, the breakthrough to the Meuse river.

The two senior commanders on the Western Front were polar opposites in personality and style. Gerd von Rundstedt was an older and far more conventional style of German commander, a member of the traditional military caste from East Prussia's landed aristocracy. Rundstedt had joined the Prussian Army in 1892 and had served as a staff officer in World War I. His moment of battlefield glory came in May–June 1940 when he commanded Army Group A, playing the central role in the crushing defeat of the French Army. He led Army Group South in the invasion of the Soviet Union in 1941, which gutted the Red Army in the encirclement battles in Ukraine. In 1942 he was brought back from Russia to take command of OB West.

Rundstedt was respected by Hitler for his competence, but was outside Hitler's circle of intimates due to his blunt honesty on military matters. He directed the fighting in Normandy in June, but his tart assessments of Germany's declining military prospects led to his relief on July 5, 1944, only a month after the start of the campaign. The disasters in Normandy in July–August 1944 forced Hitler to recall him to service in September 1944, hoping to restore some confidence in the leadership of the shattered Army of the West. Unlike Jodl, Rundstedt was not afraid to tell Hitler his misgivings about his more outlandish scheme, and as a result, his impact on the planning for the Ardennes operation was very limited.

A generation younger than Rundstedt, Walter Model had been born in Saxony into a family with no military tradition at all; his father was a music teacher. He served as a young officer in World War I, and at the start of World War II he served as a chief of staff at corps and field army level in the Polish and French campaigns. He led the *3.Panzer-Division* in the invasion of Russia in 1941 and steadily rose in command due to his exceptional performance. In contrast to Rundstedt's gentlemanly demeanor, Model was brash, unconventional, and ruthless. He was abusive to his staff, but he accomplished his assigned missions. Rundstedt had become disenchanted with Hitler, while Model had become beholden to the Führer after receiving a string of awards and advancements.

By 1944 Model had become Hitler's miracle worker. When all seemed hopeless and defeat inevitable, Hitler called on the energetic and undefeated Model to save the day. In March 1944 he became the

Wehrmacht's youngest field marshal when assigned to the key position of leading Army Group North Ukraine. When Army Group Center was shattered by the Red Army's Operation Bagration in the summer of 1944, Model was assigned by Hitler the almost hopeless task of restoring order, which he accomplished. In mid-August, after German forces in France had been surrounded in the Falaise Gap, Hitler recalled Model from the Eastern Front and assigned him command of Army Group B. Even he could not save such a hopeless situation, but he helped extract the army from its summer disaster and establish a precarious defense along the German frontier in September–October 1944.

Both Rundstedt's OB West and Model's Army Group B were instructed to draw up a preliminary plan based on the OKW Watch on the Rhine outline plan. The OB West plan was code-named Plan

Generalfeldmarschall Walter Model, Army Group B commander (left); *Generalfeldmarschall* Gerd von von Rundstedt, commander of OB West (center); and *General der Infanterie* Hans Krebs, chief of staff of Army Group B (right), discuss the Autumn Mist plan.

Martin (Fall Martin) and more closely resembled Jodl's Small Solution than Hitler's Big Solution. Plan Martin envisioned an attack out of the Ardennes to trap American forces southwest of the Meuse. Model's Army Group B plan was code-named *Herbstnebel* (Autumn Mist) and likewise was a more modest offensive than Hitler's Big Solution.

Regardless of their merits, these plans did not satisfy Hitler's ambitions. For all of Hitler's many faults, he did have a strategic vision for a decisive operation that could change the course of the war. The Small Solution was tactically feasible, but even if it succeeded, it would not have any strategic consequences. The problem with the Big Solution was its resources, not its ambitions.

On November 3, 1944, Rundstedt's headquarters received Jodl's letter of instruction for Watch on the Rhine that provided far more detail than the earlier drafts. This letter rejected both Plan Martin and *Herbstnebel*. The key aspects of the OKW plan were clearly labeled as "unalterable." Rundstedt's and Model's headquarters were expected to amplify, but not alter, the instructions to prepare their own detailed battle plans. The tentative time schedule was to have the forces in place by November 21 and to launch the Watch on the Rhine offensive on November 25, 1944.

The Watch on the Rhine plan envisioned the use of three field armies. The focal point of the attack was in the north, by the *6. Panzer-Armee*, also called by Hitler the *6. SS-Panzer-Armee* since its core consisted of *Waffen-SS* panzer corps. The *6. Panzer-Armee* was nearest to Antwerp, and so was provided with the strongest concentration of panzer forces to conduct the attack.

The center of the Ardennes offensive was the *5. Panzer-Armee* that was assigned to seize the key road junction at Bastogne and fan out over the Meuse river to Antwerp and Brussels with an aim to shield the western flank of the *6. Panzer-Armee* from Allied counterattacks. The third field army assigned to the operation was the smallest and weakest. The *7. Armee* held the left (southern) flank and was intended solely to shield the other two field armies from American counterattacks from that direction. It had no major panzer forces and no major offensive objectives.

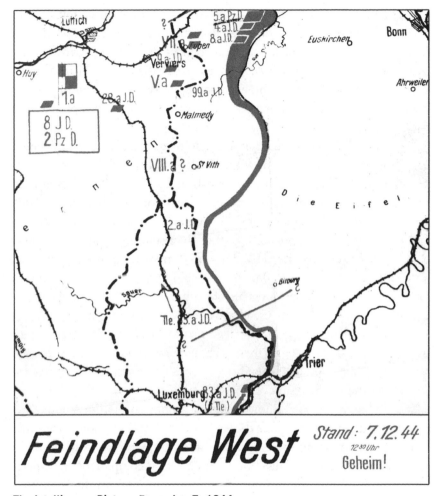

The Intelligence Picture: December 7, 1944

This is an excerpt from the December 7, 1944, Enemy Situation–West (Feindlage-West) map of the German Armed Forces High Command (OKW) showing the Ardennes and Eifel sector where Operation Autumn Mist was staged. As can be seen, the German intelligence picture for the Ardennes was not well detailed, though it was basically correct. The location of the 99th Division was accurately located, but details of other divisions are lacking.

The Watch on the Rhine plan also included an optional fourth field army, Army Group Student, located to the north of *6. Panzer-Armee*. Once the Ardennes attack had succeeded in its mission, Army Group Student would be committed against the British 21st Army Group, with its mission to be determined at some future date depending on the circumstances. It was anticipated that it would be used to exploit any of the successes won by the *6. Panzer-Armee*.

Rundstedt was insulted that Jodl had responded with such detailed and "unalterable" instructions without adequately considering the viewpoints of OB West and Army Group B. It had been the longstanding tradition in the German army to give local commanders greater initiative in executing battle plans. He understood that this was due to Hitler's intransigence, not Jodl. Rather than sending a detailed protest that would be ignored, he crafted a more limited response hoping that some modest changes would be permitted. He sent his response to Jodl late on November 3, outlining his objectives to the plan and especially the inadequacy of the forces. He made several specific suggestions to improve the plan, including the need to conduct Army Group Student's attack at the same time as the main offensive.[10] Hitler rejected even these modest suggestions when he approved the operations directive for Watch on the Rhine on November 10, 1944.

If he had been careful not to express an honest opinion about Hitler's plan during the war, after the war Rundstedt was far more scathing: "Any officer attending the General Staff school who dared to submit a plan such as [Watch on the Rhine], basing it on completely inadequate means, and intentionally disregarding the discrepancies and capabilities between the enemy and friendly forces, would never have made the grade as a General Staff officer."[11]

In the event, the plan to launch Watch on the Rhine in late November 1944 was frustrated by a string of Allied offensives. The British 21st Army Group conducted a large operation along the Scheldt estuary to free the port of Antwerp from German interference. In mid-November, Gen. Omar Bradley's 12th US Army Group launched Operation Queen north of Aachen to try to reach the Roer river, while at the same time continuing the bitter fighting in the Hürtgen forest. These actions had the greatest impact on the Ardennes force since they occurred closest to the Ardennes. The American attacks forced the commitment of some divisions earmarked for the offensive. To the south, Patton's Third US Army launched Operation Madison to clear the Metz fortified area and to push toward the Saar region. Farther south, Lt. Gen. Jacob Dever's 6th Army Group pushed over the Vosges mountains toward Strasbourg and through the Belfort Gap, reaching the Rhine river. These operations tied down several divisions that were originally assigned to the Ardennes offensive. As a result of these Allied initiatives, the launch date for Watch on the Rhine was continually pushed back into December 1944.

Hitler considered that surprise was essential to the success of Watch on the Rhine. Should the Allies understand the intent of the buildup west of the Rhine, they could readily reinforce the Ardennes sector. As a result, discussion of the plans was kept to a bare minimum of senior commanders, who swore an oath of secrecy on pain of death. Hitler had lost trust in the generals since the July 20, 1944, bomb plot and apparently considered a leak from a disloyal officer to be the main threat rather than Allied interception of radio messages. The plans were not transmitted by radio or teletype and instead were shared among the senior commands by means of couriers. As a result, the Allies never discovered the plans until after the attack was launched.

Hitler's insistence on absolute secrecy also impacted tactical preparations for Watch on the Rhine. On November 18, 1944, Jodl sent out a directive on assault tactics based on Hitler's conceptions. This covered seven main issues: the time for the start of the offensive, artillery preparations, organization of assault forces, the breakthrough, the post-breakthrough phase, *Luftwaffe* cooperation, and flak and supply issues. This seemingly mundane directive would in fact have profound consequences to the conduct of the offensive, as will be detailed later.[12]

The senior commanders remained very uneasy about the prospects for the Ardennes mission, and debate continued well into November. Rundstedt considered the Big Solution to be completely impossible in view of the limited forces available, and that even the Small Solution would have modest chances at best. Model was equally skeptical of the plan, calling it "damned fragile." Rundstedt and Model continued to push for the Small Solution plan through the end of November 1944. Nevertheless, Hitler refused to change course.

The final, detailed version of the plan was drafted by Model's Army Group B headquarters on November 29, 1944, and adopted as Operation Order (*Operationsbefehl*) "Autumn Mist" on December 9 after Hitler had made some minor changes.[13] Movement would begin on December 10, and X-Day was scheduled to be Saturday, December 16, 1944.

Schwerpunkt

THE *SCHWERPUNKT*, OR FOCAL POINT, OF THE ARDENNES OFFENSIVE WAS the *6.Panzer-Armee* on the northern flank of the assault. Hitler habitually referred to this command as the *6.SS-Panzer-Armee*, though it was not officially designated as such until January 1945. Its affiliation with the *Waffen-SS* was one of the reasons it was selected to be the focus of the attack. Since the July 1944 bomb plot, Hitler had increasingly turned to the *Waffen-SS* for the most difficult missions since he was increasingly distrustful of the leadership of the regular army, the *Heer*. The *Waffen-SS* was the military arm of the Nazi Party, inculcated with its ideology. The *Waffen-SS* was given preference for equipment, and its commanders were selected more for political reliability than battlefield expertise.

Generalfeldmarschall Gerd von Rundstedt, commander of OB West, and beside him, his son *Leutnant* Hans Gerd von Rundstedt.

From a tactical standpoint, the *6.Panzer-Armee* was the focal point since its sector was seen as the most essential for the success of the mission. Hitler's first draft of the plan described the mission of the *6.Panzer-Armee*: "6.SS-Panzer-Armee will boldly seize the crossings over the Meuse river astride Liège to secure them in cooperation with Operation S; it will establish strong defensive positions facing north on the Vendre river including the eastern fortifications of Liège; it will reach the Albert Canal between Maastricht and Antwerp and secure the area north of Antwerp."[1]

The *6.Panzer-Armee* would launch its attack from the forested Eifel region into the Ardennes south of Monschau. The *6.Panzer-Armee* sector was significantly closer to the main objective of Antwerp than was

Generalfeldmarschall Walter Model, Army Group B commander, on the right chats with *General* Hasso von Manteuffel, commander of *5.Panzer-Armee*, on the left. The figure in the center is *Generalleutnant* Horst Stumpf, the inspector of panzer forces on the Western Front.

the start point for the neighboring *5.Panzer-Armee,* located farther south near Bastogne. Its proximity to Antwerp was essential since the Ardennes plan relied on speed. Even Hitler appreciated that time was on the Allied side, and he expected that German forces could reach Antwerp within a week from the start of the offensive.[2] If the German spearheads were not quick enough in reaching their objectives, the Allies could mobilize greater forces to block their path. The shorter the route, the more likely its success.

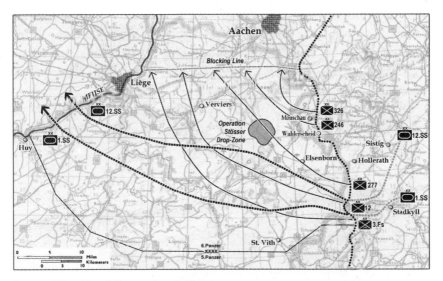

Autumn Mist: The *6.Panzer-Armee* Plan
This map shows the objectives of the *6.Panzer-Armee.* The two spearhead *SS-Panzer* divisions aimed to cross the Meuse river south of Liège before proceeding to Antwerp, while the supporting infantry divisions would conduct the initial break-in, followed by a northward swing to establish a blocking line south of Aachen to shield the *SS-Panzer* divisions from attack by the Ninth US Army to the north.

THE *6.PANZER-ARMEE* COMMANDER

The *6.Panzer-Armee* was led by *SS Oberstgruppenführer* Josef "Sepp" Dietrich. Unlike the other senior German commanders in the Ardennes, he had no formal officer training. Senior German commanders regarded him as an uncouth lout and a dim sycophant of the Führer. His military talents were damned with faint praise as those of a "splendid sergeant." Rundstedt was very uncomfortable relying on the *6.Panzer-Armee* as the *Schwerpunkt* of the offensive due to Dietrich's limitations as a commander. He judged Dietrich as "decent but stupid."[3]

Rundstedt knew very well that Hitler would not countenance Dietrich's replacement, but he did insist that Dietrich's current chief of staff, *Generalleutnant* Alfred Gause, be replaced by "the ablest and most outstanding Panzer army chief-of-staff to be found on the Eastern Front."[4] There was some hope that if a skilled commander could be appointed as Dietrich's chief of staff, this might make up for Dietrich's limitations. In the event, *Generalmajor der Waffen-SS* Fritz Krämer was appointed to this position at the beginning of December 1944.[5]

During its expansion in 1943, the *Waffen-SS* suffered from a shortage of formally trained staff officers. Krämer was a former regular army

SS *Oberstgruppenführer* Josef "Sepp" Dietrich, commander of the *6.Panzer-Armee*, in the Ardennes in 1944.

(*Heer*) staff officer who was seconded to the *Waffen-SS* in 1943, initially serving as Dietrich's chief of staff when leading the *I.SS-Panzer-Korps* in Russia. Krämer was probably not Rundstedt's ideal choice, but he had served ably as Dietrich's chief of staff in the *I.SS-Panzer-Korps* in Normandy. Given the short preparation time before the offensive, it was more prudent to rely on a proven partnership than to risk the potential clash between two unacquainted and headstrong commanders.

Dietrich was a jovial, hard-drinking, and down-to-earth commander who was very popular with his troops. Brutal to opponents, he was maudlin and sentimental with his own soldiers. Dietrich had won the Iron Cross in World War I in a storm troop unit, and served in one of the few German tank units during 1918. He fought against the Poles with the Silesian militias in 1921 and returned to Bavaria to serve as a policeman since there were few opportunities in the army.

Dietrich joined the Nazi Party in 1928 and was promoted to command of the Munich SS (*Schutzstafflen*), a group of toughs formed as a personal guard for Hitler in the rough-and-tumble street politics of the fractious Weimar Republic. Hitler's trust in Dietrich as a reliable enforcer led to his appointment as the head of the enlarged *SS Leibstandarte Adolf Hitler* (Adolf Hitler Bodyguard) after he became chancellor in 1933. Dietrich demonstrated his loyalty to Hitler by rounding up his brownshirt comrades for summary execution in the "Night of the Long Knives" in 1934, when Hitler ordered the SA (*Sturmabteilung*) crushed to curry favor with the army.

The *Leibstandarte* was committed to combat for the first time during the 1939 Polish campaign, gradually shaking off their reputation as "asphalt soldiers." Dietrich was a charismatic fighter, but unprepared in intellect or training to command a large formation. So the practice began of placing him in a prominent position while at the same time assigning a talented officer as his chief of staff to carry out the actual headquarters and staff functions.

Later evaluations of Dietrich by US Army interrogators tended to reflect the opinions of German commanders from the *Heer*. He was described by American interviewers as "a crude, loquacious, hard-bitten, tough man whose statements are often inaccurate—yet also a man having a great deal of common sense. His fellow officers, the more class-conscious of whom are often shocked at Dietrich's language and behavior, attribute his meteoric rise in the army to his [Nazi] party connections."[6] 1Lt. Robert E. Merriam remarked, "Dietrich is regarded in low esteem by his fellow officers. He did not seem to have a grasp of the operations of his Army in the Ardennes and was unable to present a comprehensive picture of the happenings, even in the most general terms."[7]

Dietrich was Hitler's alter ego—a common soldier of the Great War, a man of the people, a man of action, and the polar opposite of the type of intellectual, aristocratic Prussian staff officer that Hitler so despised. He was awarded the Iron Cross 1st and 2nd Class for the undistinguished performance of the *Leibstandarte* in Poland, and the Knight's Cross for their modest role in the French campaign. These were the first of many preposterous awards and rank increases that Hitler used as much to rankle the bluebloods of the German military establishment as to reward Dietrich.

In 1943 Dietrich was ordered to form the *I.SS-Panzer-Korps*. The corps was first committed to action in Normandy, where it earned a formidable reputation for its obstinate and skilled defense of Caen against British tank assaults. On August 1, 1944, Dietrich was elevated to *SS Oberstgruppenführer*, and a few days later Hitler added Diamonds to his Iron Cross, one of only twenty-seven soldiers so decorated during the war. On September 14, 1944, Hitler instructed him to begin the formation of the *6.Panzer-Armee*. Dietrich had grown increasingly despondent over the conduct of the war, but he was too inarticulate to convey his views, and too beholden to his Nazi sponsors to press his complaints with any conviction. He drank heavily, and vaguely blamed the setbacks at the front on "sabotage." He was unwilling to recognize that the source of the problem was the regime he so ardently served.

Organization of the *6.Panzer-Armee*

Dietrich's *6.Panzer-Armee* consisted of three corps: *I.SS-Panzer-Korps*, *II.SS-Panzer-Korps*, and *57.Armee-Korps*. The front assigned to the

6.*Panzer-Armee* was quite narrow, only about 20 kilometers (13 miles) wide. The plan was to begin the attack with the *I.SS-Panzer-Korps* attacking toward Elsenborn and the Losheim Gap while the *57.Armee-Korps* on its right flank would push into the Monschau forest. The *II.SS-Panzer-Korps* would wait until the *I.SS-Panzer-Korps* had secured the breakthrough, and then exploit the penetration in a race to Antwerp.

The *57.Armee-Korps*, under the command of *General der Infanterie* Otto Hitzfeld, was by far the weakest of the three corps and had the least ambitious mission. In many respects, it mirrored the role of the *7.Armee* to the south: to shield the shoulder of the offensive using a modest infantry force. The First US Army was very active in the Monschau area as part of its bloody campaign to reach the Roer river dams, and Hitzfeld's corps was assigned to keep the American infantry in this sector tied down and away from the main attack sector farther south.

Wehrmacht Commands in the Elsenborn Sector, December 1944	
OB West	*Generalfeldmarschall* Gerd von Rundstedt
Army Group B	*Generalfeldmarschall* Walter Model
6.*Panzer-Armee*	SS *Oberstgruppenführer* Josef "Sepp" Dietrich
I.SS-Panzer-Korps	*General der Waffen-SS* Hermann Priess
II.SS-Panzer-Korps	*SS-Obergruppenführer* Wilhelm Bittrich
57.Armee-Korps	*General der Infanterie* Otto Hitzfeld

AUTUMN MIST TACTICS

The tactics of the Autumn Mist plan were textbook 1944 pattern, with the infantry divisions executing the tactical breakthrough of the American defenses, followed by the operational breakthrough by the panzer divisions. The *I.Panzer-Korps* had three infantry divisions assigned to the initial breakthrough mission. Once this operation was completed, these units were expected to make a wide swing to the northwest to create a blocking line from Liège to Monschau to prevent Allied divisions from interfering on the right flank of the panzer breakthrough.

This blocking line would include the three infantry divisions assigned to the *I.Panzer-Korps* as well as two infantry divisions in Hitzfeld's *57.Armee-Korps*.

The two panzer corps were expected to bear the burden of the attack. The *I.SS-Panzer-Korps* was assigned as the spearhead to conduct the initial breakthrough by way of Elsenborn and the Losheim Gap and race to the Meuse river crossings. At this point, the *II.SS-Panzer-Korps* would be injected into the battle. In the event that the *I.SS-Panzer-Korps* had suffered heavy losses in the breakthrough phase, the *II.SS-Panzer-Korps* would follow behind to conduct the exploitation phase beyond the Meuse river. In the event that the *I.SS-Panzer-Korps* was still relatively intact, both corps would proceed in parallel, with the *II.SS-Panzer-Korps* most likely forming the right flank of the attack from the Elsenborn area toward Antwerp. At this stage, Army Group Student would also be available to further amplify the attack in the northern sector out of the Aachen area.

Aside from the narrowness of the attack front, the other reason the two panzer corps were scheduled to attack in sequence was that the road network in this area was not suitable for a concentrated panzer attack. The front lines in this sector ran along the International Highway (Reichsstrasse 258), with a significant forest immediately to the west. This area along the German-Belgian border has relatively good north–south roads emanating from Aachen, but the east–west road network was poor until reaching the road network emanating from Liège. The forest in this area was used for logging and so was relatively free of underbrush and traversable by infantry. However, the road network through the forest consisted mainly of paths and firebreaks that were only marginally suitable for vehicular traffic. For the attack plan to succeed, the American defenses in the forest had to be rapidly overwhelmed to permit the mechanized columns to reach open farmland on the other side of the woods.

A total of five routes, called *Rollbahn*, were assigned to the two panzer divisions of the *I.SS-Panzer-Korps*. These routes were reserved for the panzer units, and the accompanying infantry divisions were explicitly instructed to avoid clogging these routes until after the panzer spearheads had passed. The five routes were labeled as Rollbahn A through E, with the three northern routes (A–C) assigned to *12.SS-Panzer-Division "Hitlerjugend"* and the remaining two to its southern neighbor, *1.SS-Panzer-Division "Leibstandarte Adolf Hitler."* Of the five routes, the northernmost, Rollbahn A, was judged to be inadequate for extensive tank use and instead was slated to be used only for a reinforced armored reconnaissance detachment.[8] In the event, Rollbahn A would take on far greater importance than envisioned in the original plan.

Within the *I.SS-Panzer-Korps*, the focal point was the center of the sector: Rollbahn D for the *1.SS-Panzer-Division* and Rollbahn C for the *12.SS-Panzer-Division*. Both of these routes passed through the Losheim Gap. This started with a narrow band of forests northwest of Losheim, exiting into open farmland with a good road network heading to the northwest.

No specific time schedule was set for the offensive, though there were some rough expectations about the likely progress of the operation. It was anticipated that the infantry divisions would fight their way through the forests on the morning of the first day, advancing to a depth of 5 to 6 kilometers by midday.[9] The original OKW plan expected that the Meuse would be reached in two days. The *6.Panzer-Armee* had less optimistic expectations. Army chief of staff Fritz Krämer expected it would take one day to break through the American defenses and one day for the spearhead panzer divisions to pass over the Hohes Venn highlands, with arrival near the Meuse on the evening of the third day and the crossing the Meuse on the fourth day.[10]

THE ARTILLERY DILEMMA

There was considerable controversy about the artillery preparation at the start of the Autumn Mist attack. Dietrich's *6.Panzer-Armee* followed the November 18, 1944, tactical guidelines from Hitler to the letter. The neighboring *5.Panzer-Armee*, led by the dynamic panzer commander Hasso von Manteuffel, had very serious reservations about Berlin's artillery instructions.

General der Panzertruppen
Hasso von Manteuffel,
commander of the *5.Panzer-Armee* in the Ardennes
campaign.

Artillery could undoubtedly soften up an enemy infantry defense if applied with enough accuracy and enough volume. Hitler's instructions undermined the value of the artillery preparation by insisting that none of the new divisional artillery battalions or supporting corps artillery could register their targets before the attack. This was to maintain the absolute secrecy essential to the attack. To ensure accuracy, field artillery batteries normally would conduct a few registration fires to make certain that the main barrage would hit where intended. Without the registration, field artillery loses its accuracy.

A further impediment was Hitler's insistence that deep reconnaissance into the American lines be curtailed prior to the offensive to create the impression that the Ardennes was a quiet front. This further weakened the potential of the artillery since the artillery fire control units lacked detailed information on the location of American defenses. Artillery observation batteries were deployed in late November and early December to collect data on US field artillery battery locations by means of flash observation and sound ranging. This precipitated a crisis on December 2, 1944, when two forward observers from *I.SS-Panzer-Korps* were captured by US patrols, leading to some fear that the Autumn Mist plans might be compromised.[11] This led to further restrictions on artillery reconnaissance.

The German artillery batteries did not have enough ammunition to bombard the entire front, and furthermore Hitler insisted that the preliminary softening of the American infantry positions be limited to an hour; it was later shortened to a half hour. In view of the lack of precise targeting information, this implied that the artillery preparation would not be accurate enough or powerful enough to significantly damage the American infantry defenses.

Besides these problems, the American forward defenses were located in the forest belt along the Belgian frontier. Forests pose a significant problem for artillery firing against defended positions. This should have been clear to both sides as a result of the brutal fighting in the nearby Hürtgen forest that had been taking place since September 1944. The artillery projectiles would usually detonate in the upper branches of the trees. This sprayed the area below with a lethal combination of blast, fragments, and wood splinters, killing or injuring any exposed infantry. But it was nearly worthless when the enemy infantry was protected. The American defenses were in many cases based in earthen bunkers with log roofs, which were nearly invulnerable to tree bursts. Unless the American infantry was caught out in the open, the artillery bombardment would be nearly useless.

Manteuffel's solution was to rely on 1918 tactics, which favored infiltration over firepower. He argued that the artillery preparation as conceived would be inadequate and moreover would only serve to alert the Americans to the impending infantry assault, giving them time to man their forward defenses. Instead, Manteuffel wanted to infiltrate at least a battalion from each infantry regiment through the weakly defended American lines, cutting off and encircling the forward American defenses. His suggestions to the OKW in this regard were rebuffed. Manteuffel conveniently ignored Berlin's orders, and the *5.Panzer-Armee* used infiltration tactics with considerable success, with the storm battalions "infiltrating like rain-drops" through the American front.[12]

Manteuffel's view on this issue was shared by the staff of Preiss's *I.SS-Panzer-Korps*:

> Corps headquarters had repeatedly requested that there be no prepa-
> ratory barrage, but that the artillery open fire at the beginning of the
> attack. This was all the more advisable because the enemy positions in
> the attack sector were deployed 7–9 kilometers deep. Their locations
> could not be determined and the amount of ammunition available
> was not enough for a rolling barrage. Moreover, corps headquarters
> believed that a one-hour artillery preparation along this completely
> quiet front would surrender the advantage of secrecy one hour too
> soon. The attack troops would thereby be deprived of the great advan-
> tage of surprise without gaining any essential fire support. Corps
> headquarters' requests in this regards were refused.[13]

Dietrich and his staff tended to be far more compliant with the
OKW instructions and lacked the tactical foresight of more skilled
commanders like Manteuffel. This would have ruinous consequences on
the first day of the attack.

General der Waffen-SS Hermann
Preiss, commander of the
I.SS-Panzer-Korps during the
Ardennes campaign.

INFANTRY SPEARHEAD

The Hollywood depiction of the Battle of the Bulge usually portrays the panzer divisions as the spearhead of the attack. This was not the case in 1944. The proliferation of infantry anti-tank weapons such as the American 2.36-inch bazooka and the German *Panzerfaust* made it very dangerous for tanks to attempt to push through dense infantry defenses because these defenses could slow the attack and lead to unacceptably high tank losses. Infantry, with armored vehicle support, was considered a more effective means to break through enemy infantry defenses. Once the infantry defenses were penetrated, the panzers would advance.

In the case of German infantry divisions, the armored infantry support came from the ubiquitous *Sturmgeschütz III* (*StuG III*). At least on paper, each German infantry division had a company of twelve *StuG IIIs* or their low-cost replacement, the *Jagdpanzer 38 Hetzer*. This was hardly enough armor support for a major offensive, so usually one or more *StuG* brigades from the corps reserve were assigned to help the infantry. This was the plan for the *I. SS-Panzer-Korps* attacks, though as will become apparent, this plan went awry.[14]

The German plan assessed American forces in this sector as weak. The 99th Infantry Division was stretched across a very wide front so the three attacking infantry divisions should be able to obtain a three-to-one advantage in the initial attack. This three-to-one ratio is a "rule of thumb" and considered by many analysts to be the magic number needed on the 1944–45 battlefield to obtain a high probability of penetrating infantry defenses.

The one intelligence gap in German planning was the location of the US 2nd Infantry Division. The 106th Infantry Division had replaced it in the Schnee Eifel sector in early December 1944, and it was presumed that it was recuperating farther to the rear, probably in Lager Elsenborn.[15] The *12. SS-Panzer-Division* intelligence summary for December 14, 1944, noted that "it may be assumed that the operational reserves in the rear of the 99th Infantry Division consist of the 2nd US Infantry Division plus the 4th and 102nd independent Cavalry Regiments."[16] Details of the disposition of the 2nd Division were lacking.

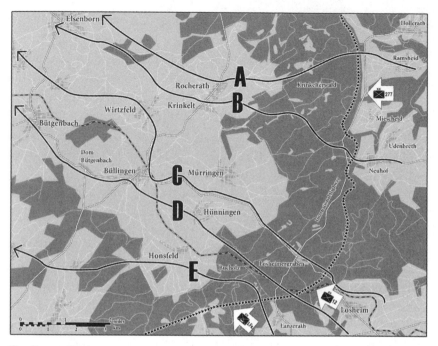

The Panzer Routes
This map shows the five *Rollbahn* routes assigned to the panzer spearheads.
Rollbahn A, B, and C were assigned to *12.SS-Panzer-Division "Hitlerjugend,"*
while Rollbahn D and E were assigned to *1.SS-Panzer-Division "Leibstandarte
Adolf Hitler."*

In the wake of the planned artillery preparation, three infantry
divisions were allotted to break through the crust of the US infantry
defenses in the *I.SS-Panzer-Korps* sector. This force consisted of the
3.Fallschirmjäger-Division in the south, the *12.Volksgrenadier-Division*
in the center, and the *277.Volksgrenadier-Division* in the north. Once
the forested border area was penetrated by the German infantry attack,
the *12.SS-Panzer-Division* would then disgorge from the woods and
head off for the Meuse river. If all went well, the *12.SS-Panzer-Division*
was expected to reach the Meuse bridges by the evening of the third day
of the attack, X+2.

Accelerating the Breakthrough

The sector assigned to the *I.SS-Panzer-Korps* was hardly ideal for a breakthrough due to the heavily forested start-line, especially in the *12.SS-Panzer-Division* sector. The *I.SS-Panzer-Korps* requested that the focus of the corps be switched to the southwest, equivalent to about two divisions' width, to take advantage of the better terrain.[17] There was also some concern over the likely concentration of US divisions recuperating in Camp Elsenborn, including the misidentified "1st Armored Division."[18] Considering the late date that this request was made, it was categorically rejected by Krämer at *6.Panzer-Armee* headquarters, knowing full well the intransigence of the higher commands to changes at such a late date.

In spite of the unfortunate terrain problems facing the *I.SS-Panzer Korps* at the start of the campaign, other actions were expected assist in its breakthrough. Two special missions were planned to facilitate its progress. Operation Stösser was a paratroop mission under the command of *Oberstleutnant* Friedrich von der Heydte to block key road junctions in the Verviers-Monschau area to prevent the reinforcement of the American defenses in the Elsenborn sector.[19] Operation Greif was a special operations mission to deploy Otto Skorzeny's *Panzer-Brigade.150* behind American lines to disrupt American defenses and seize key bridges. *Panzer-Brigade.150* was manned by troops speaking English, wearing American uniforms, and using captured US vehicles and German armored vehicles disguised as US Army vehicles.[20]

The *Hitlerjugend* Division

HITLERJUGEND'S PREPARATIONS

The *12.SS-Panzer-Division "Hitlerjugend"* was so named since it was originally created in 1943 on the basis of volunteers from the Nazi Party's *Hitlerjugend* (Hitler Youth) youth organization. The *Hitlerjugend* included young men in the fourteen-to-eighteen-year age bracket, though recruitment for the new *Waffen-SS* division was only among those born in 1926 and so seventeen to eighteen years old in 1943–44. The *Hitlerjugend* recruits served initially as enlisted men, with the NCOs and officers coming from the *1.SS-Panzer-Division "Leibstandarte Adolf Hitler."*

The *12.SS-Panzer-Division* was first committed to combat in Normandy in June 1944, initially fighting against the Canadians around Caen.[1] The division quickly earned a reputation for mindless brutality after massacring Canadian prisoners of war and French civilians during the Normandy campaign.[2] Few other divisions saw as much combat in Normandy as the *Hitlerjugend*, and it was repeatedly committed in the Caen sector against the British and Canadian forces. By the end of the campaign, the division had been effectively destroyed as a fighting force, losing nearly all of its armored vehicles and most of its *Panzergrenadier* infantry strength. From a starting strength of 20,540 men, it suffered casualties of about 9,000 men in Normandy, and was withdrawn from combat on September 3, 1944.[3]

Through the autumn of 1944, it was a "torso" division. It still had a significant personnel strength, perhaps as many as 12,000 men, but its actual combat strength was low since it had lost most of its tank crews, grenadiers, reconnaissance troops, Pioneers (engineers), and artillery in the Normandy fighting. Although these combat arms accounted for about 60 percent of the division's troops, they suffered 90 percent of the division's casualties. The level of casualties varied from unit to unit. For example, *SS-Panzer-Regiment.12* suffered about 85 percent casualties and *SS-Panzergrenadier.Regiment.26* about 75 percent. The most intact elements of the division were the administrative, supply, and support units.

12.SS-Panzer-Division Casualties June–September 1944	
SS-Panzer-Regiment.12	1,521
SS-Panzergrenadier-Regiment.25	1,692
SS-Panzergrenadier-Regiment.26	2,373
SS-Panzer-Aufklärungs-Abteilung.12	547
SS-Panzer-Pionier-Abteilung.12	506
SS-Panzer-Artillerie-Regiment.12	1,041
Other	852
Total	**8,532**

During the Ardennes campaign, the *Hitlerjugend* was commanded by *SS-Brigadeführer* Hugo Kraas, thirty-three years old at the time. He was quite young compared to his American counterparts, who were a generation older.[4] Kraas joined the Nazi Party at age twenty-two, served a brief time in the army in 1935, and switched shortly after to the SS. He attended the *SS-Junkerschule Braunschweig* and was commissioned as an NCO in 1938. He began his long association with the *Leibstandarte Adolf Hitler* (LAH) in 1938, becoming a first lieutenant (*Oberscharführer*) in the spring of 1939. The *Leibstandarte* started out as the personal bodyguard formation for Hitler, but in 1939 it was committed to combat, starting as a modest infantry formation but gradually morphing into a panzer division.

Kraas received the Iron Cross for his leadership in the Polish campaign in 1939 and again after the battle of France in 1940. He led the LAH motorcycle reconnaissance company in 1941 during the Operation Barbarossa invasion of the Soviet Union and reached captain's rank (*Hauptsturmführer*) in early 1942. Kraas was one of the first members of the *Waffen-SS* to be decorated with the German Cross in Gold on

Oberführer Hugo Kraas, commander of *12.SS-Panzer-Division "Hitlerjugend"* during the Ardennes campaign.

December 26, 1941. He was widely regarded as one of the best infantry commanders in the expanding LAH, becoming a major (*Sturmbahn-führer*) in April 1942 and a lieutenant colonel (*Obersturmbannführer*) in June 1943. He was decorated for his leadership in the fighting around Kharkov in 1943 with the Knight's Cross.

Kraas was appointed to the command of *SS-Panzergrenadier-Regiment.2* of the *1.SS-Panzer-Division "LAH"* in June 1943 shortly before the battle of Kursk, and was decorated with the Knight's Cross of the Iron Cross with Oak Leaves in December 1943 for his leadership during the 1943 campaign in Russia. He was promoted to colonel (*Standartenführer*) in January 1944, and after recovering from wounds, he attended a division commander's course in September–October 1944 before being transferred to the *12.SS-Panzer-Division "Hitlerjugend."*

This was a fairly common career path, with many of the senior *Hitlerjugend* commanders coming from the LAH. The intention had been for Fritz Krämer to command the rebuilt *Hitlerjugend* division, but when Rundstedt insisted that Dietrich receive a more experienced chief of staff, Krämer went to the *6.Panzer-Armee* and Kraas was appointed to command the *Hitlerjugend* division. Kraas had considerable battle experience, but his training as a divisional commander was very modest. This reflected the perennial shortage of experienced and trained senior officers in the *Waffen-SS* in 1944.

DIVISIONAL RECONSTRUCTION

Although units such as the *Hitlerjugend* are sometimes described as "battle-hardened," by September 1944 the division was in fact completely shattered. Its combat formations had to be essentially reconstructed from scratch, with only a brittle skeleton of battle-weary survivors. A quick survey of the small-unit combat leaders gives a sense of the extent of rejuvenation needed.[5] Of the battalion commander and four tank company commanders of *I./SS-Panzer-Regiment 12*, only two of the five still commanded his unit between the start of the Normandy campaign and the start of the Ardennes offensive. Casualties in the *Panzergrenadier* regiments were far more severe. Of the three battalion commanders and twelve rifle company commanders

Two companies of *SS-Panzer-Regiment. 12* were equipped with the *Panther Ausf. G* tank, arguably the best German tank of this campaign. This particular example was knocked out by the 393rd Infantry, 99th Division during the campaign in Germany in 1945.

in *SS-Panzergrenadier-Regiment.25*, only one of the fifteen was the same between Normandy and the Ardennes. In *SS-Panzergrenadier-Regiment.26*, three of the fifteen were the same. Not all of these officers had been killed; some were wounded or captured, and some went on to other command positions in other units. However, the lack of continuity in command undermined the battle experience of the division.

In view of the plans for the Ardennes offensive, the *12.SS-Panzer-Division* began its reconstruction on October 14, 1944, with explicit instructions that it would be held back from combat commitment until the start of Watch on the Rhine. The initial plans called for it to be completely equipped with heavy weapons, according to the KStN (*Kriegsstärkenachweisungen*; war establishment strength), and 75 percent of machine guns, individual weapons, trucks, and other vehicles. Artillery prime movers would be provided as available due to extreme shortages. The intention was to raise the division to full strength by October 31, 1944, an objective that proved to be hopelessly optimistic.

In terms of personnel, the previous practice of relying exclusively on *Hitlerjugend* volunteers ended, simply as a matter of expediency. While available *Hitlerjugend* volunteers were incorporated into the division, much of the strength, especially in the *Panzergrenadier* regiments, came from the usual sources available in the autumn of 1944, namely surplus personnel from the *Luftwaffe* and *Kriegsmarine*. In spite of other shortfalls, there were sufficient replacements to bring the division to full strength. Indeed, it was over-strength at the beginning of the Ardennes offensive, about 23,245 men versus the authorized establishment of 18,550. The problem with manpower was not quantity but quality. The divisional commander, Hugo Kraas, later wrote:

> The young replacements consisted of volunteers whose training had been very short. Only a small cadre of the combat force were front-experienced, older soldiers. Most officers, especially the staff officers, lacked front and leadership experience. These shortcomings were most apparent with the *Panzergrenadier* regiments which were in no way ready for immediate action, nor sufficiently well organized, and so not suited for offensive action.[6]

Training of the tank crews was short and cursory due to the lack of time, the late delivery of new tanks, and the general lack of fuel. In the case of *I./SS-Panzer-Regiment.12*, the unit started reconstruction in September 1944, mostly from *Hitlerjugend* troops returning from the hospital, new recruits from replacement centers, and small cadres from the *1.SS-Panzer-Division*. Unlike the infantry units, the *Waffen-SS* panzer divisions received exclusively German troops. The average age in the *Hitlerjugend* panzer companies was eighteen years old. Lacking any tanks for the first two months, initial training in September–October 1944 was ordinary infantry training and basic tank tactic theory. There was also a heavy dose of political indoctrination, and the usual *Waffen-SS* inculcation of its culture of brutality in combat. The troops were told by the divisional commander that "I ask you and expect of you not to take any prisoners with the possible exception of some officers who must be brought to [intelligence] without delay."[7]

The other two companies of *SS-Panzer-Regiment.12* were equipped with the workhorse of the German panzer force, the *PzKpfw IV*. Although a bit outdated by 1944, it was still a formidable tank with an excellent gun.

Much of the early training was away from established training camps, and the units were deployed in small towns and villages in western Germany. For example, the *3.Kompanie, SS-Panzer-Regiment.12* was located in Haßbergen, north of Hanover, in October 1944; instructional training was conducted in a restaurant in town due to a lack of facilities.[8] Tanks were finally delivered starting in the last days of October 1944, and the tank companies had about two weeks of training on the vehicles in early November. This was largely static training, with very few live-fire opportunities except for machine-gun fire, and very little driver training due to fuel shortages. One tanker in *3.Kompanie* complained that the company commander insisted on pistol proficiency for self-defense but that even pistol ammunition was in short supply. Three final weeks of training were completed through the end of November

The *Panzer IV lg.(V)* tank destroyer was the most common medium armored vehicle of the *Hitlerjugend*, serving in both *SS-Pz.Jg.Abt.12* and *s.Pz. Jg.Abt.560.* It was a derivative of the *PzKpfw IV* medium tank, with a fixed casemate and the same long 75mm gun that armed the *Panther* tank. This particular example was from the neighboring *SS-Pz.Jg.Abt.1* of *Kampfgruppe Hansen, 1.SS-Panzer-Division,* near the Poteau crossroads on December 18, 1944.

in Neurath before the battalion was deployed to staging areas in the Cologne area, where the units stayed until the final move to the Eifel region opposite the Ardennes starting December 12–13, 1944.

Tank shortages led to a truncated organization. In Normandy, the division had the usual 1944-pattern tank regiment with a battalion of *Panther* tanks and a battalion of *PzKpfw IV* tanks. In late summer 1944, the Allied bombing campaign had finally begun to target the German tank industry. The main *Panther* plant, MAN at Nurnberg, was hit hard on September 10, 1944, which cost the *Wehrmacht* the equivalent of over four months production, or about 645 *Panther* tanks.[9] Due to the tank shortages caused by the summer 1944 losses and the bombing campaign, the usual two battalions were merged into a single mixed battalion, *I./SS-Panzer-Regiment.12*, equipped with 41 *Panther* and 37 *PzKpfw IV* tanks, for a total of only 78 tanks instead of the 184 to 195 in a full-strength panzer regiment. The chart below compares the standard organizational strength of an *SS-Panzer* division against the actual holdings of the *Hitlerjugend* at the start of the campaign.

Hitlerjugend Armored Vehicle Strength in December 1944		
	Authorized	Actual
PzKpfw IV	116	37
Panther	79	41
Jagdpanther	0	17
Panzerjäger	31	50
Other AFV*	522	185

*includes armored half-tracks, armored cars, etc.

To make up for the tank deficiency, the *schwere Panzerjäger-Abteilung.560* (heavy tank destroyer battalion) was attached to the division. This unit had originally served on the Russian Front, equipped with Hornisse self-propelled 88mm anti-tank guns. After suffering heavy losses, the battalion was sent back to Germany for reconstruction in May 1944. However, it only began to receive its equipment in

October–December 1944. Its three companies consisted of *9.Kompanie* with seventeen *Jagdpanther* tank destroyers, and *10.* and *11.Kompanien* with a total of twenty-eight *Panzer IV lg.(V)* tank destroyers.[10] The *Jagdpanther* was a tank destroyer version of the *Panther* tank, armed with the same long 88mm gun as the *Tiger II* heavy tank. The *Panzer IV lg.(V)* was the tank destroyer version of the *PzKpfw IV* medium tank, but armed with the same long 75mm gun of the *Panther* tank in a fixed casemate rather than a turret.[11] The *Panzer IV lg.(V)* was actually the most common armored vehicle in the *Hitlerjugend* since it also equipped the divisional anti-tank unit, *SS-Panzerjäger-Abteilung.12*. This battalion was supposed to have thirty-one tank destroyers, but in fact received only twenty-two.

Both of these types of tank destroyers were extremely effective anti-tank vehicles when used in their intended role. They were expected to employ their powerful guns in long-range ambushes against enemy tanks and armored vehicles, and were not configured to mix it up in close combat with enemy infantry. Lacking a turret, they were far less

The *s.Pz.Jg.Abt.560* had one of its companies equipped with the *Jagdpanther* tank destroyer. It was based on the *Panther* tank chassis, but with a fixed casemate, and armed with the same long 88mm gun used on the *Tiger II* heavy tank.

versatile than tanks for most other missions. Their exceptionally long guns were a major hindrance during travel, since they could easily fall victim to accidents.

Kraas instructed *Hauptsturmführer* Brockschmidt, commander of *SS-Panzerjäger-Abteilung.12*, that he expected to use the battalion in the fashion of an assault gun (*Sturmgeschütz*) battalion for direct-fire support of the *Panzergrenadier* regiments since there was little expectation of encountering significant numbers of American tanks. The use of the *Panzer IV lg.(V)* in close combat against infantry was troublesome, since it lacked a coaxial machine gun or a hull-mounted machine gun for self-defense against enemy infantry except for simple firing ports. As a result, *SS-Panzerjäger-Abteilung.12* obtained twin machine-gun mounts from grounded *Luftwaffe* bombers and mounted these to the right of the loader's hatch on the roof of the vehicle to provide additional close-combat defense. The battalion also attempted to create an "escort company" (*Begleit Kompanie*) from the *Panzergrenadier* regiments, trained in close support of the tank destroyers.[12] Without these close-support troops, the *Jagdpanzers* would fight nearly blind and would be especially vulnerable to American infantry in close terrain such as forests.

Kraas was not happy with this awkward assortment of vehicles delivered to the *Hitlerjugend* division: "This diverse combination considerably weakened [the panzer regiment], the strongest weapon of the division's arsenal. The commitment of the Panzer regiment would prove to be tactically as well as technically difficult since it consisted of four assorted tank types."[13] In spite of the equipment shortcomings, Kraas felt that *I./SS-Panzer-Regiment.12* was better than average compared to the rest of the reconstructed division since it was manned by "good and front-experienced enlisted men, NCOs, and officers."[14]

Although not immediately apparent from this list of equipment, the development of specialized armored vehicles for the German panzer divisions had atrophied through the course of the war due to a lack of resources. Because the *Wehrmacht* was on the defensive since 1943, the accent shifted to armored vehicles such as tank destroyers. Offensively oriented armored support vehicles, especially armored engineer vehicles, were largely lacking.[15] By this stage of the war, the Soviet, US, and British armies were all operating armored mine-rollers, an essential tool in armored offensives for rapidly breaching minefields while under fire. German tanks were not fitted with dozer blades for dealing with anti-tank obstructions, and the supply of dedicated armored recovery vehicles such as the *Bergepanther* was not generous. As will become evident later in this book, the lack of this type of specialized equipment would handicap the panzer divisions in the Ardennes.

Besides the panzer and *Panzerjäger* units, the *Hitlerjugend*'s other major armored unit was an armored reconnaissance battalion. *SS-Aufklärungs-Abteilung.12* was equipped with seven *Sd.Kfz.234* heavy armored cars, nine *Sd.Kfz.222/223* light armored cars, thirteen *Sd.Kfz.250* light half-tracks, and twenty-four *Sd.Kfz.251* medium half-tracks. This was about 75 percent of the authorized vehicle strength.

Fire support for the *Panzergrenadier* regiments came from the *Sd.Kfz.251/9*, a version of the standard armored half-track fitted with a short L/43 75mm gun.

Divisional commander Hugo Kraas characterized this battalion as "very weak" and barely equivalent to a light armored infantry company.[16] This was a significant concern since this unit had been expected to act as the fast divisional spearhead to reach the Meuse bridges once the penetration of the American defense had been accomplished. In the event, it was never used as such.

The bulk of the division's strength was in its *Panzergrenadier* (mechanized infantry) regiments. Kraas himself had served with the *Panzergrenadiers* for most of the war and was widely regarded as one of the premier *Waffen-SS Panzergrenadier* commanders. In contrast to US armored divisions, the German panzer divisions had about twice as much infantry, six battalions versus three battalions.

In spite of the popular image of the *Panzergrenadier* fighting from an armored half-track, the shortage of armored half-tracks meant that the majority of *Panzergrenadier* units, even in the *Waffen-SS*, relied on trucks. On paper, the division was supposed to have 400 *Sd.Kfz.251* medium half-tracks but in fact had only 114. As a result, only one of the six *Panzergrenadier* battalions was equipped with armored half-tracks. *SS-Panzergrenadier-Regiment.25* relied entirely on trucks for transport. One battalion in *Panzergrenadier-Regiment.26* used the standard *Sd.Kfz.251* armored half-track. Of the 114 medium armored half-tracks in the *Hitlerjugend*, *SS-Panzergrenadier-Regiment.26* had only 63 at the start of the campaign, equipping *III./SS-Panzergrenadier-Regiment.26 (gep.)*.[17] The others were used elsewhere in the division.

In terms of support vehicles and trucks, the division was near overall strength. Once again, the main problem was quality rather than quantity. The division was authorized 782 all-terrain field cars but only had 262, with the shortfall made up by ordinary commercial automobiles with no cross-country capability. Likewise, it was authorized 914 trucks, 933 cross-country trucks, and 147 Maultier half-track trucks; in fact, it received 1,220 trucks but only 214 cross-country and 88 Maultier trucks with half-track rear suspensions. The situation with half-track prime movers was far worse, with only 90 of the allotted 227 actually on hand.[18] A staff officer later complained that the unsuitability of the

Mobile anti-tank firepower for the *Panzergrenadier* units came from the *Sd.Kfz.251/22*, a derivative of the standard armored half-track but fitted with a 75mm PaK 40 anti-tank gun. This particular vehicle was knocked out on December 18, 1944 during fighting between the 30th Infantry Division and battle groups of the *1.SS-Panzer-Division.*

trucks was a major factor in traffic problems that bedeviled the initial attack: "The (6.Panzer-Armee) was unable to master traffic jams on the few, narrow, steep, and windswept roads. These difficulties were mainly caused by the vehicles that were not fit to traverse the Eifel terrain and which should have never been on the battlefield."[19]

Aside from the issue of vehicle stocks, the matter of fuel supply was of critical concern to the division. There is a popular perception, fostered no doubt by films such as *The Battle of the Bulge*, that German panzer units in the Ardennes started the offensive with inadequate reserves of fuel and so were expected to depend on capturing fuel stocks from the US Army. This was not in fact the case. Although German fuel reserves were strained, enough fuel had been stockpiled for the offensive to carry out the mission.[20] The problem was not so much the amount of fuel in *Wehrmacht* stockpiles but the challenges of getting the fuel forward to the spearhead panzer units.

The reconnaissance units of panzer divisions used these *Sd.Kfz.250/8* half-tracks, armed with a short 75mm gun.

Although the popular image of the *Panzergrenadier* regiments pictures them using armored halftracks, most divisions only had a single battalion equipped with the *Sd.Kfz.251* half-track. In the case of the *12.SS-Panzer-Division*, it was the *III./SS-Panzergrenadeir-Regiment.26*.

The panzer divisions were allotted five *Verbrauchersätzen* (consumption units) of fuel for the Ardennes mission.[21] A *Verbrauchersätze* was enough fuel to move a panzer division a distance of 100 kilometers on the road. The actual number of gallons for each battalion varied by tank type; a *Panther* tank had a higher fuel consumption than a *PzKpfw IV*, so the consumption unit in a *Panther* battalion was higher. On paper, three fuel units were supposed to be available in the panzer regiments, and the remaining two within the divisional supply column. In fact, on December 15, 1944, the day before the start of the Ardennes offensive, the *12.SS-Panzer-Division* had only a 0.6 fuel unit, due in part to problems in moving fuel supplies into place in time and also to unexpectedly high consumption rates moving the division forward from the Cologne area over the several days prior to the launch of the offensive. Allied bombing on both sides of the Rhine interrupted transport columns in mid-December.[22]

This critical shortage was reported to the *I.SS-Panzer-Korps* headquarters on Friday, December 15. *Generalfeldmarschall* Model happened to be present at the corps headquarters, and he immediately ordered an emergency resupply. As a result, prior to the start of the offensive on Saturday, December 16, the *12.SS-Panzer-Division* had 1.3 fuel consumption units, theoretically capable of moving the division 130 kilometers. In practice, the actual range that this fuel allotment provided was heavily dependent on terrain. Extensive cross-country travel by the tanks cut the actual range by about half compared to road travel. The corps headquarters was concerned that the panzer divisions did not have enough fuel to reach the Meuse with the stocks on hand, though more was promised.[23]

12.SS-Panzer-Division "Hitlerjugend"

12.SS-Panzer-Division "Hitlerjugend"	Oberf. Hugo Kraas
SS-Panzer-Regiment.12	Stubaf. Herbert Kuhlmann
I./SS-Panzer-Regiment.12	Stubaf. Jürgensen
II./SS-Panzer-Regiment.12	Hstuf. Siegel
SS-Panzerjäger-Abteilung.12	Hstuf. Brockschmidt
SS-Panzergrenadier-Regiment.25	Stubaf. Siegfried Müller
I./SS-Panzergrenadier-Regiment.25	Hstuf. Ott
II./SS-Panzergrenadier-Regiment.25	Ostuf. R. Schulze
III./SS-Panzergrenadier-Regiment.25	Hstuf. Brückner
SS-Panzergrenadier-Regiment.26	Stubaf. Bernhard Krause
I./SS-Panzergrenadier-Regiment.26	Hstuf. Hein
II./SS-Panzergrenadier-Regiment.26	Hstuf. Hauschild
III./SS-Panzergrenadier-Regiment.26 (gep.)	Hstuf. Georg Urabl
SS-Panzeraufklärungs-Abteilung.12	Stubaf. Gerhard Bremer
SS-Panzer-Artillerie-Regiment.12	Ostubaf. Oskar Drexler
I./Pz.Art.Rgt.12	Stubaf. K. Müller
II./Pz.Art.Rgt.12	Stubaf. Neumann
III./Pz.Art.Rgt.12	Hstuf. Fritsch
SS-Werfer-Abteilung.12	Stubaf. W. Müller
SS-Flak-Abteilung.12	Stubaf. Loenicker
SS-Panzer-Pionier-Abteilung.12	Hstuf. Taubert
SS-Panzer-Nachrichtunen-Abteilung.12	Hstuf. Krüger

Waffen-SS Officer Rank Equivalents

Abbreviation	*Waffen-SS* Rank	German Army (*Heer*)	US/British Equivalent
Ostuf.	*Obersturmführer*	*Oberleutnant*	First Lieutenant
Hstuf.	*Hauptsturmführer*	*Hauptmann*	Captain
Stubaf.	*Sturmbannführer*	*Major*	Major
Ostubaf.	*Obersturmbannführer*	*Oberstleutnant*	Lieutenant Colonel
Staf.	*Standartenführer*	*Oberst*	Colonel
Oberf.	*Oberführer*	–	Brigadier

47

HITLERJUGEND'S BATTLE PLANS

The *12.SS-Panzer-Division "Hitlerjugend"* planned to deploy five battle groups (*Kampfgruppen*, or KG) to take advantage of the three road networks assigned to the division.[24] The northernmost, assigned to Rollbahn A, was *Kampfgruppe Ott*, consisting of *I./SS-Panzergrenadier-Regiment.25* and *SS-Panzerjäger-Abteilung.12*. This particular route started at the "Hollerath Knee," the bend in the International Highway near Hollerath. Upon leaving the Krinkelterwald forest, it exited near the "Twin Villages" of Krinkelt-Rocherath and continued on to Elsenborn. This was not an easy start point for mechanized units due to the absence of any decent roads except for some marginal forest paths before reaching the farmland around Krinkelt-Rocherath. In reality,

The *Sd.Kfz.251* armored half-track was used by most panzer divisions in the Ardennes, but usually in only one battalion per division. This is a radio-equipped *Sd.Kfz.251/3* command half-track of *Oberst* Johannes Bayer, leader of *Kampfgruppe Bayer* from *Panzer-Regiment.16, 116.Panzer-Division* in the Ardennes in mid-December 1944.

the divisional plan had little expectation that this battle group would have much success in advancing along Rollbahn A on the first day.[25] Its real mission was to serve as reinforcement for the *277.Volksgrenadier-Division* to help push it through the forest into Krinkelt-Rocherath.[26]

The attack along Rollbahn B was assigned to *Kampfgruppe Müller*. This consisted of the remainder of *SS-Panzergrenadier-Regiment 25*. The initial portion of Rollbahn B emanated from Udenbreth along one of the few good roads through the forest, a Class 3 road that exited the forest to the northwest of Rocherath before proceeding to Elsenborn.[27]

The strongest of the three columns was assigned to Rollbahn C, which began near Losheimergraben and then proceeded to Mürringen and Bütgenbach. The majority of divisional strength, a total of three

Many of the grenadiers in the *Hitlerjugend* were quite young, seventeen or eighteen years old. These two soldiers of the *12.SS-Panzer-Division* were captured in late December 1944.

battle groups, was assigned to Rollbahn C. *Kampfgruppe Kühlmann* was the most powerful battle group in the division and was composed of most of the division's panzer strength, including both *I./SS-Panzer-Regiment.12* and *s.Panzerjäger-Abteilung.560*. Besides these two units, *KG Kühlmann* also included a battalion from *SS-Panzergrenadier-Regiment.26*, a *Sturmgeschütz* battery, and a *Pionier* (engineer) company. The second column in this sector was *KG Bremer*, which consisted mainly of *SS-Panzer-Aufklärungs-Abteilung.12*, the mechanized reconnaissance battalion of the division. Finally, the third column was *KG Krause*, which contained the remainder of *SS-Panzergrenadier-Regiment .26* along with some supporting units. It was expected that the three battle groups would head along Rollbahn C in succession until reaching the open ground around Mürringen, at which point the columns could fan out to exploit the more open countryside.

In spite of the formidable training and equipment problems facing *I.SS-Panzer-Korps* in the execution of the Ardennes plans, there was a certain degree of optimism that the mission could succeed. The *Hitlerjugend* commander, Hugo Kraas, later wrote:

> The plan of attack for a penetration as far as Antwerp was ambitious, considering the forces at our disposal. It could only succeed if tactical surprise was complete, if the Allies had only small reserves at their immediate disposal, and if they did not take active counter-actions immediately. Nevertheless, in view of the promised support and the buoyancy displayed by the troops, the corps considered that there was every possibility of reaching the Meuse.[28]

Metal Storm

Although the focus of this book is the combat performance of the *12.SS-Panzer-Division* in the Ardennes, it is essential to understand the other elements of the combined-arms team that conducted the initial Ardennes attacks on December 16, 1944. This is especially true regarding the infantry and artillery. Since the infantry divisions of *I.SS-Panzer-Korps* were expected to make the initial penetration of the American defenses, their performance was critical to the

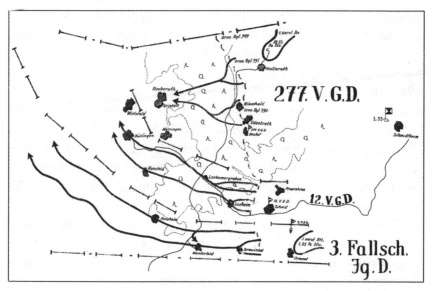

Break-In of the 99th Division Defenses, X-Day
This is the map prepared by the chief of staff of the *I.SS-Panzer-Korps*, Rudolf Lehmann, for the US Army Foreign Military Studies B-779 report showing the objective of the corps' three infantry divisions on X-Day, the initial day of the Ardennes offensive.

prospects of the *Hitlerjugend* to carry out their mission. The units most closely associated with the *Hitlerjugend* in the Ardennes were the *277.Volksgrenadier-Division*, which was supposed to open up Rollbahn A and B on the first day of the attack, and the *12.Volksgrenadier-Division*, assigned to the critical Rollbahn C.

THE *VOLKSGRENADIER* DIVISION

The two divisions leading the way for the *Hitlerjugend* were organized under a new configuration, the *Volksgrenadier* division. This new organization stemmed from the takeover of the Replacement Army (*Ersatzheer*) by Heinrich Himmler, the head of the Gestapo and the SS. The headquarters of the Replacement Army had been at the heart of the bomb plot against Hitler in July 1944. Himmler volunteered to root out dissident generals.

In September 1944, Himmler proposed to organize some of the new infantry divisions in the *Volksgrenadier* (People's Grenadier) configuration. The name stemmed from the Nazi Party's affection for applying the term *Volks* to all manner of things, such as the *Volks Artillerie-Korps*, *Volkssturm*, *Volksjäger*, and so on. The term became ubiquitous in late 1944. The *grenadier* portion of the new name came from Hitler as an allusion to the elite Grenadier troops of Frederick the Great.

In contrast to its glorified name, the *Volksgrenadier* was in effect a cheap alternative to conventional infantry divisions. Although Himmler was responsible for the name, the concept of a shriveled infantry division was inevitable in late 1944 due to the declining manpower available to the *Wehrmacht*.

The *Volksgrenadier* divisions were intended primarily for defensive missions on elongated fronts. They were not optimized for offensive missions due to inadequate transport. Due to manpower shortages, the organizational structure was cut back. Instead of the traditional nine infantry battalions in three infantry regiments, the structure was reduced to only six battalions. To make up for the smaller number of troops, the firepower of the division was supposed to be enhanced. This included plans to equip a larger portion of the riflemen with the new

Sturmgewehr 44 assault rifle. This was the ancestor of the modern assault rifle and gave the infantryman considerable more firepower than the usual bolt-action 98k rifle. The *Volksgrenadier* divisions were supposed to be favored in the appointment of regimental and battalion commanders and assigned young, combat-proven officers with a minimum of the German Cross in Gold, and preferably holders of the Knight's Cross or Iron Cross.

These changes sounded good on paper, but given the disastrous conditions in the autumn of 1944, most of the innovative features had to be sacrificed. There were not enough assault rifles to go around, and likewise, combat-experienced combat leaders were too few in number and in great demand.

Due to manpower shortages, an increasing number of men came from older age groups. This led to the joke among officers that the *Volksgrenadier* should be renamed the *Metalsturm*: "lead bones, gold teeth and silver hair."[1] *Metalsturm* (Metal Storm) was a mocking reference to the newly created *Volkssturm* militia, notorious in the army for its reliance on young boys and old men.

Morale in the German infantry was still good considering the circumstances. One of the staff officers from Model's Army Group B headquarters later recalled:

> The German soldier continued to fight on. He no longer had any great ideals. He still had a spark of faith in Hitler. He fought because there was nothing else to lose, and he was still searching for a last chance. By the autumn of 1944, there was scarcely a German family which had not suffered a casualty within the immediate family, or had not been bombed out and lost all their possessions. The German soldier was loath to have less conviction than those on the home front. Another motivation was the ever increasing amount of propaganda flowing from Hitler's headquarters to all the officers and troops. This propaganda was not based on fact: it was announced that in the near future there would be new weapons, masses of German fighter plans going into combat, U-boats in all the oceans . . .[2]

277.Volksgrenadier-Division

The original *277.Infanterie-Division* had been formed in November 1943 and was first deployed in southern France. At the end of June 1944, it was transferred to the Normandy front, fighting against the British in the Tilly sector near Caen. The division was encircled and largely destroyed in the Falaise pocket in August 1944, and the survivors were sent to Hungary to form the core of a reconstructed division.[3]

The number of survivors reaching Hungary is not clear. A divisional report from September 1 suggest that about 2,330 men, including about 1,000 infantrymen, were part of the initial rail transport back to the rear.[4] The divisional commander estimated their strength at 2,500, of whom about 1,000 were from the combat units and the remainder from administrative and support units; about 120 were officers.[5] The division's chief of operations recalled that the division reached Hungary "1,500 strong equipped with only rifles and a few machine guns."[6]

The division had a few experienced commanders such as the leader of *Grenadier-Regiment.990*, *Oberstleutnant* Josef Bremm. He had been decorated with the Oakleaves of the Knight's Cross of the Iron Cross on December 23, 1942, due to his exemplary leadership as an infantry battalion commander on the Russian Front. He was only the 165th recipient of this high award at the time.

The *277.Volksgrenadier-Division* was supposed to be ready by October 10, 1944, but this proved impossible due to the lack of replacements and the poor training facilities available in Hungary. Most of the replacement troops did not arrive until the last two weeks of October 1944. Up to this point, the infantry troops had received minimal training, and the divisional staff considered that the quality and training of the recruits was poor.[7] The division was instructed to move to the Eifel region in western Germany on October 30, 1944, well before it had reached full strength or was adequately trained. This process took far longer than expected since the rail lines from Hungary through Vienna had been disrupted by Allied bombing.

By November 10, 1944, about a third of the trains had arrived in western Germany, and the division began to be moved to the

Blankenheim sector in the Ardennes to relieve the *347.Infanterie-Division*. It was deployed along the old Westwall defense line in a sector 45 kilometers (28 miles) wide, far more than was judged prudent in usual infantry doctrine. While deployed on the Westwall, the divisional strength was increased by transfers of young sailors and naval personnel from the *Kriegsmarine*.

Commander of the *277.Volksgrenadier-Division*, *Generalmajor* Wilhelm Viebig.

The *277.Volksgrenadier-Division* spent much of its time in late November and early December pulling companies out of the line in the hopes of providing the inexperienced troops with some minimal amount of tactical training. The divisional commander, Wilhelm Viebig, described the status of their training:

During the four weeks of deployment on the Westwall, the division became well versed in defensive missions. Several companies were trained for small scale offensive missions, namely counter-attacks. There was still a serious shortage of small unit commanders [squad and platoon]. The Volksdeutsche and Alsatians were an untrustworthy element, and the fighting spirit of some of the [Austrian] men originating from the Vienna area was also low.[8]

The *Volksdeutsche* mentioned by Viebig were supposed to be ethnic Germans who lived in areas outside of Germany and were eligible to be drafted into the *Wehrmacht*. The manpower situation in 1944 had become so desperate that non-Germans who lived in regions annexed to Germany, such as Poles from Pomerania and Silesia, were also recruited.[9] Often, they spoke no German. They deeply resented German army service after enduring years of brutal practices during the German occupation of their homelands. Alsatians were also drafted in 1944. Alsace had changed hands three times between Germany and France since the 1870 Franco-Prussian War and World War II, so national identification was complicated. Although there were few problems with Alsatian troops on the Russian Front, their deployment to the Western Front was more troublesome, usually leading to many desertions. The situation became serious enough in the weeks before the Ardennes offensive that some units were told to keep their Alsatian troops away from the front lines for fear that they would desert and reveal the planned attack.[10]

Since the *277. Volksgrenadier-Division* was raised in the lands of the old Austro-Hungarian empire, it had a significant Austrian content. The German army was skeptical about Austrian recruits since they generally lacked the pre-induction paramilitary training conducted in Germany, and they were regarded as less enthusiastic soldiers than Germans. Friction also arose when young Austrian lieutenants were put in charge of platoons with experienced German NCOs.

This was also evident from American reports of deserters from the unit. A typical example from late November 1944 was a group of five deserters from the division's *Grenadier-Regiment.989* near Losheim.[11] Of the five, one was German, four were Austrians. Three were drafted

The intended armament of the *Volksgrenadier* divisions was the StG 44 assault rifle. However, production in 1944 was too small to meet the demand, and it remained a relatively rare weapon at the time of the Ardennes offensive.

early in the war, fought in France in 1940, and then were released for "essential industry," two to farming and one to industry. They were then brought back into service due to the shortage of infantry. Two others remained in the army, were wounded or hospitalized for service injuries such as frostbite, and then brought back into infantry service after extensive hospital stays. The five men formed an isolated outpost in Losheim, and after not having received food for three days, they decided to desert.

Even the troops from Germany could be a problem. As in many units at this time, the German replacements came from idle *Kriegsmarine* units. Viebig later noted that "it was easier and quicker to train a young civilian than a naval petty officer who had spent four years sitting on a warship in port and who could not understand why he should die the death of an infantryman in the last year of the war."[12]

When committed to combat in the Ardennes on December 16, 1944, the division had been brought to a strength of 7,249 men, about 72 percent its authorized strength.[13] In April 1944, the Wehrmacht adopted a simplified method for rating the combat value (*Kampfwert*) of divisions on a sliding scale of 1 to 4.[14] *Kampfwert* 1 indicated suitable for offensive missions; 2 indicated limited suitability for offensive missions; 3 was suitable for defense; and 4 was limited suitability for defense. At the start of the Ardennes offensive, the *277.Volksgrenadier-Division* was rated at *Kampfwert* 3, suitable for defense.[15] This assessment is significant since it was a tacit admission that the division was unprepared to conduct its offensive mission at the start of the Ardennes attack.

277.Volksgrenadier-Division Organization, December 1944	
Division Commander	*Oberst* Wilhelm Viebig
Division Operations Officer	*Oberstleutnant* Horst Freiherr von Wangenheim
Grenadier Regiment-989	*Oberst* Georg Fieger
Grenadier-Regiment.990	*Oberstleutnant* Josef Bremm
Grenadier-Regiment.991	*Oberstleutnant* Otto Jaquet
Divisions-Füsilier-Kompanie.277	*Hauptmann* Gerhard Hellige
Artillerie-Regiment.277	*Major* Karl-Erich Kienzler
Panzerjäger-Abteilung.277	*Hauptmann* Heinz Grawunder
Pionier Bataillon.277	*Major* Georg Bienert
Nachrichtungs-Abteilung.277	*Hauptmann* Schildt
Versorgungs-Regiment.277	*Major* Schaab

Viebig and the divisional staff were briefed on the Autumn Mist plan during the first week of December 1944. Details were confined to the senior officers. The mission was to penetrate the American main line of resistance in the forests between Hollerath and Udenbreth in advance of the *12.SS-Panzer-Division* and to capture the Twin Villages of Krinkelt-Rocherath. Once these initial missions were accomplished, the division was to push over the Elsenborn Ridge toward Verviers.

Having been stationed in this sector for several weeks, Viebig made several comments on the plan: "In my report regarding the enemy and our positions as well as the difficult terrain conditions, I emphasized that success could only be expected with very strong artillery support. The main prerequisite was elimination, or at least suppression, of the enemy artillery positions that we had [already] encountered."[16]

Viebig was assured that his attack would be preceded by a heavy artillery preparation and that the division would receive the support of *Sturmgeschütz* assault guns from the corps reserve.

In the weeks prior to the start of the Ardennes offensive, the division stretched from Huppenbroich in the north to Udenbreth in the south. Most of its positions corresponded to those of the American 99th Infantry Division, who would be their opponents in the Ardennes fighting a month later. This sector was relatively quiet, with both sides conducting reconnaissance patrols and occasional artillery duels.

12. VOLKSGRENADIER-DIVISION

In contrast to the anonymous and uncelebrated *277.VGD*, the *12.Volks-grenadier-Division* was one of the most famous German infantry units in the West. It was the only infantry division that Hitler specifically earmarked to take part in the Ardennes offensive.

The original *12.Infanterie-Division* was one of the oldest divisions in the *Wehrmacht*, formed in 1934 and continuously engaged in combat in the 1939 Polish campaign, the 1940 French campaign, and the 1941 invasion of the Soviet Union. The division remained on the Russian Front for most of the war, fighting in the Demyansk pocket in 1942 and eventually being overrun and destroyed in the summer of 1944 during the Red Army's Operation Bagration offensive.

Some of the staff from the old division escaped the encirclement in Belarus, including two of its regimental commanders, *Major* Wilhelm Osterhold and *Oberstleutnant* Heinz-Georg Lemm. Both officers had been decorated with the Knight's Cross. During an August 1944 meeting at the Führer Headquarters, they were able to convince the new army chief of staff, *General* Heinz Guderian, to reconstitute the division. They also urged Guderian to assign Gerhard Engel as the new commander. He had been a military aide to Hitler in 1941–43 and had commanded *Füsilier-Regiment.27* before Lemm.[17] Osterhold later explained their interest in Engel's appointment:

> He had influence, he knew everybody, he knew [defense minister Albert] Speer and we will be equipped with more weapons than he can bear. In that context he was useful. Otherwise, he was a man of ordinary talents . . . he was not an overwhelming man. He was a nice man and gave us more influence. We wanted him and that gave us more independence and influence on the decisions of the division.[18]

Generalfeldmarschall Walter Model, commander of Army Group B, having a chat with *Generalmajor* Gerhard Engel, commander of the *12.Volksgrenadier-Division.*

The division was re-created in East Prussia in the late summer of 1944 and sent to the Roer front in western Germany in mid-September 1944. US intelligence assessments consistently rated the division higher than average, a testament to Osterhold's and Lemm's success in leveraging better-quality troops and equipment as a result of Engel's connections.

The division fought along the Westwall as part of the *7.Armee*, and in early October 1944 it was committed to the defense of Aachen. Hitler was particularly interested in Aachen's fate due to its symbolic importance. Not only was it the first German city threatened with capture, but it was once the seat of power of Charlemagne. The *12.Infanterie-Division* particularly distinguished itself in the fighting, and Hitler decided to change its name to the *12.Volksgrenadier-Division* in honor of its performance.

Hitler's interest in the division was both a blessing and a curse. It did receive far better equipment than the average infantry division, including a large supply of the new *Sturmgewehr 44* assault rifles. This was the world's first assault rifle and significantly increased infantry firepower. At the same time, Hitler used the division as his fire brigade, deploying it to the hottest sections of the Western Front. In November and December 1944, it took part in the fighting along the Roer river near Düren and Jülich and suffered such heavy losses during the seventeen days of fighting that it was withdrawn from combat on December 2–3, 1944. Engel later described the conditions in the division at the time:

> The 12th was badly battered and fit for neither offensive or defensive action at the time of being relieved. Most of its infantry units had lost two-thirds of their strength. All its other units had also suffered severe losses in the course of the third battle of Aachen . . . We had lost up to 90 percent of the infantry's automatic weapons and losses in mortars, infantry guns and anti-tank weapons amounted to similar percentages. The Panzerjäger Abteilung was down to six assault guns instead of the twenty authorized and these were not only partially fit for service.[19]

The division needed relief, because after 17 days of major fighting, it was completely exhausted. In the infantry, all [three] regiments were worn out, having no replacements during the battle. The companies had a combat strength of 15–20 men at most [of an authorized strength of 128 men]. Experience on both the Eastern and Western Fronts had proven it unwise to combine units since only by keeping the cadres intact was it possible to reconstruct the units. The total strength of the infantry regiments, including the heavy weapons units, was between 200 and 300 men [of an authorized strength of 1,911 men]. The casualties of the division since 16 November totaled 2,500 men wounded and killed; the number of men missing-in-action, however, was strikingly low [meaning few soldiers surrendering to the Americans]. The artillery was more intact than other combat arms. Of the 12 guns per battery, they averaged 3 operational . . . The anti-tank gun company had only 2 of its 12 anti-tank guns.[20]

The division was kept in the Roer area for rebuilding. About 500 wounded troops returned to the division from the hospital along with about 3,000 new replacements.

These replacements consisted mainly of men taken from staffs, from the Replacement Army, and men previously labeled as indispensable [to industry]. They were by no means sufficiently trained. Supplies of materiel also arrived, and small arms as well as heavy infantry weapons were replaced comparatively quickly. But as far as anti-tank weapons were concerned, the situation was more difficult. The urgently-requested assault guns, indispensable as close-support weapons for the infantry, did not arrive . . . In spite of all the difficulties, the rest period was used by the infantry companies for training on a modest scale, and occasional small arms practice with live ammunition to accustom the new men to actual fighting.[21]

When committed to combat in the Ardennes on December 16, 1944, the division had been brought to a strength of 9,517 men, about 94 percent its authorized strength. On December 11, Engel and the

Many of the infantry in the *6.Panzer-Armee* were quite young. These two soldiers, both under seventeen years old, were probably from *3.Fallschirmjäger-Division*. They were captured near Weywertz, west of Bütgenbach, by the 3rd Battalion, 16th Infantry, 1st Infantry Division.

other divisional commanders were summoned to Rundstedt's OB West headquarters at Bad Neuheim for their first briefing on the role of their divisions in the forthcoming Autumn Mist offensive. Hitler personally explained the goals of the offensive.

Engel's division was given one of the most important assignments of the infantry units of *I.SS-Panzer-Korps*, to push up from Losheim through Losheimergraben. This would provide the access for *12.SS-Panzer-Division* to Rollbahn C, which was by far the best road network in the area. As mentioned earlier, the majority of the mechanized units of the *Hitlerjugend* were expected to use Rollbahn C to reach the Meuse river. It was essential that this objective be captured quickly for the schedule to be maintained.

The German infantry remained dependent on horse transport throughout the war. This is a *Grosser Gefechtswagen Hf. 7/11,* which had a carrying capacity of up to 1,700 kilograms.

12. Volksgrenadier-Division

12. Volksgrenadier-Division	*Generalmajor* Gerhard Engel
Füsilier-Regiment.27	*Oberstleutnant* Heinz-Georg Lemm
Grenadier-Regiment.48	*Oberstleutnant* Wilhelm Osterhold
Grenadier-Regiment.89	*Major* Otto Benzin
Artillerie-Regiment.12	*Oberstleutnant* Erwin Böhm
I./Artillerie-Regiment.48	
Pionier-Bataillon.12	
Panzerjäger-Abteilung.12	

Assessment

The ability of the *12.SS–Panzer–Division* to fulfill its mission and reach the Meuse river objective was highly dependent on the ability of the *277.Volksgrenadier–Division* and *12.Volksgrenadier–Division*, with heavy artillery support, to overcome the American main line of resistance. The probability of accomplishing this mission was substantially undermined by the shortcomings of the infantry divisions assigned to the initial breakthrough. The *277. Volksgrenadier-Division* was assessed as only being suitable for defensive missions, lacking trained troops and sufficient small-unit combat leaders to be effective in an offensive mission. The *12. Volksgrenadier-Division*, while somewhat stronger on paper, had been exhausted in previous fighting and hastily reinforced without adequate time to train or integrate its new replacements.

Fire Waltz

THE DECLINING QUALITY OF GERMAN INFANTRY DIVISIONS INCREASED the need for powerful artillery support. Viebig pointed this out, as mentioned in the previous chapter, and this view was widely shared among the senior German commanders. Indeed, field artillery proved to be a decisive arm in the Ardennes campaign, so it is worth taking a more detailed look at this often-ignored combat arm.

15 CM SCHWERE
FELDHAUBITZE sFH 18

10.5 CM LEICHTE
FELDHAUBITZE LFH 18/40

German infantry division field artillery included three light battalions of the 10.5cm IFH 18/40 and one medium battalion of the 15cm sFH 18, with each battalion having twelve field guns.

Gerhard Engel, commander of the *12.Volksgrenadier-Division*, reflected on the dominance of artillery in the previous fighting against the US Army along the western German frontier in November–December 1944:

The battle soon demonstrated that this was not primarily a battle between the front-line [infantry] troops, but one of materiel. The German troops could hardly have been expected to succeed in the defense had it been appreciated beforehand the amount of weapons and ammunition the enemy expended against them. On the German side as well, the battle was not dominated by the infantry. Although our stockpiles were insufficient, our fights had to be conducted with materiel. So the third battle of Aachen was dominated by artillery. While completely acknowledging the heroic struggle of the infantry, it still must be recognized that the success of the defense was achieved by artillery in practically all cases. Under strict and skillful direction, our artillery smashed enemy concentrations; with well-controlled barrage fire it stopped enemy attacks; during the final days of the battle it halted the enemy attacks with direct fire.[1]

The head of artillery under Rundstedt's OB West headquarters further emphasized this perspective:

Owing to the bloody losses and uninterrupted, maximum psychological strain in the heavy defensive battles often several weeks in duration, the German infantry continuously lost combat power. More and more, the defense depended upon artillery. It many cases, it decided the issue. It was estimated that the artillery bore sixty to eighty percent of the combat burden. The battles around Aachen in the winter of 1944 were the same.[2]

Artillery support for the initial break-in phase of the Ardennes offensive came from two principal sources: divisional artillery and heavy artillery at corps and field army level, sometimes called GHQ (General Headquarters) artillery.

German and American infantry divisions contained their own artillery units. These were very similar in caliber and numbers of guns. German infantry divisions typically deployed an artillery regiment that included four artillery battalions. Three of these were usually equipped with some variant of the 105mm *leichte Feld Haubitze 18* (light field

The backbone of the German field artillery was the 105mm *leichte Feld Haubitze 18*. This is the basic horse-drawn variant used through the war. There were usually three battalions of these per infantry division.

howitzer Model 1918), typically in its modernized lFH 18/40 form.[3] There were twelve of these howitzers in each battalion, for a total of thirty-six per division. The fourth battalion was typically equipped with the heavier 150mm *schwere Feld Haubitze 18* (heavy field howitzer Model 1918), with twelve per battalion. In contrast to regular infantry divisions, the first battalion in each *Volksgrenadier* artillery regiment was equipped with three batteries of eighteen of the 75mm *Feldkanone 40* instead of the usual twelve 105mm howitzers. This field gun never reached the production stage, and so the standard 75mm PaK 40 antitank gun was substituted instead. The *277.Volksgrenadier-Division* followed this pattern.

The basic IFH 18 105mm field gun was upgraded with a new carriage to permit motorized towing as the IFH 18/40. This version was in widespread service with the *Volksgrenadier* divisions in 1944.

The *12.SS-Panzer-Division* on paper was authorized self-propelled guns for its artillery regiment, but these were no longer in production. As a result, it had three battalions of truck-towed 105mm lFH 18/40 and one battalion of half-track-towed 150mm sFH 18. The *Waffen-SS* panzer divisions had an additional complement of artillery beyond that in *Heer* divisions, including an additional battery of four 100mm guns and a separate *Werfer* battalion equipped with twenty-four multibarrel *Nebelwerfer* rocket launchers.[4] Another difference from infantry artillery regiments was that each of the artillery battalions had a specially equipped tank for its forward observer, called a *Beobachtungspanzer IV*. This was essentially the same as the *PzKpfw IV* tank, but had additional optical devices and radios for its mission. Usually there were four in the artillery regiment, one for each battalion.

CORPS ARTILLERY

Beyond the divisional artillery, there was usually an additional grouping of artillery at corps and field army level. German artillery was highly centralized as a means to maximize its firepower and effectiveness. Under ideal circumstances, the divisional field artillery and the separate corps artillery formations were coordinated under a corps-level headquarters called the *Artilleriekommandeur* (ARKO). This command system could offer the corps commander an artillery fire plan to provide supporting fire along the whole corps so that the individual batteries and battalions would mutually support each other. Thanks to the unity of command provided by the Arko, it was possible to quickly direct a large number of batteries to a specific target from several directions.

The standard heavy cannon of German divisions was the sFH 18 150mm howitzer. There was usually a single battalion of twelve of these in each infantry or panzer division. This was the second-most-common type of field gun in German service, with 129 in use by units of the *6.Panzer-Armee* in the Ardennes in 1944.

In the case of the *6.Panzer-Armee* in the Ardennes, this was taken one step further with all the divisional and corps firepower concentrated at the field army level under a single HARKO (*Heeres Artilleriekommandeur*, or army artillery commander) led by *Generalleutnant* Walter Staudinger. The aim was to create an extremely powerful artillery reserve that would be concentrated on the *Schwerpunkt*.

Several innovations in German artillery saw their debut in the West in the Ardennes. Among these were the *Volks-Artillerie-Korps* (VAK) and *Volks-Werfer-Brigade* (VWB). The name for the VAK was far grander than its actual composition. In reality, it was a reconfiguration of the of the 1944 artillery brigade, and not a corps-size formation as its name would suggest. The VAK came in different configurations, and those assigned to the *6.Panzer-Armee* included two of the fully motorized type and one of the semi-mobile type. Usually there were three light battalions and two or three heavy battalions in these units.[5]

The specific composition of the artillery attached to the *6.Panzer-Armee* is detailed in the accompanying charts. One problem that was encountered when trying to create these units was that there was an insufficient supply of German guns for the heavy battalions. Instead, war-booty Soviet guns were used, including the 122mm sFH 396(r) (Soviet M-30) and 152mm *Kanone 433(r)* (Soviet ML-20). While these cannon were of good quality, ammunition supply was a problem. According to *Generalleutnant* Staudinger, "The difficulties of supplying and transporting the ammunition for the non-German guns resulted in the unfortunate and inevitable consequence that almost always, one or two of the VAK battalions were out of action on account of the lack of ammunition."[6]

The *Volks-Werfer-Brigade* was a new type of multiple-rocket launcher unit and generally included three battalions (twelve batteries) with a total of seventy-two 150mm light multiple rocket launchers and one or two battalions (six batteries) totaling thirty-six heavy 210mm launchers. As in the case of the VAK, they came in both fully motorized and semi-mobile configurations.

The *6.Panzer-Armee* was supported by three *Volks-Artillerie-Korps* and three *Volks-Werfer-Brigaden*. These were supplemented with four heavy mortar batteries that employed very heavy siege guns or heavy mortars, usually three per battery. There was also a single *Festung-Artillerie-Batterie* in the area with two 240mm guns from the old Westwall defenses. About two-thirds of the non-divisional artillery of the *6.Panzer-Armee* was committed to support the *I.SS-Panzer-Korps* on the opening days of the Ardennes offensive, including two *Volks-Artillerie-Korps* and two *Volks-Werfer-Brigaden.*[7]

6.Panzer-Armee GHQ Artillery, December 1944[8]

*Volks-Artillerie-Korps.388 (mot.)**	*Oberstleutnant* Hermann Grusche
Volks-Artillerie-Korps.402 (mot.)	*Oberst* Erich Schmidt
Volks-Artillerie-Korps.405 (t. bew.)	*Oberst* Reismüller
Volks-Werfer-Brigade.4 (mot.)	
Volks-Werfer-Brigade.9 (mot.)	*Oberstleutnant* Martin Beyrich
Volks-Werfer-Brigade.17 (t. bew.)	
Heeres-Mörser-Batterie.428 (mot.)	
Heeres-Mörser-Batterie.1098 (bo.)	
Heeres-Mörser-Batterie.1100 (bo.)	
Heeres-Mörser-Batterie.1120 (bo.)	

(mot.)= motorized; (t. bew.) = semi-mobile; (bo.)= static

Volks-Artillerie-Korps Weapons[9]

VAK.388	VAK.402	VAK.405
7 x 75mm *Feldkanone*	16 x 75mm *Feldkanone*	18 x 75mm *Feldkanonen 40*
18 x 88mm PaK		
17 x 105mm IFH	18 x 105mm IFH	18 x 105mm IFH 18/40
12 x 122mm sFH 396 (r)	12 x 100mm *Kanone 18*	12 x 100mm *Kanone 18*
22 x 150mm sFH	12 x 122mm sFH 396 (r)	12 x 122mm sFH 396 (r)
6 x 210mm *Mörser 18*; 3 x 170mm *Kanone 18*	10 x 152mm FH 433 (r)	12 x 152mm FH 433 (r)

6.*Panzer-Armee* Divisional and GHQ Artillery by Type[10]	
Type	Total
75mm FK40	95
88mm PaK 43	18
100mm K18	41
105mm lFH 18/40	324
122mm sFH 396 (r)	22
150mm sFH 18	129
152mm KH433 (r)	22
170mm K18, Mrs L	3
210mm Mrs 18	6
220mm Mrs 531 (f)	3
240mm K3	2
305mm Mrs (t)	3
355mm M1	3
600mm Mrs	2
Artillery subtotal	**673**
Rocket Launchers	
150mm *Werfer 41* (6–8 tube)	214
210mm *Werfer 21* (5 tube)	108
300mm *Werfer 42* (6 tube)	18
Rocket subtotal (# tubes)	**340 (1,996)**

Overall, divisional field artillery represented about 65 percent of the artillery available to the 6.*Panzer Armee*, while the various GHQ artillery units represented the rest as well as nearly all of the rocket-launcher artillery. During the opening phase of the Ardennes battle, the German artillery outnumbered the American artillery about three to one, 1,013 to 314.

One of the most serious problems in the German artillery during the Ardennes campaign was a severe shortage of trained officers. Officer staffing was about 60 percent of authorized strength and NCO staffing about 70 percent.[11] Furthermore, many of the officer and NCO replacements were not adequately trained.

For specialized long-range firepower, the corps artillery of the *Wehrmacht* used the heavy 170mm *Kanone 18*, which had an effective range of 28 kilometers (17 miles). This was not a common weapon, and the *6.Panzer-Armee* had only three in *Volks-Artillerie-Korps.388*.

Aside from the actual field pieces, the combat effectiveness of field artillery depended on many other factors including command and control, mobility, and ammunition supply. Divisional artillery in the *Volksgrenadier* divisions relied primarily on field telephones for communication between the batteries and higher headquarters. This was a tried-and-true method since the Great War, and was fairly reliable except for occasions when enemy artillery managed to cut lines during counter-battery exchanges.

The German artillery did employ radios to link the forward observers and forward infantry units with the divisional artillery, but this was not especially effective in the initial fighting in the Ardennes in 1944. Although the *Wehrmacht* led the way in radios for command-and-control at the start of the war, they had fallen badly behind by 1944. One of the reasons was that German industry could simply not produce the massive number of dry-cell batteries needed for daily operation of thousands of small tactical radios. The infantry company was not allotted radios until the October 1943 KStN, which authorized two Feldfu. b (*Feldfunksprecher* b) radios.[12] This was a backpack AM radio weighing 13 kilograms (29 pounds) with an effective range of about a kilometer. The December 1943 KStN increased the authorization to four, with the allotment usually being one to each platoon. The usual practice for requesting artillery support would be for the close-combat units such as platoons and companies to use couriers or radio or field telephones to contact artillery liaison officers via the infantry battalion headquarters, with the requests then passed up the line. The process was more time-consuming than that of the US Army, which had a far larger number of tactical radios that accelerated the fire support process.

Regardless of the official tables of equipment, the *Volksgrenadier* divisions suffered from a frequent shortage of radios, so many units never even received the authorized amount.[13] The German infantry radios were relatively low-power.[14] Their performance in wooded areas was often poor, and so infantry troops would lay field telephone wire as they advanced to provide a continuous link with higher headquarters. This was essential to permit the advancing troops to call in artillery fire and other support.

The use of artillery forward observers during offensive campaigns was not as widespread in the German army as in the US Army, partly due to the heavier weight of German tactical radios, which encumbered the forward observer. This was noted by a senior German artillery commander: "A forward observer attached to an attacking infantry battalion or regiment is taxed beyond his physical power since he must carry a two-way radio, binoculars, compass, map, and firing table, side arm and entrenching tool, etc. while at the same time observing the terrain and protecting himself from enemy small arms fire."[15]

At corps and field army level, a number of innovations were introduced around the time of the Ardennes campaign aimed at improving the coordination of multiple battalions and batteries. The *Kopplungs-gerät* was introduced into the corps-level fire control batteries late in 1943. This device computed range and deflection in connection with a firing table or map for several batteries and automatically transmitted the data via wire or radio teletype, which considerably sped up target plotting and coordination. This formed the basis for the new fire control batteries that were introduced after February 1944 to assist in massing fires in the corps artillery. However, the *6.Panzer-Armee* had only one of these batteries in the Ardennes in 1944, hampering the ability to coordinate massed fires. In addition, the artillery headquarters that was supposed to coordinate the various batteries and battalions of the corps artillery did not have its own communications network and was forced to rely on the overburdened signals regiment of the *6.Panzer-Armee* headquarters.[16]

German artillery intelligence at the start of the Ardennes campaign was poor. As mentioned earlier, the November tactical instructions from Berlin forbade the conduct of deep reconnaissance in the Ardennes and also reduced the tempo of tactical patrolling and raids to secure prisoners to maintain the pretense that the Ardennes was a quiet front. The *6.Panzer-Armee* had four artillery observation battalions assigned to it, which attempted to gather targeting data prior to the start of the campaign.[17] The general lack of *Luftwaffe* photo reconnaissance and instructions to avoid using artillery-spotting balloons limited the collection of targeting data before the start of the offensive. As a result, older, traditional forms of targeting were used, primarily sound and flash ranging, to locate American field artillery positions. Since the American infantry defenses in the Elsenborn sector were located in the woods, the German field artillery had no accurate data on the location of major strongpoints. Artillery preparation at the start of the offensive was limited to fire strikes against likely locations, which wasted much of the ammunition, or fire strikes against predictable targets such as road junctions and other fixed terrain features.

Mobility in German divisional artillery units was old-fashioned and not as extensively motorized as in the US Army. There was a general lack of cross-country vehicles in December 1944. The artillery regiments in the *Volksgrenadier* division used a mixture, with the standard establishment including 99 motor vehicles and 285 horse-drawn vehicles.

Ammunition supply at the start of the Ardennes campaign was not generous. German artillery ammunition allotments were measured as *Ausstattung*, which was a standardized figure for the amount of ammunition needed for three days of average fighting or one day of intense fighting.[18] This is roughly equivalent to the US Army term "unit of fire." A single unit of fire (*1.Munition Ausstattung*) for a 105mm light field howitzer was 225 rounds, or 2,700 rounds for a twelve-gun battalion. The unit of fire for the 150mm sFH 18 field howitzer was 150 rounds, for a total of 1,800 rounds per battalion. As a result, the unit of fire for a divisional artillery regiment was 9,900 rounds.[19] The unit of fire for the *Volks-Werfer-Brigade* was 4,000 150mm rockets and 1,000 210mm rockets.

The most common German artillery multiple rocket launcher was the six-tube 150mm *Nebelwerfer 41*. This fired a 34-kilogram (75-pound) rocket to a range of about 7 kilometers (4 miles). There were 214 of these in the *Volks-Werfer-Brigaden* of the *6.Panzer-Armee* in the Ardennes.

Generally, an artillery regiment would carry one unit of fire in the regiment's own vehicles, and a second would be carried on the divisional supply train. The Autumn Mist plan allotted two units of fire for the start of the campaign, but in practice only one was on hand at the start of the offensive.[20] Of this, a half-unit of fire was assigned to the initial thirty-minute artillery preparation, except at corps level where there was up to three-quarter unit.[21] Most of the artillery officers thought that this was inadequate for the mission, especially in light of the lack of precise targeting information. The total campaign allotment was promised for fourteen days, but only ten days was actually provided, much of it stored in ammo dumps in the Bonn area.[22] These ammunition reserves were frequently inaccessible during the course of the campaign due to the traffic jams that will be described in more detail later.

The *Volks-Werfer-Brigaden* were allotted three units of fire at the start of the offensive, totaling 12,000 rounds of 150mm rockets and 4,000 rounds of 210mm rockets.[23] The shortages were most severe in the heavy howitzer units of the GHQ artillery. Army Group B had been promised 116,500 heavy howitzer rounds, but only 30,000 rounds were delivered by the start of the attack.

In general, the US artillery was not impressed by its German opponent. A 1945 assessment prepared by the VII Corps artillery summarized the American view:

> The German artillery has not been able to cope with American artillery. It lacks especially the organization for massing of fires, the communications, and the airplane observation which characterizes American artillery. He is now terrifically handicapped by transportation trouble due to the loss of motors and horses and shortage of gasoline. The counter-battery fire received from German artillery to date has been negligible. Massed fires are rare and brief. Harassing programs have been inaccurate and incomplete. It has been obvious again and again that an observer must be close to his guns in order to conduct fire. German artillery fires which fell ineffectively in plain view of German OP [observation post] positions with good visibility, and which with slight correction would have been very damaging for

us, have continued to fall into the wrong place. The most common form of fire has been the single gun. The accurately adjusted fire of one battery, which would usually mean slightly more difficult communications from one observer to battery than fire by a single gun, has been much less frequent. A concentration by more than one battery has been rare, even in the Aachen area at a time when there were approximately 25 battalions of German artillery in front of VII Corps.[24]

A German artilleryman loads a 150mm rocket into a *Nebelwerfer 41*.

After the Ardennes campaign, the artillery commander of the *6.Panzer-Armee*, *Generalleutnant der Waffen-SS* Walter Staudinger, offered his lessons about the artillery in the Ardennes campaign:[25]

1. The training of *Waffen-SS* artillery officers was inadequate, and the *Waffen-SS* lacked the cadre of trained artillery officers that the *Heer* (regular army) enjoyed.

2. The enlisted personnel of the *Waffen-SS* artillery were not well trained and there were too many *Volksdeutsche* not even conversant in German.

3. The supply of artillery equipment prior to the offensive was slow and wasteful, depriving the new troops of training time. Lack of fuel impaired driver training.

4. The Autumn Mist plans degraded the tactical potential of the artillery.

5. The lack of targeting intelligence and the prohibition against registration fires prior to the offensive was a problem.

6. The decision to begin the preparation fires in the predawn darkness removed any chance for fire adjustment during the preparatory barrage.

7. The lack of artillery-spotting aircraft or balloons squandered ammunition and diminished accuracy.

8. The failure of the *Luftwaffe* to provide air support allowed the Allied air force to attack German artillery. Air attacks slowed the movement of German artillery units, and combined with ammunition and fuel shortages, led to catastrophic conditions.

9. The supply situation was debilitating, with units having to send their trucks back more than 100 kilometers to collect needed ammunition.

10. Ammunition supplies were completely inadequate, seldom more than two to three *Kampfsätz* (combat sets; e.g., six rounds for a 105mm howitzer).

11. No effort was made to provide snowplows or other snow-clearing equipment.

12. The lack of a prime mover reserve made it very difficult to move the GHQ artillery.

13. There had been no preparation of artillery positions.

14. The centralization of artillery command under the HARKO and ARKO had proven to be correct.

15. The prohibition against splitting up the *Volks-Artillerie-Korps* and *Volks-Werfer-Brigaden* had proven to be correct.

ARMORED FIRE SUPPORT

Armored support for the German infantry divisions was less generous than in the US Army. Each infantry division was supposed to incorporate a single *Panzerjäger* battalion, which contrary to its name, was not simply a tank destroyer unit but rather a general-purpose fire support unit. It usually included a company of assault guns and a company of towed anti-tank guns. Due to a shortage of the standard *StuG III* assault gun, most *Volksgrenadier* divisions received its cheap substitute, the *Jagdpanzer 38*, sometimes called the *Hetzer*. This vehicle was built at one of two factories in the occupied Czech Republic and consisted of a chassis derived from the prewar Czech *PzKpfw 38(t)* light tank fitted with a fixed casemate and armed with a 75mm gun. Its *Jagdpanzer* name was a complete misnomer foisted on the army by its new chief of staff, Heinz Guderian, who had been involved in a running feud with the infantry branch over the gradual absorption of more and more armored vehicle production away from his favored tanks and to the infantry's favored assault guns. In the event, the *Jagdpanzer 38* was intended from the outset as an assault gun for infantry support. It was never a very popular vehicle compared to the *StuG III* assault gun since it was very cramped inside and had poor side armor.

A few assault-gun units were usually attached at corps or army level, generally less than one per infantry division. This was similar to the US Army pattern of deploying separate tank and tank destroyer battalions at corps level and then doling them out to the infantry divisions as they were needed. Although the pattern was the same, the German allotment of armored vehicles to the infantry was invariably less generous than in the US Army due to a perennial shortage of vehicles. On February 14, 1944, the army instituted a cosmetic change to the assault-gun unit designation, renaming them from *Abteilung* (battalion) to *Sturmgeschütz Brigade*. This was purely a propaganda move, and there was no change in unit strength. These brigades contained thirty-one assault guns (three batteries of ten vehicles plus one command vehicle), though a handful were expanded to an enlarged configuration with forty-five assault guns (three companies with fourteen vehicles plus one staff vehicle).

These brigades were assigned to the infantry divisions as needed rather than permanently attaching them to the units. The advantage of this arrangement was that a larger mass of assault guns could be employed to support a particularly vital operation. The disadvantage was that assault-gun brigades did not regularly interact with the infantry formations they supported, often making tactical coordination more difficult. During the critical first days of the Ardennes offensive, the assault-gun brigades were often absent from the battlefield since they were given a lower priority in road traffic compared to the panzer divisions.

Most of the assault-gun brigades were equipped with the *StuG III*, a *PzKpfw III* tank chassis with a fixed casemate, armed with a 75mm gun.

The five-tube 210mm *Nebelwerfer 42* fired a 112-kilogram (245-pound) rocket to a range of about 8 kilometers (5 miles). There were 108 of these in the *Volks-Werfer-Brigaden* of the *6.Panzer-Armee*.

A few were equipped with the *StuG IV*, essentially the same vehicle but on a *PzKpfw IV* chassis. A few specialty support units were attached to the *6.Panzer-Armee*, including a *Sturmpanzer* battalion equipped with the *Sturmpanzer IV*. This was armed with a short 150mm gun. There was also a single *Sturmtiger* company. The *Sturmtiger* consisted of a *Tiger* tank chassis with a fixed casemate, armed with a 380mm rocket-assisted demolition projectile.

6.Panzer-Armee Armored Support Units

Sturmgeschütz-Brigade.394
Sturmgeschütz-Brigade.667
Sturmgeschütz-Brigade.902
Sturmpanzer-Abteilung.217
Sturmmörser-Kompanie.1000

ASSESSMENT

Due to the weaknesses in the German infantry assigned to the *6.Panzer-Armee*, the ability of the *12.SS-Panzer-Division* to fulfill its mission and reach the Meuse river objective was highly dependent on fire support from the German field artillery. This was all the more the case when promised *Luftwaffe* air support failed to arrive. The German artillery, while numerous, started the campaign with very modest stocks of ammunition. The main drawback was a lack of targeting data, which meant that most of the ammunition fired in the initial preparatory barrage would inevitably be wasted. These factors were widely appreciated by senior German commanders before the start of the Ardennes attack, which led to considerable pessimism about its chances for success.

A dismounted radio team of a *Panzergrenadier* heavy infantry gun company in action in the Recht-Poteau area at the start of the Ardennes offensive in December 1944. This team connected the self-propelled battery to the forward observer.

The Battleground: Winter Mud

Hitler's inspiration for the Ardennes offensive was the astonishing victory over the French Army in 1940. At the heart of the 1940 victory was a bold plan, code-named Case Yellow, to push the panzer divisions through the Ardennes, thereby cutting off the best French and British divisions in Belgium. This precipitated the evacuation of the British Expeditionary Force at Dunkirk and the eventual defeat of the entire French Army in a lightning war lasting barely six weeks. Hitler hoped that the Autumn Mist offensive would replicate the surprise 1940 victory, creating a "New Dunkirk."

The muddy conditions along the forest tracks in the Ardennes presented mobility problems for soldiers and vehicles alike.

In spite of Hitler's connection between 1940's Case Yellow and 1944's Autumn Mist, there were significant and critical differences. Among the most important were geography and weather. These differences were an important contributory factor in the eventual defeat of the 1944 Ardennes offensive.

The 1940 offensive was waged on a much broader front than the 1944 Ardennes offensive. The focal point of the 1940 attack, Rundstedt's Army Group A, struck primarily through Luxembourg, passing through the High Ardennes in southwest Belgium before finally exiting in the Sedan region of northeastern France.

The 1944 Ardennes battlefield was traversed in May 1940 by Gunther von Kluge's *4.Armee*. This 1940 formation consisted of only four infantry corps made up of seven infantry divisions and two panzer divisions. In contrast, this sector in 1944 was host to a far larger force including two panzer armies, six corps, nine infantry divisions, and seven panzer divisions in the first wave alone. As a result, in 1944 many more vehicles were funneled through this narrow sector than in 1940.

The *6.Panzer-Armee* sector in 1944 stretched from Monschau in the north to the Losheim Gap in the south, a distance of roughly 50 kilometers (30 miles). The front lines ran along the pre-1940 Belgian-German frontier. The Belgian side of this sector was the source of contention between Germany and Belgium over the centuries because many of the towns on the Belgian side of the border were German-speaking. This area was part of Germany prior to World War I, came under Belgian control after the Great War, and was reabsorbed into Germany after the 1940 campaign. This was of some significance in 1944 due to the geographic effects of the 1919–40 border zone.

Unlike the contemporary European Union, there was no mass tourism in the area prior to 1940, nor were there free and open borders. The number of cross-border roads between Belgium and Germany was very limited since both governments established tollhouses on the border to regulate commerce and to impose taxes. This was an expensive proposition and so border crossing points were few in number, especially in rural areas such as this region. In the *6.Panzer-Armee* attack sector, there was

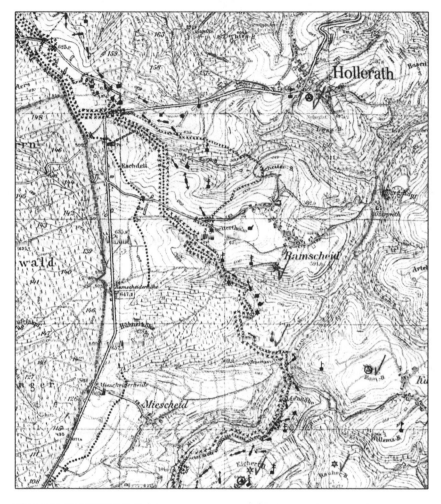

Westwall: The Hollerath Knee

This German army construction map shows the layout of Westwall bunkers along the Belgian border near Hollerath. A thick belt of dragon's teeth anti-tank obstructions can be seen in the upper left corner near the "Hollerath Knee," where the International Highway abruptly turns south. The small *X*s indicate belts of dragon's teeth, the small dots indicate minefields, and the other symbols indicate bunkers and other defensive structures. These belts of obstructions slowed the approaches to Rollbahn A during the start of the Ardennes offensive.

only a single border crossing at Losheimergraben, where both countries established tollhouses. As a result, this was the only good cross-border road south of Monschau.

Although there was an adequate road network on the German side of the border, this network largely ended on the Belgian side, which consisted mainly of forests. On the German side of border, there was a major road, usually called the International Highway in American accounts and Reichstrasse 258 in German accounts. It headed west from Hollerath and then abruptly turned south on reaching the Belgian border, creating a perpendicular road bend called the "Hollerath Knee" (*Hollerather Knie*). At this point the road paralleled the border until reaching Losheim, where the road bifurcated with one road heading across the border into Belgium at Losheimergraben and the other continuing southwestward along the border.

The forest on the Belgian side of this area is referred to in this book as the Krinkelterwald (Krinkelt forest), though in fact the forest area had a variety of names for different segments based on local ownership and taxation. "Krinkelterwald" is used in this book as a more convenient way to identify the forest. The Krinkelterwald formed a natural barrier along the German-Belgian border. Aside from the one cross-border road through Losheimergraben, there were no major roads on the Belgian side of the border until reaching the small towns on the western side of the Krinkelterwald. The Krinkelterwald was a pine forest that was harvested for wood. As a result, some small logging roads and firebreaks ran through the forest. However, these were not regularly used for normal road traffic and so were not paved.

Further complicating the geography of the border zone was the erection of the Westwall on the German side in the late 1930s, the German equivalent of France's Maginot Line. This consisted of a row of dragon's teeth anti-tank obstacles and minefields along the border, as well as a network of small pillboxes and personnel bunkers. As a result, vehicle transit across the border was impossible except at a few key locations such as Losheim, where there were access points through the Westwall barriers. In the autumn of 1944, after the retreat back to

The Krinkelterwald is typical of the pine forests on either side of the Belgian-German border, with the neighboring German Eifel being essentially the same. The forest was harvested for wood, so it was relatively accessible for foot soldiers, though not for vehicles. STEPHEN ANDREW

the Westwall, the *Wehrmacht* thickened the minefields along the border, and the Americans did the same on their side of the battle line.

A further interruption of cross-border traffic was the demolition of several bridges in the area, especially in the vital Losheim-Losheimergraben corridor. On the German side of the border, the Reichsstrasse 258 / International Highway passed over the cross-border railway line about a kilometer outside Losheim. This overpass had been knocked down in 1944, providing a major barrier to road traffic westward. In addition, the US Army had demolished several other overpasses west of Losheim with the intention of preventing easy transit down this corridor. In other words, the only major route over the German-Belgian border in this area was blocked to ordinary road and rail traffic.

While these geographical details might seem tedious and obscure, they had major implications in the conduct of the 1944 Ardennes offensive. The transit of German mechanized units up to the Belgian border was relatively straightforward. However, on reaching the Belgian border, the road network essentially ended. In this 50-kilometer stretch of frontier, there was only a single good-quality road passing through the Westwall obstructions and the forest at Losheim-Losheimergraben. The other routes for the most part were dirt forest tracks. Trying to push several panzer divisions across the border at this point was an invitation to a major traffic jam.

German planning for Autumn Mist did include provisions for various engineer units to conduct minefield clearing operations at the start of the operation, followed by the erection of special ramps over the dragon's teeth. There were also plans to bridge the collapsed over-pass on Reichsstrasse 258 outside Losheim. On a map, in a comfortable headquarters office in Berlin, everything seemed very simple. But in war, even the simplest thing proves to be very difficult.

Early Winter Weather

Hitler chose to stage the Autumn Mist offensive in November–December 1944 specifically to minimize the effectiveness of Allied air-power by staging it when the skies were most likely to be overcast. The Ardennes region is notably wet and overcast during these months, as described in a later US Army assessment:

> The weather that occurs in the Ardennes and Eifel terrain during the winter generally is severe, and it was in 1944. This is mountainous country, with much rainfall, deep snows in the winter, and raw, harsh winds sweeping across the plateaus. The heaviest rains occur in November and December. The mists are frequent and heavy, lasting well into the late morning before they break. Precise predictions by meteorologists are difficult because the Ardennes lies directly on the boundary between the northwestern and central European climactic regions and is affected by the conjuncture of weather moving east from the British isles and the Atlantic with that moving westward out of Russia.[1]

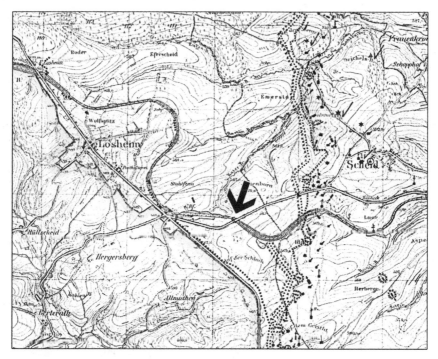

Westwall: Approach to Losheim
This German army construction map shows the Westwall construction on the
approaches to Losheim. Road traffic had to be channeled down a relatively
narrow approach through gaps in the belt of dragon's teeth. The arrow superim-
posed on this map points to the road overpass over the railway tracks that had
been knocked down prior to the Ardennes offensive, causing major traffic jams
in this area until it was repaired.

In this respect, Hitler's intentions were largely realized during the
first week of the fighting, since there was nearly complete overcast
over most of the battlefield. The overcast conditions strictly limited the
number of air support missions that could be conducted by US fighter-
bombers over the Ardennes. These conditions continued through the
night of December 22–23, 1944, when a high front arrived from Russia.
This brought freezing temperatures and clear skies, permitting a return
of US airpower to the Ardennes battlefield.[2]

In this respect, Hitler's decision to stage the Ardennes offensive in the early winter of 1944 did give the German army a temporary reprieve from air attacks for the first week of the fighting. But the advantage was short-lived.

THE MID-DECEMBER THAW

If Autumn Mist had started during the first week of December 1944 as originally planned, the ground would have been frozen and snow-covered. However, by the time it started in the third week of December, a thaw had begun that had some important consequences for battlefield conditions. At the time, there was a low-pressure system in the area with slightly higher than average temperatures, usually above freezing, with frequent periods of fog and light rain. The weather reports from the Elsenborn area are shown in the accompanying chart.

Weather Conditions near Elsenborn December 15–22, 1944[3]				
	Min. Temp (F)	Max. Temp (F)	Precipitation (mm)	Visibility (km)	Cloud cover*
Dec. 15	27	39	0.6; rain	4; morning fog; wet drizzle	10
Dec. 16	27	37	–	4; morning fog; rain	10
Dec. 17	34	46	4.3; rain	7	9
Dec. 18	45	50	2.6; rain	7	10
Dec. 19	32	48	–	5; drizzle; fog	10
Dec. 20	36	45	–	1; fog	10
Dec. 21	36	41	6.1; rain	2; fog	10
Dec. 22	36	41	3.0; rain	6; drizzle	10

*10 = total overcast; 1 = clear

What Hitler did not consider in his quest for cloud cover was the related weather conditions of rain and snow. Rain has a largely unappreciated impact on mechanized operations, especially in rural areas with a poor road network. The autumn of 1944 was much wetter than usual, and November had more than double the normal rainfall, as can be seen in the chart below. There are several military implications for heavy rain accumulations in rural areas, the most important of which is the problem for the conduct of mechanized offensives when confronted with deep mud on fields and non-metalled roads.

Autumn Precipitation in Belgium[4]				
	Sept.	Oct.	Nov.	Dec.
Average monthly precipitation 1931–60 (mm)	74.4	73.6	75.5	73.6
Monthly precipitation in 1944 (mm)	107.5	110.2	161.6	89.5

Hitler and his planning staff were not particularly sensitive to the problems posed by the wet autumn of 1944, since the *Wehrmacht* was largely on the defensive. In contrast, the US Army conducted two major mechanized offensives in November 1944 that were both badly affected by the wet conditions. Operation Queen was the offensive by the First US Army and the Ninth US Army in the area near Aachen, north of the Ardennes. The aim of this offensive was to push these field armies up to the Roer river prior to an eventual offensive to the Rhine. The 12th Army Group commander, Lt. Gen. Omar Bradley, expected that Operation Queen would be a great success on the order of the Operation Cobra breakthrough battle in Normandy in July 1944. Operation Queen, however, largely failed in its mission.[5] One of the key reasons was the unusually wet weather and the difficulty of conducting combined tank/infantry operations in the mud.

In a similar vein, Patton's Third US Army attempted to envelope the German defenses around the fortified city of Metz during Operation Madison in November 1944. The results of the operation were more satisfactory than Operation Queen, but not as extensive as planned. This was in no small measure due to the flooding in the area which engorged the local rivers, making crossing operations over the Moselle very difficult.[6] In addition, the armored divisions had a great deal of difficulty in advancing due to the deep mud in the fields.

The US Army experiences in November 1944 led to a new expression to describe the battlefield conditions: "a front one tank wide." Simply put, this meant that operations could only be conducted on good roads.

Deep mud made it very difficult to conduct tank operations off the roads. Once tanks tried to move off-road to travel cross-country, they quickly became bogged down in the deep mud. The situation was even worse for wheeled vehicles such as supply trucks. Attacks inevitably were channelized down the available road network. This made it much easier for the defending German troops, since tank advances could be readily frustrated by positioning anti-tank guns to fire on the limited number of roads. A few guns could control the advance along an otherwise wide front.

The thaw that took place in the third week of December 1944 turned many of the small country roads in the Elsenborn region into sodden, muddy trenches. Here, *Waffen-SS* troops of *I.SS-Panzer-Korps* attempt to extract a radio command car from the mud in the Elsenborn area during the Ardennes offensive.

The second impact of these muddy conditions was the increased importance of small villages and towns along the road. These modest, built-up areas could readily be converted into strongpoints bristling with anti-tank rockets and anti-tank guns. The usual tank tactics in normal weather conditions would have been to bypass the villages. But when the battlefield was covered in deep mud, the villages had to be captured since they could not be outflanked. Capturing these villages often proved to be a time-consuming and costly process. The architecture of the Ardennes enhanced this effect since the buildings were mainly constructed of stone, making them particularly suitable as improvised fortifications. Forests were likewise a major hindrance to advance since the handful of roads through the woods could be easily defended.

The popular image of the Battle of the Bulge imagines the Ardennes battlefields covered in snow. There was snowfall in the Ardennes in late November and early December 1944. However, the weather warmed up in the days before the December 16 attack, and the thaw led to a return of rain and slush. Some snow lingered in shady areas of the woods, but it tended to melt or turn to slush in many areas. Significant snow cover did not return until after December 23 and the arrival of hard winter weather.

The wet, muddy weather in mid-December had a significant impact on the battles that are the focus this book. During the first of these, the fighting in the Krinkelterwald forest on December 16–17, the German forces had considerable difficulty providing armored support to the infantry due to the limited number of forest roads and the muddy conditions on the few available paths. The weather more strongly influenced the next two battles, at Krinkelt-Rocherath and then at Dom Bütgenbach. In both cases, the *12.SS-Panzer-Division* was forced to fight for small villages that controlled the local roads. Attempts to bypass these American strongholds were frustrated by the deep mud in the fields.

These two battles consumed far too much time, and ultimately led to the failure of the *6.Panzer-Armee* mission to reach the Meuse. While weather alone did not determine the outcome of the battles for the

Elsenborn sector, the weather combined with the geography constrained the ability of the *Wehrmacht* to conduct a fast mechanized assault.

It is worth noting that the two major panzer advances during the Battle of the Bulge, the *II.SS-Panzer-Korps* advance toward Manhay and the *5.Panzer-Armee* advance to the Meuse at Dinant, occurred after the December 22–23, 1944, freeze, when the ground became hard enough to facilitate cross-country maneuver. From the American perspective, Patton's lightning drive to relieve Bastogne also began after the freeze had returned.

Battle Babes: The Defenders

THE AMERICAN MAIN LINE OF RESISTANCE IN THE ELSENBORN SECTOR was held by the 99th Infantry Division. This division had arrived in the European sector only in November, so it had not seen much combat beyond patrolling.

The 99th Division was activated in November 1942, and its first major test came in the 1943 Third Army maneuvers in Louisiana in September 1943. The performance during the maneuvers was rated as "excellent" and the division was declared "ready for combat" on November 15, 1943. Deployment to combat was delayed for nearly a year due to the Army practice of stripping trained riflemen from Stateside divisions

A rifle squad of the 393rd Infantry, 99th Infantry Division on the march.

to make up for personnel shortages in the Eruopean theater. The shortage of trained riflemen adversely affected the readiness of the division. The 99th Division was stripped of about 3,000 riflemen in March 1944 to flesh out units already committed to combat. Their places were filled by young men from the Army Specialized Training Program (ASTP), an effort by the army chief of staff, Gen. George C. Marshall, to divert the smartest young soldiers into advanced academic training. At a time when less than 5 percent of young men went to college, Marshall did not want to waste their talents and had them sent to further schooling rather than the battlefield.

ASTP came to an abrupt end in 1944 when rising casualties created an immediate need for troops, so 100,000 ASTP college students were transferred to active service. Some were sent as engineers to the secret atomic bomb program, others to technical branches of the army,

Maj. Gen. Walter Lauer, (right) commander of the 99th Division, talks to Lt. Joseph Carnevale, leader of the 2nd Platoon, B Company, 393rd Infantry about the defenses being established in Rocherath on November 14, 1944, shortly after the division arrived in this sector.

but most ended up as riflemen. The large number of ASTP troops in the division led to its nickname "Battling Babes," or "Battle Babies." The new replacements led to another round of field exercises, including regimental exercises in southern Oklahoma in July 1944. The 99th Division was brought up to full TO&E strength in July 1944.[1] It began to be transferred to the European Theater of Operations (ETO) in mid-September 1944, arriving in the Dorsetshire region of England in October 1944.

99th Infantry Division	Maj. Gen. Walter Lauer
393rd Infantry Regiment	Lt. Col. Jean D. Scott
1st Battalion	Maj. Matthew Legler
2nd Battalion	Lt. Col. Ernest Peters
3rd Battalion	Lt. Col. Jack Allen
394th Infantry Regiment	Col. Don Riley
1st Battalion	Lt. Col. Robert Douglas
2nd Battalion	Lt. Col. Philip Wertheimer
3rd Battalion	Lt. Col. Norman Moore
395th Infantry Regiment	Col. Alexander J. Mackenzie
1st Battalion	Lt. Col. Charles Hendricks
2nd Battalion	Maj. Stevens
3rd Battalion	Lt. Col. McClernand Butler
99th Division Artillery	Brig. Gen. Frederick Black
370th Field Artillery Battalion (105mm)	Lt. Col. John Brindley
371st Field Artillery Battalion (105mm)	Lt. Col. Jones
372nd Field Artillery Battalion (155mm)	Lt. Col. Frank Mostek
924th Field Artillery Battalion (105mm)	Lt. Col. Logan Clarke
324th Engineer Combat Battalion	Maj. Justice Neale
324th Medical Battalion	Lt. Col. P. R. Beckjord

The division continued its training in Britain in October 1944 for about a month before being sent into combat in Belgium. One of the lessons of the summer 1944 fighting was that infantry units sent immediately into intense combat tended to suffer very high casualties in their first few weeks due to their inexperience. No matter how well trained, many battlefield lessons could not be easily taught. A better alternative was to deploy a green division into a relatively quiet sector of the front to learn basic combat skills such as patrolling and preparing defenses. Once these divisions became acclimated to the battlefield, their performance in combat was generally better.

In the case of the 99th Division, they were directed to the Ardennes. This was considered a quiet sector of the front and had been called the "kindergarten and old-age home of the army." The two divisions in the Bastogne area, the 4th and 28th Infantry Divisions, had suffered heavy casualties in the bloody Hürtgen forest fighting, and had been transferred to the Ardennes to rebuild and recuperate. The other two "kindergarten" divisions, the 99th and 106th Infantry Divisions, were both new divisions with no combat experience.

House number 129 in Krinkelt was used as the command post for the 393rd Infantry Regiment. "Dakota" was the regiment's radio call-sign. This gives a good sense of the durable stone construction of many of the buildings in Krinkelt-Rocherath, which influenced the fighting there in December 1944.

Troops of a headquarters company of the 393rd Infantry, 99th Division during the Ardennes fighting in 1944–45.

The 99th Division arrived in the Ardennes in November 1944 and took over the sector formerly held by the 9th Infantry Division. The division's three regiments were in place by November 12, 1944, and troops engaged in their first firefight with an enemy patrol the following day. The unit began the routine of patrolling, small skirmishes, and preparing trench-work. Their opponents were the equally inexperienced *277.Volksgrenadier-Division*, described in an earlier chapter.

In comparison to the *277.Volksgrenadier-Division*, the 99th Division was a full-strength division with the traditional configuration of three regiments, each with three battalions for a total of nine battalions. As mentioned previously, the *277.Volksgrenadier-Division* had only six battalions. In terms of artillery, both divisions were similar.

The usual deployment pattern for a US infantry division in the defense was to place two of its infantry regiments in the main line of resistance and to keep one infantry regiment back to serve as a reserve.

This was not the pattern with the 99th Division in the Ardennes in December 1944, since it had an elongated 19-mile front to cover and it was considered a quiet front. As a result, all three infantry regiments were in the forward line. The deployment pattern had the 395th Infantry Regiment on the division's left flank near Hofen, the 393rd Infantry Regiment in the center in the Krinkelterwald, and the 394th Infantry Regiment on the right flank to the south, on either side of Losheimergraben.

AMERICAN FIRE SUPPORT

On November 20, 1945, Lt. George S. Patton stood in front of a board of forty senior American commanders to discuss the performance of US infantry divisions in the European Theater of Operations. He remarked:

> The infantry component of the division, which is 65.9% of the total personnel, inflicts on the enemy by means of small arms, automatic weapons, mortars and hand grenades approximately 37% of the [enemy] casualties. In order to inflict 37% of the casualties, the infantry sustains 92% of the casualties of the division. The artillery, which comprises 15% of the division, inflicts on the enemy 42% of the total casualties for which it pays but 2%.[2]

Patton's estimate that the artillery accounted for 42 percent of enemy casualties may in fact be low. Other studies have suggested that artillery, including the infantry's mortar, may have accounted for 80 percent of enemy casualties. The importance of artillery on the World War II battlefield has generally been neglected in most published histories. The role of other technologies such as tanks has attracted far more attention. Field artillery is more closely associated with the advent of industrialized warfare in World War I. Nevertheless, it remained a vital element on the World War II battlefield. As will become apparent in subsequent chapters, it determined the outcome of many of the engagements in the Ardennes fighting.

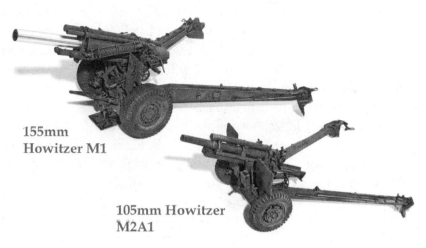

155mm Howitzer M1

105mm Howitzer M2A1

This illustration provides a size comparison between the two standard cannon of the divisional artillery, the 105mm M2A1 howitzer and its larger counterpart, the 155mm M1 howitzer.

The backbone of the US Army field artillery was the M2 105mm howitzer. There were usually three battalions of these in each infantry division, with twelve cannon per battalion.

The 99th Division had the standard American configuration for divisional artillery, consisting of three 105mm howitzer battalions and one 155mm howitzer battalion. Each of these battalions had twelve cannon. Although the number of howitzers was similar in US and German divisions, there were many significant differences. The US Army divisional artillery had several advantages over their German counterparts, most notably their complete motorization. This meant that not only were all howitzer motor-drawn, but ammunition supply was also motorized. In general, US Army artillery battalions had a much greater chance to remain stocked with ammunition during prolonged combat since the artillery could depend on a steady stream of ammunition supply.

The other advantage enjoyed by the US Army artillery in the Ardennes was that the ammunition supply was nearby, while German divisions frequently found that their nearest resupply points were much farther away in the Rhine area.

The heavy firepower in the infantry division's field artillery came from the M1 155mm howitzer. There was one battalion containing twelve of these in each division.

Heavy firepower at corps level was often provided by the M1A1 155mm gun, nicknamed the Long Tom. This weapon had an effective range of over 14 miles.

While it was not immediately apparent at the outset of the campaign, within a few days after the start of the German attack, the artillery of three infantry divisions was concentrated in the Elsenborn area, creating a formidable mass of firepower. The units on hand are listed on the following page.

V Corps Divisional Artillery in Elsenborn Sector

1st Infantry Division Artillery
5th Field Artillery Battalion
7th Field Artillery Battalion
32nd Field Artillery Battalion
33rd Field Artillery Battalion

2nd Infantry Division Artillery
12th Field Artillery Battalion
15th Field Artillery Battalion
37th Field Artillery Battalion
38th Field Artillery Battalion

99th Infantry Division Artillery
370th Field Artillery Battalion
371st Field Artillery Battalion
372nd Field Artillery Battalion
924th Field Artillery Battalion

Divisional artillery fire control in the US Army was somewhat more centralized than in German infantry divisions due to the adoption of a fire direction center (FDC) at battalion level in 1935.[3] This encouraged the development of new tools and techniques to facilitate the concentration of fire by all the batteries within a battalion. In addition, it led to improvements that allowed the divisional artillery headquarters to rapidly coordinate the fires of the four battalions within the division and to link them to corps-level fire artillery.

One artillery tactic that stemmed from these innovations was the "Time on Target" (TOT).[4] This received different nicknames in different units, such as "Serenade" or "Stonk." A TOT meant a fire mission where all the batteries were coordinated so that their fire arrived on the target simultaneously rather than sequentially. This could include all the batteries of a single battalion, or a division, or even a corps. The reason this tactic was so effective was that the lethality of an artillery strike declined rapidly after the first bursts since enemy infantry would quickly take cover in trenches or other shelters. Enemy infantry was most vulnerable to artillery when in the open and fully exposed to the blast and fragmentation effects of the initial artillery strike.

The German army was not unaware of the advantages of centralized fire control innovations, and this was at the root of the new *Kopplungsgerät* that saw its debut in the Ardennes as mentioned previously. However, the German army did not have as robust a communication network as the US Army, particularly in regard to radio networks. Such tactics were heavily dependent on a redundant and robust network, including both traditional field telephones and tactical radios.

One technical innovation that saw its debut in the Ardennes was the VT (variable time) fuze, which was the cover name for the

The M1 8-inch howitzer was another common weapon in the corps artillery battalions. It was related to the similar 155mm gun, but used a different gun tube. It had less range than the 155mm gun, about 10 miles versus 14 miles, but fired a projectile twice as heavy, 20 pounds versus 10 pounds.

revolutionary proximity fuze. This fuze contained a miniaturized radar. As the projectile approached the ground, it could be set to detonate at a predetermined height. Airbursts are particularly lethal against infantry since they maximize the blast and fragmentation effects compared to a normal groundburst using a conventional impact fuze. When an artillery projectile detonates upon impacting the ground, a good deal of the energy, blast, and fragmentation is absorbed by the ground, and only a fraction goes against its target.

The US Army delayed releasing the VT fuze for fear that the Germans would find a dud and copy the design. VT fuzes substantially improved the lethality of anti-aircraft artillery, and there was considerable concern about the losses that a German proximity fuze would inflict on Allied heavy bomber formations over Germany.[5] In the Ardennes, the VT fuze was released for use by field artillery on December 18, though it does not appear to have been used extensively during the Battles for Elsenborn Ridge covered in this book.[6]

CORPS ARTILLERY

The 99th Division was part of Lt. Gen. Leonard Gerow's V Corps. This corps contained an additional three field artillery groups, with a total of nine field artillery battalions. This added firepower was allotted as needed, and on occasion the entire weight of the corps artillery would be used to assist single divisions.

The most common role for corps artillery at this time was counter-battery, interdiction, and harassing fire. Counter-battery missions were directed against enemy artillery. This was based on specific intelligence such as ground or aerial reconnaissance as well as from sound detection conducted by the corps observation battalion. US divisional and corps artillery had light observation aircraft that was used for artillery spotting. Interdiction and harassing missions were usually based on known road networks and other fixed geographical targets. The corps artillery would periodically strike main road junctions, railroad stations, and other likely targets at night to prevent resupply. The corps artillery would be instrumental in the fighting in the Ardennes in the Elsenborn sector.[7]

V Corps Artillery, December 15, 1944[8]	
HQ, V Corps Artillery	
17th Field Artillery Observation Battalion	
190th Field Artillery Group	
190th Field Artillery Battalion	155mm gun
997th Field Artillery Battalion	8-inch howitzer
187th Field Artillery Group	
187th Field Artillery Battalion	155mm howitzer
953rd Field Artillery Battalion	155mm howitzer
941st Field Artillery Battalion	4.5-inch gun
406th Field Artillery Group	
186th Field Artillery Battalion	155mm howitzer
955th Field Artillery Battalion	155mm howitzer
200th Field Artillery Battalion	155mm gun
272nd Field Artillery Battalion	240mm howitzer

ARMORED SUPPORT FOR THE INFANTRY

Besides artillery support, US infantry divisions tended to receive more armored support than their German adversaries. The official doctrine was to place the separate tank battalions and tank destroyer battalions under corps command, with an armored group headquarters and tank destroyer group headquarters coordinating their activities. It was discovered in Normandy that this was far from ideal, and that it was better to semipermanently attach tank and tank destroyer battalions to specific infantry divisions. Prolonged cooperation in combat operations significantly improved the performance of the tank-infantry team once both units became familiar with one another. As a result, the usual practice by late 1944 was to attach a tank battalion and a tank destroyer battalion to each infantry division when involved in offensive operations.[9]

The main problem was a shortage of armored units, since there were not enough tank and tank destroyer battalions in the theater to allot one of each to the available infantry divisions. As a result, "quiet" theaters such as the Ardennes tended to have fewer separate tank battalions than active theaters. In the Ardennes, divisions would only receive one or two companies of tanks, rather than an entire battalion. These allotments are covered in more detail in subsequent chapters.

The 741st Tank Battalion was the first US tank unit ashore on D-Day and served for much of the war in support of the 2nd Infantry Division. This M4A1 seen here on a treadway bridge in Germany on March 9, 1945, was the only survivor of the original tanks that landed with the battalion at Normandy.

The separate tank battalions each included four tank companies, three of these equipped with M4 Sherman medium tanks and the fourth, D Company, equipped with the M5A1 light tank. Ideally, the pattern was to deploy a medium tank company with each infantry regiment. Due to tank battalion shortages in V Corps, the 99th Division did not have a tank battalion attached during the fighting described here. In some cases, its units were supported by the 741st Tank Battalion, attached to the 2nd Infantry Division through mid-December. At the start of the German offensive of December 16, the 741st Tank Battalion had forty-three M4 medium tanks, of which four were in repair; six M4 105mm assault guns; and seventeen M5A1 light tanks, with one in repair. The 745th Tank Battalion, attached to the 1st Infantry Division, had forty M4 medium tanks, ten M4A3 (76mm) medium tanks, six M4 105mm assault guns, and eighteen M5A1 light tanks.[10]

The 745th Tank Battalion supported the 1st Infantry Division for most of the campaign in Europe. This is a M4A3 tank of the battalion supporting the 16th Infantry, 1st Infantry Division during the fighting near Amel, Belgium, on January 24, 1945.

The tank destroyer battalions were of mixed configuration. Although the tank destroyer battalions through mid-1943 were generally equipped with the M10 3-inch GMC, Army Ground Forces believed from experiences in North Africa that towed guns were suitable for this role. As a result, a portion of the battalions were re-equipped with the new towed 3-inch anti-tank gun. Generally, the battalions attached to infantry divisions received the towed guns, while those attached to armored divisions retained self-propelled tank destroyers.

The deployment of the towed guns proved a serious mistake. Weighing 2.4 tons, the guns were too unwieldy to be maneuvered by their crews, and it was not safe to leave their half-track prime movers near them on the battlefield. Furthermore, the guns could not reliably penetrate the frontal armor of many German tanks and armored vehicles. Their lack of utility in the tank destroyer role led to requests to return to the use of self-propelled tank destroyers. In the meantime, some units retired their towed tank destroyer battalions to the divisional artillery, where they were used as field guns. The poor performance of the towed anti-tank guns in the Ardennes signed their death knell, and they were withdrawn in 1945.

In the case of the 99th Division, the 801st Tank Destroyer Battalion was attached to the division in November and remained through the beginning of February 1945. The 801st was equipped with the towed 3-inch anti-tank gun at the time. The 2nd Infantry Division had the 612th Tank Destroyer Battalion, another towed battalion, attached to it through the war. During the Ardennes fighting, it had companies of the 644th Tank Destroyer Battalion attached to it, equipped with the M10

One of the least popular weapons in US Army service in 1944 was the 3-inch towed anti-tank gun. These replaced the self-propelled M10 3-inch GMC in tank destroyer battalions earmarked for attachment to infantry divisions in 1943. They were not powerful enough to frontally penetrate German tanks such as the *Panther*, and they were extremely unwieldy to move on the battlefield. This is an example with the 801st Tank Destroyer Battalion, which supported the 99th Infantry Division in the Ardennes in December 1944.

3-inch GMC. The 1st Infantry Division had the 634th Tank Destroyer Battalion attached to it for most of the campaign, equipped with the M10 3-inch GMC. During the fighting around Bütgenbach described in this book, it had some companies of the 703rd Tank Destroyer Battalion attached to it. This battalion had begun to receive the new M36 90mm GMC. This was by far the best tank destroyer in use by the US Army, and the only one capable of penetrating the frontal armor of most German tanks.

FIRST BLOOD

The 99th Division began its first combat patrols on November 12, 1944. There were no large-scale engagements, simply the daily routine of patrols, preparation of defenses, and training. Some of the division's

The 1st Infantry Division was supported by the 634th Tank Destroyer Battalion for much of the campaign in Europe. This is a column of M10 3-inch GMCs of Company A, 634th Tank Destroyer Battalion on the outskirts of the German city of Aachen on October 14, 1944.

An improved derivative of the M10 tank destroyer appeared in Europe in October 1944 as the M36 90mm GMC. This is a M36 90mm GMC of the 703rd Tank Destroyer Battalion in Belgium on December 16, 1944. Elements of this battalion supported the 1st Infantry Division in the fighting around Bütgenbach in December 1944.

forward rifle platoons suffered 30 percent casualties by the end of November 1944, more than half of the casualties due to trench foot. Total combat casualties in November were 187 men, of which there were 21 killed, 13 missing, and 153 wounded. The 99th Division was in the line for nearly a month prior to the start of the German Ardennes offensive. This provided the troops with a good appreciation of the terrain.

The advent of cold weather also prompted the construction of numerous log shelters behind the trench line to provide some measure of relief from the snow and rain. These were used as sleeping shelters, and some of the larger ones were constructed as drying shelters with small woodstoves to allow soldiers to dry out their boots and clothing as a means to avoid trench foot. These log-covered entrenchments would later provide important cover for the forward rifle platoons during the initial German artillery bombardment on December 16, 1944, at the start of the offensive.

The 99th Division held a sector 19 miles wide. This was wider than was considered prudent in tactical doctrine, but considered acceptable along a quiet front. As a precaution, the division dug a second defense line about 5,500 yards behind the forward lines in an arc to the south and east of Mürringen and Hünningen. The terrain in this sector was described in a later Army report:

> The forward positions of the 393rd and 394th Infantry Regiments were in the thick woods. This area, all part of the Monschau forest, is as densely wooded in many places as was the Hürtgen Forest. It is an area pitted with rocky gorges, small streams, abrupt hills and extremely limited road net. The routes to the forward positions, with the exception of the one main road running southeast of Losheim, consisted of narrow, rutted, firebreak trails. During most of the period prior to 16 December, these routes were quagmires of mud. Drainage was almost impossible owing to the fact that these trails were lower than the ground immediately around them. Even the corduroy log base on the route leading to the CP [command post] of the 2nd Battalion, 394th Infantry, which had originally been built by the 9th Division Engineers, did little to help. It did make movement possible by providing a firm base. But this was covered by a sea of mud, knee deep. Vehicular movement was slow and tortuous. Visibility was limited to 100–150 yards at a maximum. Fields of fire were equally limited and poor. Fire lanes for automatic weapons could not be cleared for any great distance without cutting down trees and thereby disclosing their position.[11]

PLAN DEWEY

December saw the first significant fighting by the division. The First US Army, commanded by Lt. Gen. Courtney Hodges, decided to stage yet another offensive to capture the Roer dams and their associated reservoirs. This had become a major operational objective in the autumn of 1944 once it was realized the dams posed a threat to any future advances to the Roer river.[12] If the dams remained in German hands, they could be opened during the course of an offensive over the Roer plains, flooding the lowlands on the approaches to the river and cutting off any units that were caught in the flooded areas. Attempts were made to breach the dams using heavy bombers, but without success.

The December attack was conducted primarily by the VIII Corps, to the north of V Corps, and the 99th Division. In early December the 2nd Infantry Division had been transferred from its position opposite the Schnee Eifel and replaced by the newly arrived 106th Division. During the Roer dam offensive, the 2nd Infantry Division was assigned to capture the Urfttalsperre dam. The mission of the 99th Division was to secure the right flank of the 2nd Infantry Division during this

Troops of the 9th Infantry, 2nd Infantry Division in the Krinkelterwald during the attack toward the Roer dams on December 13, 1944.

A squad from the 2nd Infantry Division rests in a snowy trench during the fighting near "Heartbreak Crossroads" in the Wahlerscheid area in the days prior to the Ardennes offensive.

operation. Indeed, the 2nd Division attack was actually conducted through the 99th Division lines, on its northern left flank, held by the 395th Infantry Regiment. The 2nd Division supply lines ran through the 99th Division sector, near their previous sector to the southwest.

One combat team of the 99th Division's 395th Infantry Regiment was assigned to push through the Westwall defenses and capture the town of Arenberg. The 395th Combat Team (CT395) consisted of the 1st and 2nd Battalions of the 395th Infantry, the 2nd Battalion of the 393rd Infantry, and supporting units. The attacks began at 0830 hours, Wednesday, December 13, 1944, and CT395 spent most of the first day of the attack trying to overcome German defenses along the Westwall. At the time of the operation, there was still deep snow in the area. On Thursday, December 15, the 2/395th Infantry captured six of the bunkers. By December 16, CT395 had penetrated the Westwall and took the town of Arenberg, completing its assigned mission.

At the same time, the division's 393rd Infantry Regiment conducted a secondary operation, called Plan Dewey, to the north of its original position to capture "Rat's Hill" (*Raths Busch*) and to straighten out its defensive line along the edge of the Krinkelterwald up to the International Highway. *Raths Busch* had been an irritant to the division because it overlooked divisional defenses. The 394th Infantry Regiment to the south conducted a "demonstration" to distract German attention from the two main efforts. Company L of 3/393rd Infantry Regiment overran Rat's Hill on the morning of the first day of the attack. The battalion also pushed out to "Purple Heart Corner," the Hollerath Knec.

Plan Dewey had unanticipated consequences when the Germans attacked two days later on Saturday, December 16. One of the 393rd Infantry Regiment's three battalions, the 2/393rd Infantry, was pulled

The December 1944 attack toward the Roer dams by the 2nd Infantry Division reached as far as "Heartbreak Crossroads" near Wahlerscheid, Germany, before being halted by the start of the German Ardennes offensive. This is a view of the crossroads after it was retaken by the US Army in February 1945. All the nearby forests have been shredded by artillery fire.

Maj. Gen. Walter Robertson was an experienced infantry commander, having served in Tunisia, Normandy, and Brittany with the 2nd Infantry Division. He is seen here on September 18, 1944, accepting the surrender of the fortified city of Brest from *Oberst* Erich Pietzonka, on the left, who commanded *Fallschirmjäger-Regiment.7.*

out the Krinkelterwald to join CT395 in the northern Roer dam mission. As a result, the Krinkelterwald was now held by two battalions instead of three. To make matters worse, the successful execution of Plan Dewey extended the front lines of the 3rd Battalion, 393rd Infantry Regiment farther to the north. It put six of the battalion's nine rifle companies oriented northward, leaving only the three rifle companies of K Company facing eastward toward the International Highway. Furthermore, it extended the frontage of K Company so that the platoon on its left side near the Hollerath Knee had to create new trenches and defenses in the two days prior to the German attack. For the most part, these defenses were more sparse than in other company areas.

Unbeknownst to the 393rd Infantry Regiment, one of the main German objectives, Rollbahn A, passed directly through this weak point in the regimental defenses.

Fighting to the north in the 395th Infantry Regiment area continued through Saturday, December 16. The 2nd Infantry Division finally captured a main road junction dubbed "Heartbreak Crossroads" near Wahlerscheid, and there were signs that the main German defenses in this sector were finally collapsing. During the predawn hours of December 16, the forward infantry battalions around Wahlerscheid heard extensive German artillery fire to the south. It was initially assumed that it was a German diversionary attack, intended to frustrate the attack toward the Roer dams. It was, in fact, the start of the Autumn Mist offensive.

Part 2

THE CAMPAIGN

Rollbahn A: Krinkelterwald on X-Day

THE AUTUMN MIST OFFENSIVE BEGAN IN THE PREDAWN DARKNESS AT 0530 hours, Saturday, December 16, 1944. In the plans, the start was designated as X-Day (*X-Tag*). Many German troops, unaware of the plans, used the usual army designation for the start of an operation: *Null Tag* (Zero Day).

In the *I.Panzer-Korps* sector, the offensive began with artillery bombardment along the main line of resistance, the edge of the forest to the immediate west of the International Highway. Searchlights had been brought forward from flak batteries deeper inside Germany. They were aimed at the low cloud cover with the intention of creating

This is a contemporary view of Rollbahn A, really nothing more than a dirt forest trail. STEPHEN ANDREW

artificial moonlight for the advancing German troops. Due to the fog, they created an eerie glow over the battlefield.

Recollections of the barrage were tempered by the observers' perspectives. Experienced German officers were pessimistic due to the barrage's short duration. Wilhelm Viebig, commanding the *277.Volksgrenadier-Division*, described the barrage simply as "brief." One of the younger officers, *Leutnant* Wingolf Scherer, who led a company of *Grenadier-Regiment.989*, recalled the scene:

> Punctually, at half past six, the barrage began . . . In a continuous succession, the lightning soon flashed closer, then distant muzzle-fire; then the Nebelwerfers started to roar; the track of their projectiles could be traced overhead. The searchlights projected their spider web of light beams over to the main line, from about six kilometers behind the main-line-of-resistance. The machine-guns chattered; the searchlights reflected off the low clouds. It was a scary-beautiful spectacle. For a while the enemy seemed surprised and silent. But when our fire subsided after half an hour, the American artillery proved that it had not been destroyed and began to take up the duel. Of course, anywhere heavy traffic could be expected, the artillery blanketed the roads with fire.[1]

Ensconced in the Krinkelterwald forest was Lt. Col. Jean Scott's 393rd Infantry Regiment. A young private from K Company, 393rd Infantry recalled the first moments of the attack:

> We were awakened by an artillery barrage that lasted nearly two hours. When it first started, I thought it was our own artillery dropping short rounds. But when the barrage stopped, German soldiers in great numbers crossed the International Highway to the right of our outpost position.[2]

American troops recall the bombardment lasting for two hours, while the German accounts usually mention a brief barrage of a half hour. Both accounts were correct, and simply a matter of perspective.

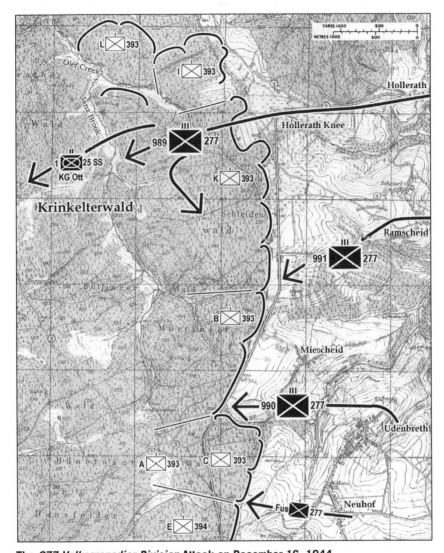

The *277.Volksgrenadier-Division* Attack on December 16, 1944

This map illustrates the attack of the *277.Volksgrenadier-Division* on X-Day against the two battalions of the 393rd Infantry, 99th Infantry Division along the edge of the International Highway and the Krinkelterwald.

Lt. Col. Jean D. Scott, commander of the 393rd Infantry Regiment, 99th Infantry Division.

The discrepancy was due to the cascading effect of the artillery bombardment. The initial preparation phase, aimed at the American main line of resistance along the edge of the woods, lasted for only a half hour, until 0600 hours. The German divisional artillery then switched to attack key road junctions and other likely concentration points farther in the woods. In the meantime, the corps artillery such as the *Volks-Artillerie-Korps* and the heavy gun batteries began counter-battery fire against expected US artillery positions as well as road networks and towns farther behind the lines. The later phases of the German barrage lasted until 0800 hours, but from the perspective of the German infantry, the only barrage that mattered was the initial half hour of artillery fire intended to crush the American defenses immediately in front of them.

For many German infantrymen, the initial preparation seemed much too brief given the density of the Krinkelterwald forest. The senior German artillery commander viewed the artillery preparation as largely a failure:

> On account of the visibility problems, observed fire was not possible when the infantry attack began and the artillery fire proceeded the advancing infantry according to a previously established schedule. As could be anticipated, the results of the artillery preparations did not meet expectations. The fire was dispersed over a great expanse. The enemy's tactics of erecting a loose network of strongpoints instead of a continuous main-line-of-resistance proved correct when faced with artillery fire. As a result of the restrictions against any previous registration fire or any preliminary terrain reconnaissance, much of the preparatory fire hit open ground without having any substantial effect. This showed yet again necessity of observed fire for the artillery.[3]

The American defenses in the main line of resistance in the Krinkelterwald consisted of two battalions of the 393rd Infantry Regiment: Lt. Col. Jack Allen's understrength 3rd Battalion in the northern portion of the Krinkelterwald opposite Hollerath, and Maj. Matthew Legler's 1st Battalion in the southern portion opposite Udenbreth. As mentioned earlier, the regiment's 2nd Battalion had been detached to support the 2nd Infantry Division in the Roer dam operation near Wahlerscheid. The authorized strength of each battalion was about 870 men but there were numerous cases of trench foot, so the line companies were understrength. As a result, the two battalions deployed less than their authorized strength of 1,740 men.

Oberst Wilhelm Viebig had no intelligence information about the composition of the American defenses beyond expecting the defense line to include a few infantry battalions of the 99th Division. His plan of attack was to deploy two of his three regiments in the initial attack.[4] *Grenadier-Regiment.989* was assigned to advance over the International Highway near the Hollerath Knee to seize Rollbahn A, a modest unpaved forest track heading toward Krinkelt-Rocherath.[5]

Grenadier-Regiment.990 was assigned to advance out of the Westwall bunkers near Udenbreth and then push over the International Highway, taking control of Rollbahn B, a narrow Class 3 road, through the positions of the 1st Battalion, 393rd Infantry Regiment that projected to the northwest before reaching the clearings outside Krinkelt-Rocherath. The division's third regiment, *Grenadier-Regiment.991*, was kept in reserve around Ramsheid along with the division's Fusilier company. Viebig intended to use *GR.991* in support of one of the other two regiments once the initial attack had been conducted.

Viebig also had *Kampfgruppe Ott*, a reinforced battalion from *SS-Panzergrenadier-Regiment.25*, nominally under his command. It was intended to be used to complete the breakthrough of the Krinkelterwald. Each of Viebig's grenadier regiments had an organizational strength of 1,911 men, but due to the manpower shortages, they were closer to 1,400 men each. Viebig had more than a three-to-one advantage in troop strength against his American opponents.

One of the problems facing German troops entering the Krinkelterwald was the Westwall anti-tank barrier on the German side of the frontier consisting of dragon's teeth and minefields. This is a contemporary view of the dragon's teeth near the Rollbahn A entrance point at the Hollerath Knee. STEPHEN ANDREW

The tactics used during the attack varied from sector to sector. The old Westwall defenses on the east side of the International Highway were lined with dragon's teeth, a type of concrete anti-tank obstacle. These posed no problems for the German infantry, but they limited the use of any armored vehicles at the opening stage of the attack until engineers could erect ramps over them. A more immediate problem was the presence of minefields in between the dragon's teeth and the International Highway. Due to the restrictions from Berlin limiting actions in this sector until the start of the offensive, the German engineers could not begin to open gaps in the minefields until the start of the offensive. In many cases, they waited until the preliminary artillery barrage lifted at 0600 hours.

Oberst Georg Fieger's *Grenadier-Regiment.989* was provided with a single engineer company to breach the minefields. Since this was a time-consuming procedure, especially due to snow cover and enemy fire, Fieger decided to open a narrow corridor through the minefield and pass his two battalions through the gap in rapid succession. Both battalions reached the edge of the Krinkelterwald without attracting much fire from American lines since American defenses in this area were so sparse. The main German attack took place on the overextended northern flank of K Company.

Lt. Col. Jack Allen's 3rd Battalion, 393rd Infantry had three rifle companies, with L Company on the southwestern side of Rat's Hill, I Company on either side of Olef Creek, and K Company facing the International Highway. Company M, the battalion's heavy weapons company, had its platoons supporting the other companies. The battalion was badly overextended, covering a frontage 5,500 yards wide, with only a single platoon, 2/L/383rd Infantry, in reserve.

Capt. Stephen Plume's K Company was spread out over a 1,750-yard front. To the north, and nearest the Hollerath Knee, was 2Lt. Robert Dettor's 3rd Platoon; in the center was 2Lt. Herman Dickman's 2nd Platoon; and to the south was 2Lt. Joseph Dougherty's 1st Platoon. The two .30-caliber machine guns of 1Lt. Joseph Mallon's 1st MG Platoon from M Company were forward deployed, including one with Dettor's platoon. Plume's command post was a short distance behind the 2nd Platoon in the center. One of the unit's officers later recalled the initial attack:

> At 0530 on the morning of the 16th, the Germans turned loose a terrific artillery, mortar, and rocket barrage which raked the Battalion front. The Germans scattered their shells in the Company areas, in the CP [command post] area, and in the rear areas; they thoroughly saturated their targets and wrecked the communications system. By 0600, wire contact with all the companies was out. Within the next half hour, radio contact, which had been established after the wire went out, was lost with K Company . . . Finally, after repeated tries, Battalion [HQ] got through to the K Co. CP for a few minutes using the Artillery FO's [forward observer's] radio. This didn't last long.[6]

The American troops kept their heads down during the artillery preparation, even after the initial thirty-minute barrage of the front lines. The forward outposts were located in the open ground immediately to the east of the woods. These outposts were simple trenches containing three or four men, 100 to 300 yards apart, in no-man's-land in front of the woods. Most had telephone links back to the platoon command posts, but as often as not, these were severed by the preliminary artillery bombardment. As a result, many platoons received no warning of the advancing German infantry, nor could they see out into the fields near the International Highway. Most of the American defenses were located farther back in the woods. The density of the trees prevented the American troops from seeing for more than a few hundred feet even in daylight. Sunrise on December 16 was not until 0839 hours, and the German searchlight radiance was not bright enough to illuminate the landscape from within the forest. Further obscuring any observation was the early morning fog.

The first wave of German infantry from *Hauptmann* Lanzke's *I./GR. 989* moved up to the dragon's teeth in front of the woods and waited for the engineers to complete their work in the minefield. Once they had received the "all-clear," the battalion began heading into the forest beyond the Hollerath Knee. They may have encountered the first outposts of the 1st Platoon, K Company at this point, but German records of the battle are scant. The regimental commander, *Oberst* Georg Fieger, later wrote: "As planned, [Lanzke's] I.Battalion attacked without delay and quickly penetrated into the forest . . . Soon, support of the attack by heavy weapons was no longer possible, since in the confusing forest terrain the exact position of our own front line couldn't be determined. The telephone wires were continually damaged and radio communication, especially with the artillery, did not function properly."[7]

Lanzke's mission was to push the battalion down the forest trail as quickly as possible to permit the *Hitlerjugend* spearheads to reach to the open farmland on the other sides of the woods by early afternoon. As a result, enough troops were left behind to keep Dettor's platoon from interfering with the mission, while the rest of Lanzke's men marched along the forest trail to the west.

Lt. Dettor's 3rd Platoon was the first element of K Company to be hit by the German infantry, about an hour after the start of the barrage. With communications out, they were isolated from surrounding units. The platoon spent the entire morning warding off German infantry probes. Dettor's notes were simple and to the point: "0540-0640-Artillery concentration on position. 0640-1230-Small arms fire fight. Sent runner to CP [command post] for reinforcements. Runner returned stating no reinforcements, stay on position and continue fighting. Communications to CP and outposts cut. No contact with men except those in foxholes in immediate vicinity. German troops to rear. Heavy machine gun to front seen captured."[8]

Some time after 0700 hours, Lanzke apparently decided to send a company of infantry southward to make certain that K Company did not cut off his battalion from the rear. With Dettor's 3rd Platoon tied down in a firefight, the German infantry moved toward the positions of 2nd Platoon and the nearby K Company command post. German infantry was able to infiltrate into the woods without great difficulty, but they began bumping into dispersed American defenses as they moved south. *Oberst* Georg Fieger, the *GR.989* commander, later wrote: "The enemy was offering tenacious resistance. His defense nests were so well camouflaged that they were difficult to detect even at close range. The terrain features were particularly unfavorable for our attacking forces. Time and time again, this deadlocked the attack."[9]

S/Sgt. Otha Langford was in the outpost of the 1st Squad, 2nd Platoon, 3rd Battalion and had observed the German troops crossing the International Highway farther to the south. When telephone lines were lost, Langford walked back to the company command post for instructions. The woods were swarming with Germans. When he returned to the outpost trench, he grabbed the two members of his bazooka team and told them to follow him back. On arriving back at the K Company CP, they met Capt. Stephen Plume:

> [Plume] apparently had been in his sleeping bag during the artillery barrage and the ensuing infantry attack, and had just slipped on his combat boots and leather jacket over his silk pajamas. He addressed Sgt. Langford: "Sergeant, we're surrounded. You'd just as well surrender." To that, Sgt. Langford said, "Captain Plume, you can go straight to hell. We're getting out of here." The 1st Squad soldiers withdrew further west to the battalion command post.[10]

Another soldier from the heavy weapons company appeared at the K Company CP and told Plume the company's whole right flank "had been swallowed up in the first rush of Germans."[11] This was not true, but lacking any communications, Plume had every reason to believe that the right platoons had been overwhelmed. Cut off from the battalion command post, Plume ordered his executive officer and supply sergeant to head back and inform Col. Allen of the situation. Plume attempted to counterattack toward the 2nd and 3rd Platoon positions "but met such stiff resistance that he was forced to fall back to the area around his company CP."[12]

The German infantry eventually reached the 2nd Platoon positions, probably from the northern flank and rear. Pfc. William Mudra, a rifleman with the 2nd Squad, 2nd Platoon, described his dugout being overrun by the German infantry:

The barrage stopped as suddenly as it had begun. There were a few minutes of silence, then [Pfc. Frank Smollen], who was nearest the entrance [of the dugout], said he heard a sound outside. He poked his head out in order to see over the top of the dugout. "They're here!" The Jerries were almost directly on top of us. I couldn't say with certainty just how many there were, perhaps twenty; each one was armed with an automatic weapon . . . We had little choice but to accept capture.[13]

Although the dugouts with their stout log roofs had been instrumental in protecting many GIs from the initial artillery barrage, they were not ideal defense positions. They had no firing ports and usually had only a single small opening to keep the heat inside. Troops were supposed to return to the neighboring trenches to defend the platoon positions once the artillery barrage was over. Many inexperienced troops preferred the dry shelter of the log dugouts to the exposed muddy

This is a typical example of the log shelters built by the 99th Division in the Krinkelterwald. These provided good shelter during the initial German artillery bombardment, but could be a hazard to their occupants once German troops arrived on foot since they had only a single entrance and lacked firing ports.

trenches while the artillery bombardment still seemed to be going on. It was not obvious to the inexperienced troops of the 2nd Platoon that the artillery was no longer aimed at their forward positions but at the rear areas. They could still hear explosions in the distance and *Nebelwerfer* rockets flying overhead, so they decided not to take chances in the exposed trenches. This often proved a fatal mistake, as German infantrymen roamed through the American positions, lobbing stick grenades into the shelters.

This problem was so widespread that after the fighting, the 99th Division posted instructions to avoid this predicament in the future:

> Improvement of a position may lead to some dangerous results. Bad weather, cold and snow made necessary the construction of living quarters on or near the positions, to permit men to get dry and warm. Such shelters are a necessity to prevent exposure and trench-foot. However, they must not take the place of properly constructed fighting foxholes. Where living shelter are too close to the foxholes, they give away the squad or platoon battle position. While huts constructed with a heavy log and dirt roof, a canvas false roof for drainage and a third roof of pine boughs for camouflage are excellent shelters, they can be easily spotted after the enemy enters the position . . . Men occupying dugouts or log shelters must have at least one man on duty outside at all times to prevent being trapped by enemy infiltrators using grenades and sub-machine guns.[14]

Lt. Joseph Dougherty, leading the 1st Platoon, saw his 2nd Squad being overrun. Realizing his position was cut off and becoming untenable, he sent a runner to Plume's company command post to request permission to withdraw there. After permission was granted, Dougherty managed to collect thirteen men and withdraw to the company command post. They were assigned to cover one sector of the perimeter.

Back at the 3rd Battalion command post, Col. Allen received Plume's news about the loss of the two platoons and the machine-gun platoon. Around 0815 hours, Allen ordered his only reserve, 2Lt. Peter Jenkisson's 2nd Platoon of L Company, to head to Plume's command post in hopes of stabilizing the sector. Jenkisson's platoon arrived there about 0900 hours and attempted to set up their defense in the kitchen and supply area. As they were doing so, they were attacked by a German infantry force. "The platoon was caught at a disadvantage and was shot up badly, disorganized and suffered what was estimated to be 25% casualties."[15]

Col. Allen had finally recognized that K Company was on the verge of being destroyed, and he ordered the remainder of Capt. Paul Fogelman's L Company to move off Rat's Hill and rally around the Battalion Command Post in hopes of restoring the situation. Before they could arrive, around 0915 to 0930 hours, Allen's battalion command post and the neighboring command post of M Company (heavy weapons) came under heavy attack by German infantry. "Every available man—mortarmen, cooks and headquarters personnel—had been thrown in front and all were fighting desperately."[16] The two rifle platoons from L Company had to fight their way through German units moving west and the German troops besieging the battalion command post. The L Company force reached the command post around 1015 hours, and were then hit by another wave of German forces from both flanks. Calling in artillery and using the mortars of M Company at point-blank range, the German attack was pushed off by 1100 hours.

With the situation still very precarious, Allen ordered his last unit, I Company, to return from the Rat's Hill area. The 1st Platoon, leading the I Company column, reached the southern side of the Olef Creek ravine but was hit with small-arms fire and forced to halt. Allen instructed the I Company commander, Capt. William Coke, to pull back and then swing wide to the west to avoid the German ambush before heading back to the battalion command post. This was accomplished later in the morning, and I Company was positioned behind the battalion command post as a reserve. The situation remained chaotic through the late morning.

By this time, the defense of the K Company command post was faltering due to continuing casualties and low ammunition. Dougherty's squad continued to defend their sector of the command post until 1030 hours, by which time their ammunition was running out. Dougherty told his men to escape on their own if they wished, but recognizing they were surrounded, he and Plume decided to surrender.

Dettor's 3rd Platoon held out longer. By this time, Lanzke's *I./ GR.989* had become stalled and Fieger sent in *Major* Friedrich Wilhelm Jörn's *II.Bataillon/Grenadier-Regiment.989* to reinforce the attack. It was probably a company from this battalion that finally overran Dettor's platoon. Dettor recalled the last stand of his platoon in his diary:

> Germans do a great deal of yelling during battle. At least one out of three Germans had automatic weapons, carried a great deal of equipment, wore camouflage suits . . . No contact with men except those in immediate vicinity. Sgt. [Paul] Phifer, Sgt. Surtorka, myself fighting from the same emplacement . . . I ordered McDowell, the runner, to destroy all letters, situation map. Capt. Gardner reported left flank cut off by German infantry troops. German troops to rear . . . Pvt. Hunter dropped back to my foxhole to state that heavy machine gun in front had fallen . . . Sgt. Surtorka yelled over that grenade thrown at my foxhole. Hunter hit by grenade. Sgt. Phifer wounded in shoulder by rifle bullet. Enemy closing in within 20 feet of foxhole. Took last report of ammunition. Sgt. Phifer had one clip left. I had four rounds. Burp gun to left rear firing at my foxhole hitting Hunter. I believe Hunter was dead . . . Ordered runner to throw box of chocolate D bars to my foxhole which I distributed to men in immediate vicinity. 12:30 PM—position overrun . . . I believed I would be shot. Ordered out of foxhole and kicked by German soldier. Artillery and mortars still firing. Opposing company of enemy started digging in on my position. My men searched and ordered to carry German wounded to German rear lines . . . Great confusion taking place. Germans firing on my position with mortars killed our men. German officer greatly irritated.[17]

Although Fieger had deployed both of his grenadier battalions into the woods, they reported back to the corps headquarters at 1400 hours that they only managed to penetrate about 600 meters into the woods.[18] By later in the day, some of the unit made it to the Jans Brook (*Jans Bach*) about 2 kilometers (2,000 yards) from the start point on the edge of the forest. The *12.SS-Panzer-Division* was expecting them to be clear of the woods by midday and on the way to Elsenborn, but the attack had bogged down. The officers and NCOs were forced to lead from the front due to the inexperience of their untrained men, and as a result, the combat leaders quickly became casualties. Without their leadership, the German infantry advance faltered.

As a result, *I.SS-Panzer-Korps* instructed the *Hitlerjugend* to activate their reserve in the area, *Kampfgruppe Ott*. This battle group consisted primarily of *I./Panzergrenadier-Regiment.25* under the command of *Hauptsturmführer* Alfons Ott. *Kampfgruppen Ott* was ordered to follow behind *GR.989* and open up Rollbahn A to the clearings opposite Rocherath. The group began to move into the woods around midday and immediately suffered some casualties in the area of the Hollerath Knee, which by this time had come under American artillery fire.

Ott ordered his dismounted *Panzergrenadiers* to advance in a column of companies, with one in the lead and the other two staggered on either side behind the first. Following the infantry were the heavy weapons section, the anti-tank gun section, and the heavy infantry gun section. These later units were delayed since the engineers had still not finished assembling special panels over the dragon's teeth obstacles near the forest entrance that blocked access to vehicular traffic. An attempt was made to tow some of the heavy weapons down the forest road by hand, but they quickly became stuck in the mud.

Scouts from *KG Ott* reached the western side of the Krinkelterwald in the afternoon, with the rest of the battalion gradually following. There was little contact with American troops until this point. A small US supply column was trapped in the clearing and captured. Curiously enough, *KG Ott* had little contact with *Grenadier-Regiment.989* during its traverse of the woods.[19] One history of *I.SS-Panzer-Korps* has gone so far as to wonder whether *KG Ott* had even deployed into the woods as claimed.[20] A more likely explanation for its lack of contact with friendly or hostile troops was that it had become lost in the forest. As had been the case with *GR.989*, once *KG Ott* was in the woods, its communication network failed. Neither radio nor field telephone links were operable. With evidence of US troops wandering to his rear, and no sign of other friendly forces, Ott instructed his battalion to take up defensive positions. He sent his adjutant back through the woods in an attempt to get further instructions from either Fieger or his own divisional headquarters.

By early afternoon, Col. Jean Scott at the 393rd Infantry command post in Krinkelt was finally getting some firm information on the status of his two battalions. Allen's 3rd Battalion seemed to be in the most trouble, while Maj. Matthew Legler's 1st Battalion farther south seemed to be coping better. Scott had telephoned the 99th Division headquarters in Bütgenbach to inquire whether any reinforcements were available, and he was promised reinforcement in the form of I Company, 394th Infantry that was in divisional reserve.

Allen sent out guides, who met the approaching reinforcements and led them to the 3rd Battalion sector by late afternoon. In the meantime, another wave of German infantry attacks struck the M Company command post, forcing Allen to commit two platoons from Company I, 393rd Infantry to help repel this attack. M Company machine guns had taken a heavy toll on the German infantry; it was later estimated that there were 200 to 300 dead in front of their positions, and "the screaming of the German wounded could be heard throughout the day and into the night."[21] The fighting largely petered out by sunset, 1637 hours, though there was mortar and artillery shelling by both sides after dark.

By evening, Allen began counting the toll of the day's fighting. Plume's K Company had been largely destroyed, with only 2 officers and 45 enlisted men remaining of approximately 185 men at the start of the day. L Company had started the day with about 170 men and had been reduced to 133 men. Of the three rifle companies, I Company was in the best shape with about 155 men. M Company (heavy weapons) had lost its 1st MG Platoon and was down to about 95 of the original 165 men.

On the German side, *Oberst* Georg Fieger's *Grenadier-Regiment.989* had taken heavy losses in both battalions, though precise statistics have not survived. *Major* Lanzke, commander of *I./GR.989*, had been severely wounded, and *Major* Friedrich Wilhelm Jörn of *II./GR.989* had been killed in action. Fieger, who had recently returned from the hospital following treatment for wounds suffered in the spring of 1944, collapsed at his headquarters and had to be evacuated. The regiment was leaderless, stuck in the woods, and had suffered such heavy losses among the officers and NCOs that there was little prospect for any further advance.

Ott's *SS-Panzergrenadier* battalion had reached the western edge of the woods by the afternoon, but was out of touch with the other commands. That night, Ott came to believe that the American forces were trying to encircle his unit (there was no such effort). He decided to pull back his battalion into the woods, apparently to a defensive position of *Grenadier-Regiment.989*. Details of the time and location of the withdrawal are lacking.

Grenadier-Regiment.989 and *Kampfgruppe Ott* had failed to clear Rollbahn A even though their path was blocked by little more than an overstretched American infantry platoon. The *Volksgrenadiere* appear to have become distracted from their mission and embroiled in fighting with other elements of K Company by mid-morning. Forest fighting while under artillery fire was very disorienting for the inexperienced troops, and the *Volksgrenadiere* seem to have suffered a crippling loss of small-unit leaders from the outset of the fighting. This small failure would have serious repercussions in disrupting the time schedule of the *Hitlerjugend* advance.

Rollbahn B on X-Day

THE GERMAN ATTACK INTO THE KRINKELTERWALD ON X-DAY WAS A two-pronged attack, with *Grenadier-Regiment.989* attempting to seize Rollbahn A and farther south, *Oberstleutnant* Josef Bremm's *Grenadier-Regiment.990* attempting to take Rollbahn B. This regiment was located in the town of Udenbreth before the attack.

Bremm led the assault with a special *Sturm Kompanie* consisting of his better troops, equipped with a heavier concentration of automatic weapons. Bremm's regiment was supported by the divisional Fusilier company under *Hauptmann* Gerhard Hellige, which contained some of the division's better infantry. Hellige's company was located near the village of Neuhof before the attack.

Since the main objective of the day's mission was to seize the Class 3 road to Krinkelt-Rocherath, the emphasis of Bremm's attack was on the triangular section of the Hünningerwald forest that projected east of the International Highway where the road started. There were two ways to access this road, by moving either down the International Highway to the main road junction or across a forest path emanating out at Neuhof that connected to the road. Bremm selected to stage his main attack on the first option, while assigning Hellige's Fusilier company the forest path near Neuhof. Both these attacks were mainly directed against the positions of C Company, 393rd Infantry.

Facing Bremm's regiment was Major Matthew Legler's 1st Battalion, 393rd Infantry Regiment. In contrast to 3rd Battalion, the 1st Battalion had all three rifle companies available. The force ratio was roughly two-to-one in favor of the Germans, with two battalions facing one battalion. Legler had two rifle companies forward and one in reserve. Capt. Thomas DeBerry's Company B was along the forest edge in the section of the woods called the Mürringerwald, facing the small village

Maj. Matthew Legler,
commander of the
1st Battalion, 393rd
Infantry, 99th Division.

of Miescheid. Capt. Aaron Nathan's C Company was in a triangle of woods, part of the Hünningerwald, located to the east of the International Highway opposite the town of Udenbreth. As mentioned above, this area was the focus of the German attack. Capt. Joseph Jameson's A Company was in the woods behind C Company, slightly north of the Krinkelt road that ran northwest in a diagonal to the main International Highway. Capt. Harry Bangs's D Company (heavy weapons) had its machine guns positioned to provide coverage along the entire 3,500-yard battalion front, and the mortars were likewise positioned to enable fire support of the entire line.[1]

The battalion S-3 (operations) officer, Capt. Lawrence Duffin, described the initial German attack:

At 0530 on the morning of the 16th, the enemy opened a tremendous barrage of artillery, breaking the entire battalion front. This barrage continued without pause until about 0700 and shortly afterwards, enemy riflemen supported by automatic weapons attacked both flanks of the Battalion front. This initial attack was repulsed with only a few casualties among the battalion troops. At approximately 0800, the enemy attacked again, this time using successive waves of infantry. The artillery forward observers estimated an almost continuous artillery barrage in front of our lines. Our own mortars and machine guns fired their protective lines. Both front lines companies reported numerous enemy dead piled up immediately in front of their positions, but at approximately 0830, C Company reported an enemy breakthrough on their right flank.[2]

Hauptmann Gerhard Hellige's *Füsilier-Kompanie.277* had attacked on either side of the small road leading from Neuhof to the edge of the forest. They were lucky enough to hit the junction between the 1/393rd Infantry and 394th Infantry, which presented a gap in the defenses. As a result, the company was able to advance up the forest path that intersected the International Highway along the southern flank of C Company. While Hellige's company had made some progress, the main attack by Bremm's *GR.990* made no headway when it attacked near the junctions of the B Company and C Company defenses. Duffin later described the situation:

> The reserve [A] Company was alerted for counter-attack, but the enemy made no attempt to penetrate the lines farther and seemed satisfied to occupy only the front-line positions. Some of the Germans got into the same foxholes with our soldiers and several were bayoneted. Others occupied positions adjacent to and in the rear of our foxholes. The defense was spread so thin that our line was mainly a series of strongpoints with gaps in between each. It is to be emphasized that our soldiers did not retreat but stayed in their positions until they were overrun.[3]

Hellige's Fusilier company stalled once it reached the International Highway. This may have been due to the casualties sustained crossing the open ground from Neuhof. In the meantime, Bremm threw in the last of his regimental reserve against the southern edge of B Company, but they failed to reach the edge of the woods and suffered very heavy casualties.

The *277. Volksgrenadier-Division* still had its *Grenadier-Regiment. 991* in divisional reserve in Ramscheid, waiting for instructions. Oberst Viebig was aware that *GR. 989* in the north was already into the Krinkelterwald on Rollbahn A. However, Rollbahn A was limited to a narrow and muddy forest road, hardly adequate for mechanized operations. The Rollbahn B road was durable enough for mechanized traffic and so Viebig decided to throw this reserve into the battle for Rollbahn B. He instructed *Oberstleutnant* Otto Jaquet to move *GR. 991* from Ramscheid and to attack on the right of Bremm's faltering *GR. 990*. His lead battalion began to form up in a gully southwest of Ramsheid after 0800 hours. Duffin described the results: "From 0800 to 0930, B Company was under constant attack by great numbers of enemy infantry. At approximately 0830, a particularly heavy concentration of enemy infantry was reported in the draw to the east of B Company's limiting point east of Ramsheid, but was broken up by artillery."[4]

The American troops had seen Jaquet's move into the gully, and called in an artillery strike on them. The lead battalion of Jaquet's *GR. 991* was badly smashed up by the American artillery barrage, but the follow-on battalion managed to advance across the open ground and finally penetrate the American lines. According to Duffin:

> At approximately 0935, B Company reported that its left flank platoon and part of the center platoon had been overrun in force. A Company, in reserve, was ordered to counter-attack to restore B Company's left flank. A Company moved out and attacked to the northeast crossing the counter-attack line-of-departure at approximately 1000. It restored approximately 300 yards of B Company's original front line positions before being stopped by overwhelming numbers of enemy infantry and heavy enemy artillery fire. A Company held this position against repeated enemy attacks for the remainder of the 16th.[5]

Unteroffizier Karl Heinz Franke, a squad leader in the *3./GR.991,* recalled the fighting and the death of his company commander, *Hauptmann* Hans Hagedorn:

> Further behind us is our Chef [boss], at his side Sergeant M., and the company runner. Several other riflemen work their way forward. So we get away from the artillery impacts and as close as possible to the enemy, now in front of us. Strong rifle fire strikes around us from the jumble of branches of two felled spruce trees. Crawling on our belly, we work our way through the snow. Sergeant M. tries a surprise rush. Followed by his runner, he charges forward. Firing from the hip, he attracts the enemy's defensive fire. Hit!
>
> Unaffected by the American sniper, our Sani [medic] goes to work. The boss is shouting something to me. I don't understand. I'm lying just in front of a tree obstruction. The foolhardy Panzerschreck [anti-tank rocket] team sets up a few meters to the left, in front of the obstacle. A quick aim, followed by a rocket blast and the heavy bang in the spruce branches. Our opponents are finished.
>
> An [American] prisoner near us wants to move to the rear, but has to drop down next to me when the artillery fire resumes. Now we're nose to nose when the explosions start. He grins gratefully when I offer him a captured Chesterfield cigarette. We think we have been given a reprieve by the destruction of the enemy strongpoint. But to err is human! Our right flank has been bypassed, and now we receive rifle fire from the right and from the front! A few meters behind us, the boss is still there. I can see him screaming orders and waving his arms when he is hit and collapses. "SANNIIIEE!" The medic scurries up, raises the head of the "old man." Dead! Desperately, I count what's left of the scattered troops. Two NCOs and seven men. Further penetration into the woods is impossible—would be pointless—suicide!
>
> We communicate by signs, we crawl, and crawl, and slide into a captured trench and form a hedgehog defense.[6]

By late morning, Viebig's divisional headquarters had lost contact with Hellige's Fusilier company. The isolated unit had established an all-around defense in the woods to the south of C Company but could advance no further. The rest of *GR.990* and *GR.991* were still trying to overcome the American defenses in the tree line near the International Highway. Viebig later complained that "the reinforcements promised by the [I.SS-Panzer] Korps in the form of assault guns and engineer equipment either failed to appear or came too late."[7]

Shortly before noon, the 1/393rd Infantry Regiment formed a counterattack group after borrowing the mine-laying platoon from the regimental anti-tank company. This was expanded with troops from the battalion headquarters company until it was roughly platoon strength, about forty men. Under the battalion operations officer, Capt. Lawrence Duffin, this scratch force advanced down the International Highway and attacked an exposed portion of Hellige's *Füsilier-Kompanie.277* on the right flank of C Company, capturing twenty-eight Germans and forcing the remainder to withdraw. By the late afternoon the front had stabilized, with the 1/393rd Infantry Regiment holding most of the same positions as earlier in the morning.

German casualties during the day were extremely high. *Grenadier Regiment.990* suffered about 350 killed and 580 wounded out of a starting strength of about 1,400 men, more than half its strength.[8] A soldier from *6./GR.990* captured after the attack said:

> Men of this particular division were very disappointed in the manner in which the attack was launched. Tanks and airplanes were promised by the hundreds. However, none were available when the attack actually started. Many died charging blindly into [American] machine gun and rifle fire. Morale dropped considerably . . . The 2nd Battalion suffered such heavy losses that the whole unit was consolidated into two companies, 50 men each . . . The estimated strength of the whole [*GR.990*] is 200–300 men.[9]

The *277.Volksgrenadier-Division* had nothing to show for their heavy losses. And Rollbahn B was still bottled up.

AFTER-ACTION ASSESSMENT

After the war, the *277.Volksgrenadier-Division* commander, Wilhelm Viebig, offered six reasons for the failure of the unit to carry out its mission on X-Day:

(1) The division was not properly trained for offensive operation in a dense forest.

(2) The division did not have sufficient forces to clear both Rollbahn A and B, especially in light of the failure of the corps to provide the promised assault guns and engineer support.

(3) The battalion and company commanders could not be properly instructed on their missions due to the tight secrecy imposed by Berlin.

(4) *Grenadier-Regiment.990* was exhausted when it reached the starting positions since its movement had been delayed by the late arrival of its replacement unit.

(5) Artillery preparation was ineffective due to insufficient ammunition and the dispersion of what ammunition was available due to a lack of artillery reconnaissance imposed by Berlin's secrecy requirements.

(6) Heavy losses of officers and NCOs took place at the outset of combat due to the need to lead inexperienced troops by example.[10]

Were other options available? Some accounts have suggested that the *6.Panzer-Armee* should have started the offensive with their panzer divisions rather than relying on weak infantry divisions. In this sector, this would have been physically impossible. The rows of dragon's teeth, reinforced by both German and American minefields along the border, could not be overcome by tanks unless there was a substantial engineer effort to create paths through the anti-tank barriers. These barriers could not be breached before the start of the attack since this would alert the Americans that an offensive was planned. The German panzer force lacked specialized armored engineer vehicles such as dozer tanks or mine-roller tanks to quickly breach the anti-tank barriers.

Beyond this, the Krinkelterwald forest in this area was too dense and the road network so poor that it would have been impossible to pass a panzer regiment quickly through the woods. The Losheim-Losheimergraben area offered better roads, though as the next chapter will describe, there were some significant problems with tank transit there as well. A further complication was that the *Hitlerjugend's SS-Panzer-Regiment.12* was still caught up in traffic on the way to Losheim, and more than a third of its vehicles had suffered mechanical breakdowns during the three-day road march to the area from their original bases in the Cologne area.

A more plausible tactical alternative would have been for the *6.Panzer-Armee* to employ the infiltration tactics used by portions of Manteuffel's neighboring *5.Panzer-Armee*. Instead of relying on the preparatory artillery barrage, Manteuffel's *Volksgrenadier* divisions created special assault battalions that infiltrated through the many gaps in the thin American defense line "like drops of rain."[11] Manteuffel's units were already in the rear of the forward American battalions before they even realized that the German attack had begun. However, these tactics were forbidden by Hitler's tactical instructions of November 18. Dietrich obeyed the instructions; Manteuffel ignored them. Dietrich's infantry was halted by the American defenses; Manteuffel's infiltrating infantry caused the collapse of the 106th Infantry Division, opening the way to the Meuse.

Rollbahn C: Losheimergraben on X-Day

OF THE THREE ROUTES ASSIGNED TO THE *HITLERJUGEND*, THE BEST was in the area northwest of Losheim, often called the Losheim Gap. This road was the main border crossing along this stretch of the Belgian-German border, with German and Belgian customhouses in Losheimergraben. Rollbahn C was a good-quality Class 2 road, part of the International Highway, going from Losheim through Losheimergraben, and exiting the woods near the village of Hünningen on the Belgian side of the frontier.[1] More importantly, this road divided near Hünningen, heading northeast toward Elsenborn and northwest toward Malmedy, and so offered more tactical opportunities. Rollbahn D was a railway line and small parallel service road cutting through Buchholz. Due to the obvious value of these routes, the *I.Panzer-Korps* plan allotted an entire division to open this portion of the Losheim Gap, *Generalmajor* Gerhard Engel's *12.Volksgrenadier-Division*.

Losheimergraben was a key entry point across the German-Belgian border, with a pair of German and Belgian government customs and tollhouses on either side of the main street. The German hotel with tollhouse is on the left, the Belgian on the right.

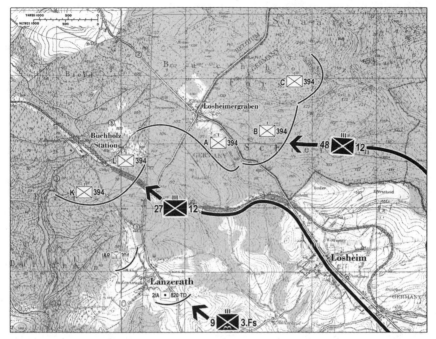

The *12.Volksgrenadier-Division* Attack on December 16, 1944
This map illustrates the attack by two regiments of the *12.Volsgrenadier-Division* and one regiment of the *3.Fallschirmjäger-Division* against two battalions of the 394th Infantry, 99th Infantry Division around Losheimergraben on X-Day.

Engel decided to use two of his three regiments in the initial assault, with *Oberstleutnant* Heinz-Georg Lemm's *Füsilier-Regiment.27* on the left flank, advancing up the railway tracks toward Buchholz, and *Oberstleutnant* Wilhelm Osterhold's *Grenadier-Regiment.48* heading up the main road from Losheim to Losheimergraben. Osterhold was reinforced with the division's only armored support, six *StuG IV* assault guns of the divisional anti-tank unit, *Panzerjäger-Abteilung.1012*. The division's Fusilier company was kept in reserve along with anti-tank guns and engineers to serve as a fast spearhead once the infantry had cleared a path through the forest. The division's third regiment, *Major* Otto Benzin's *Grenadier-Regiment.89*, was held in reserve near the village of Frauenkron.

149

The railyard was called *Bahnhof Losheimergraben* by the Germans, but it was better known as Bucholz Station to the US Army.

Facing Engel's *12. VGD* were the 1st and 3rd Battalions of the 394th Infantry Division. The 394th Infantry, commanded by Col. Don Riley, had all three of its battalions in this sector. Lt. Col. Philip Wertheimer's 2/394th Infantry connected to the 1/393rd Infantry near Udenbreth and occupied the forested area to the north. In the center, Lt. Col. Robert Douglas's 1st Battalion stretched 3,500 yards from an arbitrary boundary in the densely wooded Staatsforst Schleiden, roughly bounded on its right flank by the Kyll river to the northeast and Losheimergraben on its left flank. To the southwest, Maj. Norman Moore's 3rd Battalion was in regimental reserve around Buchholz Station, with only a modest outpost line in place. The regiment's I&R (Intelligence and Reconnaissance) platoon, under Lt. Lyle Bouck, held an isolated outpost on the

Lt. Col. Robert Douglas, commander of the 1st Battalion, 394th Infantry, 99th Infantry Division marches alongside a 1.5-ton WC62 truck.

hill overlooking the village of Lanzerath, about a thousand yards out-side of the regiment's southern perimeter. Beyond the I&R platoon was a no-man's-land, sporadically patrolled by a cavalry screen from Task Force X of the 14th Cavalry Group.

Unlike the other regiments of the 99th Division, the 394th Infantry had most of its strongpoints deep in the woods, not at the forest edge. There were some small outposts along the forest edge for observation. Since the road leading from Losheim to Losheimergraben was good enough to permit the use of armored vehicles, the regimental anti-tank company deployed towed 57mm anti-tank guns to cover key locations. Two of these were located north of the Losheim-Losheimergraben road and one south. The battalion had been in its position for about a week before the start of the German offensive.

There was some concern that the Germans could advance from Lan-zerath across the railway tracks into the southwest side of Losheimergra-ben. The bridge on the International Highway running from Lanzerath to Losheimergraben was demolished. The second road bridge over the railway tracks that ran from the International Highway to Hüllscheid had a 1,500-pound TNT charge positioned on it by engineers on the night of December 15. Lt. Col. Douglas wanted it blown up immediately to block any German approach from this direction. However, this required regimental approval, which did not come in time.[2]

FIRE POWER

As in the other sectors, the attack began with a heavy barrage. There was a strong contrast in the opinions from both sides regarding the intensity and effectiveness of the barrage, with the American side considering it enormous and the German side deprecating its effectiveness.

According to an American account:

The attack . . . began at 0530 on 16 December with an artillery concentration which, for the enemy, was of unprecedented ferocity. Men who had been through campaigns in North Africa, Italy, Normandy, and eastern France stated it was the heaviest they had ever experienced. Guns and mortars of all calibers, supplemented by multiple-barreled rocket projectors, plastered the battalion area unceasingly until about 0730. From that time on, the enemy artillery and mortar fire, though never again reaching the sustained concentration it had attained in that initial saturating preparation, was constant in its interdiction of road junctions, roads, and our possible assembly areas. Intermittent harassing fire would erupt in a barrage of volcanic fury.[3]

According to a German account:

At 0530 on 16 December, the brief but intense fire concentration commenced. All available artillery and Nebelwerfers were directed against identified enemy positions, traffic points, village entrances and exits. It would soon become evident, however, that our fire had little effect owing to the lack of reconnaissance, particularly air reconnaissance, and because the American strong points in this sector were only weakly manned.[4]

Of the two accounts of the barrage, the German account was the more sober. The American account is odd in comparing the barrage to past experiences, considering how few of the troops of 1/394th Infantry had been in combat before. There is very little data on the number of casualties inflicted by the barrage, but the American losses do not appear to have been especially heavy. K Company, 394th Infantry had no casualties because "most of the artillery fire in this area resulted in tree bursts and all positions had been constructed with overhead cover during the previous week."[5] As in other sectors, the most important tactical consequence of the barrage was that it ripped up the wires for the field telephone network, shutting down most of the communications network except for radios.[6] The 1/394th Infantry commander, Col. Robert Douglas, later recalled: "One of the early casualties of December 16 was a new telephone line completed up to the front line. It was a shame to find the gleaming copper wires, once so neatly stretched between erect poles, on the ground in a tangled mess."[7]

Engel's two lead regiments began advancing in the predawn darkness around 0600 hours. The division had only arrived in the area on the nights of December 15 and 16, so had no details of American defensive dispositions. Lemm's *Füsilier-Regiment.27* had been assigned to take the railway station in Buchholz. This was called *Bahnhof Losheimergraben* by the Germans and Buchholz Station by the Americans. The Buchholz name is used here to avoid confusion with the village of Losheimergraben that was about 1,500 yards to the northeast of the station and separated by the forest.

To reach its objective, Lemm's *Füsilier-Regiment.27* marched from Hallschlag along the railway lines through Losheim before veering off to the west to Buchholz Station. Lemm reported back to headquarters around 0900 hours that the regiment had captured Losheim, though in fact it had not been occupied by American troops. Losheim had been in no-man's-land between the 99th Division and the *277.Volksgrenadier-Division*, with German and American outposts near the town. It was not strongly held by either side.

The lead company of Lemm's column approached Buchholz Station, bumping into an outpost of L Company, 3/394th Infantry. American reports place the time of the first encounters between 0745 and 0930; the discrepancy in times is unexplained.[8] The lead column, initially estimated at about forty to fifty men, was first spotted on the railway line 1,000 yards south of Buchholz Station by an outpost of L Company. The ground was enveloped in thick morning fog, and at first it was thought that the column might be from the 4th Platoon of L Company troops heading into Buchholz for morning chow. The German formation was in closed route march column formation, with no signs of lead scouts or other security measures. There was a brief exchange of fire once the American outpost realized that the troops were German.

The 3rd Battalion headquarters ordered the outposts back to the main L Company positions near the railway station while an ambush was prepared. Maj. Moore, the commander of 3/394th Infantry, directed the A&P (Ammunition and Pioneer) platoon to take up positions on high ground overlooking the station. The German column continued to advance toward Buchholz Station, still without any forward security. It turned out that the column was larger than originally reported. A mortar observation post from the neighboring 1/393rd Infantry was on a hilltop overlooking the railway line from the east and estimated the German column as a battalion-strength formation of 300 to 400 men. This was one of the battalions from Lemm's *Füsilier-Regiment.27*.

When the Germans reached a line of boxcars about 200 yards from the company headquarters, the American troops opened fire with small arms and machine guns, supported by 81mm mortars of M Company. The German column was completely surprised. About sixty German soldiers made a mad dash for cover inside the boxcars, but the wooden-walled railway cars offered little protection from infantry weapons. The boxcars proved to be tempting targets for bazookas and a 57mm anti-tank gun. Some of the surviving German infantrymen fled the boxcars, but were brought under rifle and machine-gun fire from three sides. The survivors eventually recoiled back from the station, leaving behind about thirty prisoners and numerous dead and wounded. Captured

German soldiers indicated that they had been told that there were no US units in the area of the station, which explained their lackadaisical security.[9] It was also evidence of the lack of experienced leadership among the small-unit commanders after the division's slapdash rebuilding the week before.

Osterhold's *Grenadier-Regiment.48* reached the Gerolstein woods around daybreak and began moving through the forest to the northwest. "They soon became involved in fierce fighting with several American outposts. Progress in this area was delayed considerably by wire and tree barriers connected to innumerable mines. [Osterhold's] regiment sustained heavy losses."[10]

As the unit entered the woods, they encountered numerous booby traps consisting of trip wires attached to mines and explosive charges. Due to the lack of training of most of the young troops, it was the officers like Osterhold himself who set about trying to neutralize this menace.

> We cut through these wires and that was dangerous because the very young soldiers saw what we did, and they cut off every wire they found. We didn't even have time to instruct them and we had to move on. They wanted to be helpful and they cut my artillery officer's telephone wire. When everything was ready and our mortars and infantry guns were supposed to give the signal for the assault, our own artillery showered my 1st Battalion with some 500 rounds of heavy caliber ammunition. The result was devastating; the major part of the rounds exploded in the tree tops and showered the ground, like a hailstorm. Only five yards from my position, my 1st Battalion commander, Major Siegfried Moldenhauer, was severely wounded in the back. With one unlucky strike the battalion lost two-thirds of its strength and the remainder had all hands busy bandaging the wounded and carrying them back to the road for ambulance pickup. The 2d Battalion under Major Gerhard Kruse had to be moved up as the new spearhead and it was this battalion that assaulted the crossroads.[11]

As Osterhold's depleted regiment was advancing through the woods, a patrol was sent up the Losheim-Losheimergraben road. This route was blocked by sections of downed overpasses and other debris that made travel difficult. As its name implies, *Losheimergraben* (Losheim Gully) is in a depression with hills on either side. In the lead of the German patrol was a captured American jeep. One minor mystery is whether the jeep was part of Otto Skorzeny's *Panzer-Brigade.150.* This unit was partly equipped with captured American vehicles and uniforms and was intended to scout ahead of *I.SS-Panzer-Korps.* Two of Skorzeny's three groups were in the rear areas of the *Hitlerjugend.* It is not clear from available accounts whether the jeep was one of those assigned to Skorzeny, or whether Engel's troops were simply using a jeep they had captured in an earlier engagement.[12]

> After the barrage had lifted an American jeep, driven by Germans, came northwest up the road from Losheim. It was observed by the AT [anti-tank] gun crew which was in position about 50 yards north of the road. The jeep halted almost under the nose of the gun, which did not fire, then turned and went back south. It returned five minutes later leading a Tiger tank up the road. As the tank came almost opposite the AT gun, the crew of the gun opened fire on the tank. The first round knocked off a track, a second round penetrated the hull and the third round set the tank on fire. The German crew bailed out and took up firing positions around the tank where they opened fire on the AT gun crew with small arms. The jeep, which had continued up the road, was knocked out by small arms fire from the men of B Company astride the road.[13]

The *Tiger* tank was in fact a *StuG IV* assault gun of *Panzerjäger-Abteilung.1012.* US troops called virtually any German tracked armored vehicle a "Tiger tank," and every artillery piece an "88." These ubiquitous misidentifications have led to numerous accounts of *Tiger* tanks taking part in the fights for Elsenborn, though in fact none were present in this sector.[14] Some of the surviving accounts suggest that this incident occurred in the early morning before 1000 hours, while others place the time at 1145 to 1200 hours.[15]

The fighting around Buchholz Station spilled over to Losheimer-graben as troops from Lemm's *Füsilier-Regiment.27* tried to escape the melee at Bucholz Station by moving through the woods toward Losheimergraben.

A *StuG IV* assault gun of *Panzerjäger-Abteilung.1012* of the *12.Volksgrenadier-Division*, knocked out near Losheimergraben while fighting with elements of the 394th Infantry, 99th Division.

Company A reported a large combat patrol of between 150–200 men had penetrated the area due west of them . . . This combat patrol had hit the 3rd Battalion [at Buchholz Station] and bounced off to the northeast in the direction of the A Company CP. Company A then organized a defensive position with the remaining platoon and Head-quarters company personnel, about 150 yards south of the company

CP. The large German force hit the A Company defensive positions, was repulsed, and turned east. Two A Company squads, sent up from the southernmost defensive positions, hit the flank of the German force and turned it right into the 81mm mortar platoon positions, hitting them from the rear. The mortar platoon, dug in, had its fields of fire to the south and east. A hot, tense, and for a few minutes, confused melee ensued. The German force did not turn north to take the CP in the small town, because at the time it was being subjected to exceedingly heavy enemy artillery fire. The mortar leader, 1Lt. John Vaughan, employed one of his mortar sections and one squad of A Company and took the German force under fire. The Germans infiltrated east through the mortar position. The mortar section and rifle squad under Lt. Vaughan fired small arms at the Germans, killing several as they worked through the platoon position . . . After the German force had passed through, they turned around and formed a line about 100 yards southeast of the position. Apparently, having found the mortars, they were coming back to get them. As they started forward, Lt. Vaughan had his mortars fire almost vertically. Rounds were dropping within 25 yards of the platoon position. The Germans were repulsed with heavy losses . . . About 75 Germans must have been killed or wounded in this melee.[16]

The fleeing columns from *Füsilier-Regiment.27* were then hit with more small-arms fire as two more A Company squads appeared on the scene. They were eventually forced back to the southeast, ending the prolonged skirmish in the early afternoon.

While the fighting was going on in the vicinity of Losheimergraben, Osterhold's battered *Grenadier-Regiment.48* had rushed the forward outposts of B Company and pushed them back in. The main effort by the Germans was near the junction of B and C Companies in a shallow ravine with a small brook running through it, called "Creepy Corner" by the American troops. It had received this nickname after several encounters with German patrols in the ravine after dark in the weeks prior to the offensive. The fighting between *Grenadier-Regiment.48* and B Company was at close range and costly to both sides.

T/Sgt. Raymond Milne with the B Company mine platoon recalled his experiences when his position was hit during the attack:

When the Germans attacked, I was in a shallow foxhole with the assistant squad leader named Davidson. The time of day is confusing to me but it was still daylight. After some fighting, our foxhole was hit by a machine gun burst. Davidson was killed and I was hit slightly in the arm and severely in the upper leg, breaking it. Shortly after that, I was knocked unconscious after a German fired a Panzerfaust directly into our hole. When I regained consciousness, it was getting dark and I was bleeding from the eyes, nose and ears. My left arm was bleeding a lot more and my leg hardly at all. Davidson's body was outside the hole and a German soldier was in with me. He was very badly wounded in the chest and stomach and in bad shape. By now the fighting was so far away from us you could barely hear it.[17]

The surge by *Grenadier-Regiment.48* swept over the forward B Company outposts and into the main defensive perimeter.

B Company was over-run, with Jerries all over the position using some of the [American] foxholes that were in the area. There were more foxholes than there were American infantry to fill them. The HMG [heavy machine gun] platoon which was in position in the B Company area, was also over-run. The platoon sergeant, T/Sgt. Eddie Dolenc, pulled his gun out of the prepared position which had too restricted a field-of-fire, and set it up in a shell hole. When last seen, he was firing the gun alone. Between 20 and 25 Germans were piled up in front of the position. B Company was forced back about 400 yards during the fighting which lasted from about 0900 to late afternoon.[18]

Dolenc was later awarded the Distinguished Service Cross.[19]

While B Company's defenses were pushed back, other elements of Osterhold's *Grenadier-Regiment.48* were attacking C Company, immediately to the east of B Company.

C Company's outposts were driven in during the first enemy infantry onslaught . . . The rest of the company was intact initially. Visibility was poor in this wooded area. Fields-of-fire for rifles and automatic weapons were about as limited as visibility, about 50–100 yards or so. About 1300, one platoon of C Company was ordered to attack the penetration [in the B Company sector] and pinch it off. The penetration in the company area was never completely driven back.[20]

Retreat from Buchholz Station

Maj. Norman Moore's 3rd Battalion, 394th Infantry was supposed to be the regimental reserve on December 16, but instead became caught up in the fighting with *12. Volksgrenadier-Division*. The battalion was understrength, missing its I Company as well as the usual attached machine-gun platoon from M Company. However, Moore's main concern was the situation in the adjacent 1st Battalion around Losheimergraben, which had suffered extensive losses during the day's fighting. If 1st Battalion was forced to withdraw, this would leave Moore's 3rd Battalion completely adrift with no substantial American force on either of its flanks and an uncertain situation to its rear.[21]

After receiving permission to do so, Moore had L Company withdraw into the woods about 500 yards northeast of the railway line in order to link up with Company A, 1/394th Infantry, abandoning the defense of Buchholz Station. K Company pulled back in line with L Company into the woods paralleling the Losheim-Losheimergraben-Mürringen road. These moves were completed shortly before dusk at about 1500 hours. The regimental headquarters evidently had second thoughts about abandoning the station, and around 1600 hours they instructed Moore to detach a platoon from K Company and send it back to the northern end of Buchholz, shown as F. Buchholz on the tactical maps.[22]

Moore was not happy to do so, feeling he would be throwing away a platoon to an exposed position at a time when every rifleman was needed. Nevertheless, the regimental headquarters insisted, and so Lt. Rose, executive officer of K Company, led 1st Platoon back toward the outskirts of the station. As Moore feared, this platoon was overrun after dark.

Around dusk, elements of Lemm's *Füsilier-Regiment.27* moved back into the railyard and reported to divisional headquarters at about 1600 hours that it was in their hands. There was little contact between Rose's platoon on the northern side of the area and the German troops in the railyard once it became dark.

THE NEED FOR SPEED

The plans for Autumn Mist were predicated on the need for the German infantry to rapidly punch through the American main line of resistance and open up channels for the *SS-Panzer* divisions to advance to the Meuse. By the end of the day, the only route that was partly opened was Rollbahn E through Lanzerath, assigned to *1.SS-Panzer-Division "LAH"* (*Leibstandarte Adolf Hitler*).

The *3.Fallschirmjäger-Division* had been assigned the task of opening Rollbahn E through Lanzerath. This should have been the easiest of the breakthroughs due to the extreme imbalance between German and US forces. Lanzerath happened to be located at the corps boundary between VIII Corps to the southwest and V Corps to the northwest. It was screened by nothing more than the 14th Cavalry Group.[23] Normally, a gap this size would be assigned to an entire infantry division, not to a unit with a deployable-strength roughly that of a single infantry battalion. Furthermore, the cavalry commander, Col. Mark Devine, decided to keep one of his two squadrons in reserve almost 20 miles behind the front.[24]

A defensive plan had been developed for the Losheim Gap when the 2nd Infantry Division was responsible for the sector earlier in December, which consisted of a withdrawal of the forward outposts to the Manderfeld ridge, preregistered artillery strikes forward of these defenses, and a counterattack toward the Schnee Eifel. When the 106th Division took over this sector on December 11, this plan went into limbo in spite of the efforts of the cavalry. In contrast to the conditions in the V Corps sector to the north, with forests along the frontier, this sector consisted of open farmland with a far better road network.

Generalmajor Wadehn's understrength *3.Fallschirmjäger-Division* was deployed with both available regiments up front. *FJR.9* (*Fallschirmjäger-Regiment.9*) was assigned to seize the small village of Lanzerath, while *FJR.5* was assigned the capture of Krewinkel, the nominal start point of Rollbahn E.

Lanzerath was occupied by a screening force from the 820th Tank Destroyer Battalion attached to the 14th Cavalry Group. They were deployed as a counter-reconnaissance screen to repulse German patrols or small raiding parties and were not expected to defend the village against a full-strength attack. The force in Lanzerath totaled about fifty-five men and consisted of four towed 3-inch anti-tank guns from 2nd Platoon, A Company, plus the 2nd Reconnaissance Platoon of the 820th Tank Destroyer Battalion consisting of about twenty men with a half-track and two jeeps. The village was hit during the German barrage. Around 0700 hours, when the screening force first saw a large column of German paratroops approaching the village, they withdrew from Lanzerath based on their previous instructions and headed back to the main battalion positions around Manderfeld.

The only other US force in the area was an understrength I&R platoon of the 394th Infantry under the command of Lt. Lyle Bouck. This unit served as the southernmost outpost of the 99th Division. Shortly after the departure of the screening force, Bouck conducted a brief scouting foray into the village. He deployed his force, only about a squad in size, in a trench line on a hill overlooking Lanzerath. Shortly after, elements of *I./FJR.9* emerged from the village in marching order. A young girl from the village warned the paratroopers about the Americans on the hill and about a hundred paratroopers deployed in a skirmish line 100 meters in front of the American positions. The paratroopers advanced uphill across a snow-covered field divided by a barbed wire fence. A slaughter ensued as paratroopers were mowed down by machine-gun fire. A truce was called around 1200 hours for German medics to clear the wounded, and then the attacks resumed, including reinforcements from *II./FJR.9*.

Through the course of the early afternoon, the Germans launched two more frontal charges with equally ghastly results. Casualties in the

I./FJR.9 were sixteen dead, sixty-three wounded, and thirteen missing.[25] Although Bouck's men held their position, most were wounded, little ammunition remained, and their machine guns had been put out of action. In the late afternoon, the German tactics changed when a veteran NCO, infuriated by the casualties, pointedly told the commander, an inexperienced rear-echelon *Luftwaffe* staff officer, that they should outflank the American position and not continue to attack it frontally. This time the American position was quickly overwhelmed and the survivors, including Bouck, captured. The fate of Bouck's platoon was unknown to the 394th Infantry, which lost radio contact with it around 1400 hours.[26]

Bouck's platoon was later awarded the Presidential Unit Citation and he and his men were decorated with four Distinguished Service Crosses and five Silver Stars, making it the most decorated unit of the war. An understrength platoon had held off a paratrooper regiment for an entire day, in turn delaying the advance of *1.SS-Panzer Division* for nearly a day.

The defense of Krewinkel was more short-lived. The village was held by a platoon from C Troop, 18th Cavalry Squadron in a series of foxholes. As at Lanzerath, *FJR.5* attacked frontally, resulting in heavy casualties. However, the American positions were so thin that German units simply continued their march westward past the defenses. The 14th Cavalry Group commander, Col. Mark Devine, asked the 106th Division to send reinforcements as per the earlier defensive plan, but the 106th Division, largely unaware of the plan, refused. In the late morning, Devine ordered his men to withdraw to Manderfeld. The cavalry began withdrawing from Krewinkel at 1100, as did neighboring garrisons in Abst and Weckerath. The garrison at Roth was overrun and that in Kobsheid had to wait until dark to withdraw. Reinforcements from the 32nd Cavalry Squadron arrived near Manderfeld in the late afternoon, but by this stage, German troops were already pouring past. The surviving elements from the 18th Cavalry abandoned Manderfeld around 1600, heading for the squadron headquarters at Holzheim.

For all intents and purposes, Rollbahn E was open. The problem was that it did not offer a very good road network.

FOR THE WANT OF A BRIDGE

One of the apparent mysteries of the fighting for Losheimergraben and Buchholz Station was the failure of *I. SS-Panzer-Korps* to reinforce the infantry assault, especially *12. Volksgrenadier-Division*, to speed the penetration of the American lines. While multiple factors contributed to this mistake, one of the main ones was the massive traffic jam that had developed during the day on the approaches to Losheim.

The best road approaching the Losheim Gap entered Losheim from the southeast. Currently highway B421, this road emanates from the larger road network around Cologne, Bonn, and Koblenz heading westward past Hallschlag and Scheid. This region was the major staging area for Autumn Mist. The road network was far from ideal for the conduct of mechanized operations, though it might have proved adequate but for the usual friction of war. In this case, it was a single bridge overpass that crossed over the railway tracks southeast of Losheim.

The bridge had been knocked down and not replaced earlier in the autumn. Although it was surrounded by relatively flat farm fields, the various tree lines, hedges, and other obstructions prevented easy access past the downed bridge to reach Losheim, especially for the type of ordinary commercial trucks in use by the *Wehrmacht*. The funnel effect was further amplified by Westwall construction in the late 1930s that created numerous anti-tank barriers along the German-Belgian border in this area. The *I. Panzer-Korps* was aware of the problem, and the Autumn Mist plan had assigned an engineer bridge battalion to deal with it. However, this engineer unit became tied up in the traffic jam itself.

Finally, *1. SS-Panzer-Division* sent its own engineers to the site to repair the bridge as well as to create a parallel access route over the train tracks for tanks and cross-country vehicles. However, this route was not opened until 1600 hours.[27] As a result, for nearly half a day, traffic directed toward Losheim became backed up on the narrow country roads in the area. The traffic jam included elements of both the *3. Fallschirmjäger-Division*, *12. Volksgrenadier-Division*, and *1. SS-Panzer-Division* and three battle groups of the *Hitlerjugend*.

Otto Skorzeny, the leader of *Panzer-Brigade.150*, was caught in this traffic jam, first becoming stuck outside Schmidtheim, which was about 21 kilometers (13 miles) from the outskirts of Losheim. His unit was intended to serve as the spearhead for the *I.SS-Panzer-Korps* advance. He later described the situation:

> The endless rows of vehicles moved in stop-and-go tempo, covering barely a hundred meters at a time. It was a wretched sight and I couldn't imagine that it was really necessary to move all these huge columns. I'd just got out onto the main road as we stopped again for a long time. I turned around and drove back to Schmidtheim and then continued along almost impassable side roads to Dahlem. It was the same picture there: backed-up vehicles and hardly a movement forwards. There was nothing left to do but get out and walk. I walked slowly towards Stadtkyll. Occasionally I was able to sort out the hopeless mess of vehicles with a great deal of effort and patience. Every time I found an officer sitting comfortably in a vehicle, I sent him onto the road to straighten things out. The traffic had come to a complete standstill in the steep valley bends outside Stadtkyll. It was even difficult for me to get through here on foot. Order had to be established here so that the essential munitions and fuel supplies could get through.[28]

Even after walking to Stadtkyll, Skorzeny was still more than 15 kilometers (9 miles) from Losheim, and the roads ahead were completely jammed with troops and vehicles. Nor was this the only downed bridge in the area. As mentioned earlier, the 99th Division had demolished the overpass bridge between Losheim and Losheimergraben. Given the strict timeline of the Autumn Mist plan, these minor obstacles soon turned into major impediments to the operation.

OPERATION ABWEHR

The *12.SS-Panzer-Division* faced similar problems, but on different roads. The initial divisional staging area was around Gruenbroich, northwest of Cologne. Operation Abwehr began on the night of December

8.[29] This was the code name for the divisions earmarked for Autumn Mist to begin moving from their staging areas near the Rhine into the Eifel area, where the offensive would start. Most of the panzer divisions had been kept away from the Eifel/Ardennes sector as part of the effort to hide the preparations for the Autumn Mist offensive. To speed along the process, the *6.Panzer-Armee* was allotted a regiment of military police, about 300 men, while each corps and division received a company of police.[30]

On the night of December 13–14, the *Hitlerjugend* began its Operation Abwehr movement to the Ardennes, reaching its second assembly area near Euskirchen by dawn. On the night of December 14–15, the division moved again to the area around Mechernich-Marmecen-Sistig-Kall. This put the division about 30 kilometers (19 miles) from Hollerath and 60 kilometers (37 miles) from Losheim for the final advance on the night of December 15–16 on the eve of the offensive.

These administrative moves led to a surprisingly high breakdown rate among the division's armored vehicles. On December 15, the *12.SS-Panzer-Division* had 46 tanks and AFVs under repair out of the 115 on hand.[31] This was due to a variety of factors including poor driver training and the declining manufacturing quality of German tanks at this stage of the war. The *6.Panzer-Armee* commander, Sepp Dietrich, later noted that about 100 of the roughly 500 tanks in the field army were broken down due to minor mechanical problems incurred during the three-day road march to the start point.[32]

By the morning of December 16, 1944, when the offensive started, the division was still approaching the Ardennes. Lead *Hitlerjugend* elements, including *I./SS-Panzergrenadier-Regiment.25*, reached Hollerath by morning and so were able to take part in the day's fighting. However, much of the rest of the division was still on the road. *SS-Panzergrenadier-Regiment.26* was still about 25 kilometers from the battlefield on December 16, east of Udenbreth, and many elements of the division were caught in massive traffic jams like those near Stadtkyll. Around noon, *SS-Panzer-Regiment.12* was still in Sistig, about 25 kilometers (16 miles) from Rollbahn C through Losheimergraben.[33] In the end, the timely execution of the Autumn Mist plan depended not only on the infantry opening the access to the *Rollbahnen*, but also on the success of traffic control in promptly moving the *SS-Panzer* divisions into their launch positions. The failure to do so was every bit as costly as the failures of the infantry to win their initial battles on December 16.

Indeed, the traffic problems were a contributing factor in the infantry failures. The infantry attacks were supposed to be supported by assault-gun brigades, but these did not arrive in time. Some assault guns began appearing late in the afternoon and evening of December 16, but they played little or no role in the day's fighting. Had *SS-Panzergrenadier-Regiment.26* reached the Scheid/Losheim area by December 16 as planned, they could have reinforced Engel's *12.Volksgrenadier-Division* in the attacks on Losheimergraben and Buchholz Station.

ASSESSMENT

The problems on Rollbahn C on December 16 were the most crucial failures for the *Hitlerjugend* at the start of the Ardennes campaign. The inability of *12.Volksgrenadier-Division* to secure the route through the forest on X Day had lingering consequences. Instead of pushing most of the *Hitlerjugend* strength up Rollbahn C and through the relatively good roads beyond Losheimergraben as was originally planned, the failures on December 16 led the division to concentrate its efforts on X+1 and X+2 through the unsatisfactory Rollbahn A in the Krinkelterwald. Not only was Rollbahn A poorly suited to mechanized travel, but it also forced the division to spend the better part of three days fighting for the Twin Villages of Krinkelt-Rocherath in order to gain access to roads beyond Elsenborn. This would impose fatal delays on the Autumn Mist plan.

Nightfall, X-Day: Command Perspectives

THE FIGHTING ALONG THE ELSENBORN FRONT FROM HOLLERATH TO Lanzerath quieted down after nightfall on December 16, in no small measure due to the exhaustion and heavy infantry casualties suffered during the first day of fighting. Both sides paused to take measure of what had happened during the day, and what needed to happen the following day, Sunday, December 17.

From the perspective of the *6.Panzer-Armee*, the day's progress had been disappointing. The initial planning had assumed that the first infantry wave would have been through the woods by midday and on the way to Elsenborn. There had been partial penetrations on either flank along Rollbahn A in the north and Rollbahn E in the south, but the attacks to gain the other three routes had been resolutely blocked all day. Of the two partial penetrations, the advance by *Kampfgruppe Ott* and *Grenadier-Regiment.989* on Rollbahn A was not understood on December 16 due to the lack of radio communication between the forward troops and higher headquarters. The penetration along Rollbahn E via Lanzerath–Bucholz Station was not complete, but this did seem to offer the best prospects for an immediate panzer advance.

Of the two spearhead divisions of the *6.Panzer-Armee*, *1.SS-Panzer-Division "LAH"* was nearest to the Losheim area, and it had been assigned Rollbahn E in the original planning. *Kampfgruppe Peiper*, consisting principally of Jochen Peiper's *SS-Panzer-Regiment.1*, was ordered to move to the Losheim area in the mid-afternoon in the hopes that one of the exits out of Losheim would be opened before dark. The main impediment remained the bridge southeast of Losheim. Around 1600 hours, it was reported that this obstruction had finally been cleared, and Preiss's *I.SS-Panzer-Korps* headquarters ordered *KG Peiper* to begin their advance.

Two companies of 3-inch towed anti-tank guns from the 612th and 801st Tank Destroyer Battalions were overrun in Honsfeld by *Kampfgruppe Peiper* in the predawn hours of December 17. The poor performance of these cumbersome weapons led to their gradual retirement after the Ardennes campaign.

In fact, when the lead tanks of *KG Peiper* arrived at the junction of the Scheid-Losheim road (Reichstrasse 421) and the railroad track around 1630 hours, the bridge construction still was not complete. However, the lead *Panther* tanks were able to maneuver around the obstruction by sliding down the railroad embankment and exiting to the other side of the tracks, back onto the road. This was fine for the lead tank group, but support vehicles would have to wait for the bridge to be repaired. Once Losheim was reached, Peiper was notified of a change of plans. Since Losheimergraben was still in American hands, he was ordered to proceed toward Lanzerath and help *FJR.9* complete their capture of the town. Movement through Losheim was slow due to road congestion caused by the movement of the horse-drawn field artillery of the *12.Volksgrenadier-Division* through the area.

As soon as the first *Panther* tank exited Losheim, it ran over a mine and was disabled. This was not an American minefield, but a German minefield laid in the area in the autumn of 1944 during the retreat to the Westwall. No one had been able to locate the minefield records, and so German engineers were obliged to spend a considerable amount of time rediscovering and removing their own minefields.[1] After engineers cleared a path, the column began to advance again, but the next tank struck another mine about a half kilometer outside Losheim. The spearhead commander, *Obersturmführer* Sternebeck, was the next to be halted by a mine, about 1,500 meters west of Losheim near the village of Merlscheid. As mentioned earlier, the *Wehrmacht* had neglected to develop or deploy mine-roller tanks, the most useful method for rapid minefield breaching for mechanized operations.

The column eventually began to pick up some momentum on reaching the Lanzerath area, since the *3.Fallschirmjäger-Division* had already spent the better part of the day dealing with the minefields in this area. *KG Peiper* gingerly made its way past Lanzerath and Bucholz Station, reaching the outskirts of the woods and the open country about 0300 hours, and reached the village of Honsfeld before dawn around 0430 hours. The nighttime journey of roughly 15 kilometers (9 miles) had taken about twelve hours from its start near Scheid to Honsfeld, even without enemy opposition, due to the mines, congestion, and poor road conditions. Peiper encountered scattered elements of the 394th Infantry in the dark around Bucholz Station, but this had little effect on his advance.

Had Autumn Mist been executed as planned, the *Hitlerjugend* spearhead, *Kampfgruppe Kuhlmann*, should have been launched alongside of *KG Peiper* down Rollbahn C at roughly the same time. However, due to the traffic jams between the *Hitlerjugend* staging area around Sistig and the Rollbahn C entrance at Losheim, this was completely impossible on December 16. Instead, *12.SS-Panzer-Division* was instructed to assist in the opening of the northern *Rollbahn* routes the following day, Sunday, December 17. This was a crucial diversion from the initial Autumn Mist plans that would have serious repercussions over the next several days. This change of plans was undertaken in haste as a means to quickly circumvent the traffic problems and was based on the assumption that once out of the Krinkelterwald, the *Hitlerjugend* columns could then rapidly pass on to Elsenborn. This failed to consider the possibility that the main road junction, Krinkelt-Rocherath, would be stoutly defended.

KG Müller, based around *SS-Panzergrenadier-Regiment.25* with reinforcements from the divisional *Panzerjäger* battalion, was assigned to clear out Rollbahn A through the Krinkelterwald. The *277.Volksgrenadier-Division* was no longer combat-effective due to the day's losses, so the least-crippled of its three regiments, *Grenadier-Regiment.991*, was teamed with the *Hitlerjugend* to open up Rollbahn A.[?] *Kampfgruppe Krause*, based on *SS-Panzergrenadier-Regiment.26*, was assigned to push down the International highway and clear it out from Hollerath to Losheim to permit access to Rollbahn B and C.

Aside from the main efforts by the panzer divisions, both special operations in the *I.SS-Panzer-Korps* sector had been delayed. Skorzeny's Operation Greif was put on hold late on December 16 for the simple reason that no exits had been cleared to permit it to proceed and its troops were still entangled in traffic jams. Operation Stösser had floundered due to the unpreparedness of the *Luftwaffe* to carry out airborne missions at this point in the war. The attempts to deliver *Oberstleutnant* Friedrich von der Heydte's airborne group on the night of December 15–16 never left the runways at Paderborn air base due to problems assembling and fueling the seventy transport aircraft. It was rescheduled for 0300 in the predawn hours of December 17. The night drop was a complete fiasco, with more than a dozen transport aircraft lost to anti-aircraft fire and night-fighters.[3] Only 320 of the planned 870 paratroopers were able to assemble through the course of December 17, and in the end, Operation Stösser fizzled out without accomplishing its mission. Its only notable consequence was the diversion of the 18th Infantry Regiment from the 1st Infantry Division to try to chase down the many rumors of German paratroopers lurking in the woods.

THE AMERICAN PERSPECTIVE

Command of the Elsenborn sector was under Maj. Gen. Leonard Gerow's V Corps. Gerow was scheduled to transfer to a new field army command, and the 1st Infantry Division commander, Maj. Gen. Clarence Huebner, had been assigned to replace him. Huebner had already arrived at the V Corps headquarters and served as an interim assistant commander until the transition occurred. The German offensive temporarily delayed this change-of-command process. In the event, this delay proved beneficial because it provided V Corps with two seasoned leaders. Gerow delegated responsibilities to Huebner during the course of the campaign, easing his own workload.

Gerow had fully appreciated the fragility of the V Corps position in the event of a German attack, and had already surveyed the area to examine its defensive potential. The Elsenborn Ridge and the associated Camp Elsenborn formed a natural defense position, occupying an elevated plateau that overlooked much of the area. The barracks and facilities at Camp Elsenborn were already in use by V Corps units. On the morning of December 16, Gerow was still focused on the main activity in the V Corps sector, namely the attack toward the Roer dams by the 2nd Infantry Division with the support of the 395th Infantry, 99th Division.

Although reports began to flow in about the German attacks against the 99th Division, this was initially assumed to be a diversionary German counterattack in response to the Roer dam attack. However, by 1100 hours, Gerow was concerned enough that he contacted First US Army headquarters in Spa and requested permission to halt the 2nd Division attacks around Wahlerscheid. If the German attacks toward Krinkelt-Rocherath succeeded, the 2nd Division could be cut off.

The First US Army commander, Lt. Gen. Courtney Hodges, refused Gerow's request, believing the German attacks to be merely diversionary.[4] The Roer dams were a primary concern for the First US Army, and Hodges did not want to sacrifice the costly capture of "Heartbreak Crossroads" only to have to fight to retake it at some later date. Hodges's war diary reveals greater concern about the German attack in the VIII Corps sector to the west than in Gerow's V Corps sector.[5]

A truck column from the service battery of the 372nd Field Artillery Battalion, 99th Infantry Division withdraw from Krinkelt to Wirtzfeld on the morning of December 17. This crossroads is covered by a M10 3-inch GMC from the 644th Tank Destroyer Battalion. M10 tank destroyers from this unit repulsed a probe by *Kampfgruppe Peiper* that day along a neighboring road.

The 2nd Infantry Division commander, Maj. Gen. Walter Robertson, first received news of the troubles in the Krinkelt-Rocherath sector in the late morning of December 16. His divisional artillery commander, Brig. Gen. John Hinds, had received a request from the 99th Infantry Division asking that some of the tank destroyers assigned to the 2nd Infantry Division be transferred to the 99th Division. Robertson and Hinds were troubled by the request and decided to drive down to Lauer's headquarters in Bütgenbach to find out what was going on. The road trip to Bütgenbach provided the first evidence to the 2nd Infantry Division officers of the extent of the German artillery effort, strongly suggesting a major German push. The *6.Panzer-Armee* heavy artillery had been pounding road junctions and other targets in the rear area of the 99th Division, and so Robertson and Hinds witnessed this firsthand.

Robertson and Hinds arrived at the 99th Division command post and found it to be chaotic. They discovered General Lauer in a corner of the building, playing the piano with a few of the divisional officers, apparently unconcerned about the severity of the situation. Another officer visiting the headquarters that day described it as "something like a Gilbert and Sullivan opera . . . a big crowd of officers all with map cases, binoculars, gas masks, etc. milling about. Nobody knew anything useful . . . even where the enemy was to any certainty."[6] Lauer told Robertson that the 393rd and 394th Infantry Regiments were under attack but that the situation was well in hand. However, Robertson suspected that Lauer had reached these conclusions without actually traveling to the front lines to get a firsthand appreciation of the situation. This left him very uneasy about Lauer's judgement.

Robertson was an experienced infantry commander, having led the 9th Infantry Regiment in Tunisia before taking command of the 2nd Infantry Division prior to D-Day. Unlike the green 99th Division, the 2nd Infantry Division had fought in Normandy, Brittany, and along the Siegfried line over the preceding six months. Robertson was very worried that his division depended entirely on the modest road network leading from Wahlerscheid southwestward through Krinkelt-Rocherath. Should the Germans push through the Krinkelterwald, his division could be cut off from its main base of supplies that were still located around Bütgenbach. At the time, the 2nd Infantry Division had its 9th Infantry Regiment heavily committed to the Roer dam attack at Wahlerscheid, the 38th Infantry in support of the 9th and the 23rd Infantry in reserve at Camp Elsenborn. Robertson ordered the 23rd Infantry to prepare moving from Camp Elsenborn to serve as a backup if the 99th Division defense failed.

By afternoon, Lauer became more concerned about the attacks against the 393rd and 394th Infantries. In the mid-afternoon, he contacted Gerow's headquarters and asked for two infantry battalions from the 2nd Infantry Division as reinforcements. Gerow responded by ordering Robertson to divert the 1st and 3rd Battalions, 23rd Infantry. Since the 1st Battalion, 23rd Infantry was configured as a truck-mobile task force with tank and tank destroyer support, this unit was sent to the more distant outpost in Hünningen. This location provided a backup for the 394th Infantry near Losheimergraben. The 3rd Battalion, 23rd Infantry marched to the edge of the Krinkelterwald to back up the 393rd Infantry and was instructed to assist in regaining any territory lost during the first day of the German offensive.

On the evening of December 16, General Huebner traveled from the V Corps headquarters to Robertson's command post to discuss the day's events. By this time, the first hints of a major German offensive had emerged after a copy of Rundstedt's order-of-the-day had been captured by the 394th Infantry from a German prisoner.[7] Not only had V Corps been hit, but the neighboring VIII Corps had been struck as

A small scout party under Werner Sternebeck from *Kampfgruppe Peiper* began probing near Büllingen on the morning of December 17, where they were ambushed by M10 3-inch GMC of the 644th Tank Destroyer Battalion. This is the *PzKpfw IV Ausf. J* commanded by *Unterscharführer* Heinz Femdling, one of two tanks that were knocked out in the skirmish along with a *Sd.Kfz.251* half-track.

This is *Oberscharführer* Wien's *PzKpfw IV Ausf. H* number 631 of *6.Kompanie, SS-Panzer-Regiment.1*, part of Sternebeck's scout patrol near Büllingen on the morning of December 17. The tank was hit by US tank destroyer fire, setting off an internal ammunition fire that blew it apart. The wreck is being inspected by troops of Anti-Tank Company, 9th Infantry.

well. Huebner told Robertson that the First US Army had transferred its reserve, Combat Command B of the 9th Armored Division, to the VIII Corps to help with the situation. Robertson made it clear that he wanted to halt the 2nd Infantry Division's mission against the Roer dams to respond to the unfolding German offensive. V Corps had not received permission to halt the Roer attack, and Hodge's First US Army headquarters seemed to be adamant that it continue.

After Huebner departed, Robertson ordered his staff to develop a plan to withdraw the division back to the southwest toward Krinkelt-Rocherath. He also ordered the commander of his two forward regiments near Wahlerscheid to halt any further advances that night.[8]

Late that evening, Gerow requested reinforcements from Hodges's First US Army, and was allotted the 26th Infantry Regiment of the 1st Infantry Division to further reinforce the hard-hit 99th Division.[9] In a phone conversation late that night, Lauer continued to offer an optimistic appraisal of the day's fighting, though admitting that his right flank, the Losheim Gap area, had him worried. He did not know at the time that *Kampfgruppe Peiper* was already well under way and approaching the forest exits northwest of Bucholz Station.

Although it was not apparent at the time, the timely and perceptive actions by Robertson and Gerow on December 16 would have a decisive influence on preventing the *Hitlerjugend* from reaching the Meuse. Although still not authorized to withdraw the 2nd Infantry Division from the Wahlerscheid attack, Robertson used December 16 to alert higher commands of the necessity of this course of action and to prepare for this eventuality once the First US Army headquarters awakened to the threat. As a result, the withdrawal from Wahlerscheid took place as well as could be expected on December 17–18, placing the 2nd Division behind the weakened 99th Division just as the American forward defenses began to crumble. When the *Hitlerjugend* finally did manage to push through the Krinkelterwald late the following day, a barrier of 2nd Division defenses had been deployed. Likewise, Gerow's timely request for reinforcements from the 1st Infantry Division would prove vital in blocking the best road from Losheim to the Meuse, via Bütgenbach.

X+1: Opening Rollbahn C

In the predawn hours of Sunday, December 17, *Kampfgruppe Peiper* erupted out of Rollbahn E after having advanced past Bucholz Station the previous night. Elements of the battle group clashed with troops from K Company, 394th Infantry in a running skirmish from 0530 to 0730 in the area around the Bucholz Station. The first panzer spearheads appeared in the village of Honsfeld. This village was in the rear area of the 99th Division and was defended by a miscellaneous force consisting of two platoons of towed guns from the 801st Tank Destroyer Battalion, some towed 3-inch guns of the 612th Tank Destroyer Battalion, and two 90mm anti-aircraft battalions on the outskirts that were part of the network defending against V-1 buzz bombs. Troop A from the 32nd Cavalry Reconnaissance Troop arrived on the night of December 16.

Honsfeld had a constant stream of American vehicles moving through it, some conducting routine supply missions, others associated with the efforts to defend the Losheimergraben area. The lead German columns slipped into the American traffic and entered the village. In the darkness, chaos, and confusion, there was no organized American resistance. Most American units simply tried to flee the town.

Peiper was then faced with a decision regarding the roads. Rollbahn E headed immediately westward toward Schoppen, but this road was in poor condition and led through a hilly, forested area. On the other hand, Rollbahn D via Büllingen-Bütgenbach had an excellent road, so Peiper detoured in that direction.

The defense of Büllingen had been assigned to the 254th Engineer Battalion, which had only reached the town a few hours earlier, around 0100. In the darkness, with snow falling, the engineers set up a hasty defensive perimeter on the roads leading into the town from the south and southeast. They managed to beat back a half-hearted

German infantry attack in the predawn hours, presumably from the *12. Volksgrenadier-Division*. Peiper's tanks appeared around 0600 hours on the route covered by B Company, 254th Engineer Battalion. Their after-action report described the ensuing skirmish:

At approximately 0600 hours, four flares, blue, white, red and white, were observed to the right of our Company B front. About five minutes later tracked vehicles were headed in our direction. These were not positively identified as we presumed that there were still some division units in front of us. The first positive identification was shouts that were heard in German. The fire order was then given by 1st Lieutenant Huff, Company B, who opened fire with rifles, rifle grenades and machine guns. The German infantry then piled off the vehicles, one panzer tank and six half-tracks, got within 15 yards of our positions before being driven back. They pulled back and reorganized and in about 20 minutes the infantry charged our Company B positions under supporting fire of the tanks. The tanks fired a few large caliber shells but most were 20mm high explosive shells and machine guns. This attack was in greater force and in spite of the tanks and shouts of their officers, they were driven back after sustaining heavy losses. The next 10 minutes gave us time to evacuate our wounded but now it was getting quite light. Then, after 10 minutes they charged again, but this time the assault was led by their tanks. As no heavy anti-tank fire was encountered, the tanks spread out and over-ran Company B positions crushing two machine guns. The men stayed in their foxholes and only three men were injured by the tanks passing over them. The German infantry was still unable to over run our positions due to the intensive small arms fire. The German infantry then withdrew and maneuvered around our flank which was exposed. In this action one tank was knocked out and two of the twelve damaged while many Germans were left lying on the battlefield.

Having been over-run, the battalion was instructed to fight a delaying action falling back on Bütgenbach, by the G-3 operations officer of the 99th Infantry Division. Orders were issued by battalion for Company C to fight back out of town and north west along railroad tracks, Company A, toward Wirtzfeld, and Company B and Headquarters down Büllingen-Bütgenbach Road.[1]

A hasty meeting of platoon leaders in 1944 with a *Haupt-feldwebel* (1st Sergeant) on the left and a *Leutnant* (2nd lieutenant) on the right. Note that the sergeant is armed with one of the new *Sturmgewehr* StG 44 assault rifles.

Peiper's column halted for a few hours in the Büllingen area due to the rich pickings in the town, including fuel supplies. Both the 2nd and 99th Divisions had their divisional aviation units based near Büllingen, and this cache along with other division fuel dumps of the 2nd and 99th Divisions provided an immediate source of fuel replenishment, totaling about 200,000 liters (50,000 gallons).

While in Büllingen, Peiper sent out a small armored scouting party from *6. Kompanie/SS-Panzer-Regiment.1* northward up the road to Wirtzfeld. Three *PzKpfw IVs* and some half-tracks appeared about 600 yards south of the 2nd Division headquarters in Wirtzfeld around 0815 hours, where they were engaged by M10 3-inch gun motor carriages of the 1st Platoon, Company C, 644th Tank Destroyer Battalion under 2Lt Owen McDermott. *Oberscharführer* Wien's *PzKpfw IV Ausf. H* began firing at Sgt. Thomas Myers's M10 No. 4, bouncing a round off the mantlet. McDermott's M10 tank destroyer took aim at Wien's tank, hitting it on the side and stopping it. McDermott then pumped another ten rounds into the tank to "set it on fire and to kill the German troops milling around the tank."[2] This caused an internal ammunition fire that blew the tank apart.

Both McDermott and Myers engaged the second tank, a *PzKpfw IV Ausf. J* commanded by *Unterscharführer* Heinz Femdling. This tank was hit on the side and also set on fire. McDermott also engaged a *Sd.Kfz.251* half-track, knocking it out. McDermott and Myers also reported engaging and hitting two *Panther* tanks about 1,000 yards away, stopping both. However, this has not been confirmed from German accounts.[3] In the event, the ambush near Wirtzfeld discouraged the German scouting in the northward direction, and surviving vehicles withdrew back toward Büllingen.

Once his tanks had loaded up on the captured fuel, Peiper directed the column back to Rollbahn E toward the southwest via Morschheck-Möderscheid-Schoppen. This was of some relief to Gerow's V Corps headquarters. If *Kampfgruppe Peiper* had moved to the north like the scouting party, instead of the south, they would have gotten into the rear areas of both the 99th Division and the 2nd Division and potentially cut them off, creating a major disaster for V Corps. Instead, V Corps now had the time to reinforce its defenses facing the Losheim Gap. While a switch in direction of *KG Peiper* toward Wirtzfeld/Krinkelt on December 17 offers an intriguing "What if?" alternative scenario for the Battle of the Bulge, Peiper was merely following plans. He was assigned to the left flank of the *I. SS-Panzer-Korps* advance, while *12. SS-Panzer-Division* was assigned the corridor through Wirtzfeld. Peiper was merely a regimental commander, with no appreciation for the larger operational picture in this sector. This option was never on his mind.

The Fight for Losheimergraben Concludes

While *KG Peiper* had already gotten behind the defenses of the 394th Infantry around Losheimergraben, the *12. Volksgrenadier-Division* continued its costly struggle to clear the forest of its American defenders and open up Rollbahn C for the *12. SS-Panzer-Division*.

The fighting resumed around dawn beginning with German artillery strikes against the American defenders on either side of Losheimergraben. Lemm's *Füsilier-Regiment.27* attempted to break through the defenses of Moore's 3/394th Infantry to the west of Losheimergraben, while Osterhold's *Grenadier-Regiment.48* attacked Douglas's 1/394th Infantry positions on the eastern side of the railway line. Although the 394th Infantry commander, Col. Don Riley, thought that there was a solid connection between L Company on the left flank of 3/394th Infantry and A Company on the right flank of 1/394th Infantry, in fact there was a significant gap. He attempted to close the gap, using two platoons from a composite company from 3/394th Battalion. Before this could be accomplished, Lemm's *Füsilier-Regiment.27* pushed through the gap and opened a path to the main road. This forced Lt. Col. Norman Moore to move the 3rd Battalion command post alongside Lt. Col. Robert Douglas's 1st Battalion command post on the other side of the railroad. These command posts were in a vulnerable position, with little defense to the west. A defense force was created using assorted men from the headquarters companies as well as the Ammunition and Pioneer (A&P) platoon.

By the late morning, elements of the *12.Volksgrenadier-Division* were already out of the forest and beginning to advance on the towns of Hünningen and Mürringen behind the 394th Infantry. As a result, the fighting during the day was extremely disjointed and chaotic. Douglas's 1st Battalion still held defensive positions in Losheimergraben and the neighboring woods, but at the same time, the German troops were able to advance past the 394th Infantry through widening gaps.

One of the most exposed positions was held by a scratch force of about fifty men under 1Lt. Dewey Plankers with assorted riflemen from B and C Companies, 1st Battalion, plus jeep drivers and others. About twenty of the men were armed only with pistols. Plankers's small force occupied foxholes about 200 yards southeast of Losheimergraben. When three *StuG IV* assault guns of *Pz.Jg.Abt.1012* showed up before noon, Plankers withdrew his small force back into the village. The assault guns were kept at bay with bazooka fire. In one of the few appearances of the *Luftwaffe* in the battle, the village was strafed. The assault guns closed in on the buildings about 1530 hours, with the US troops claiming to have knocked out two and damaged a third with bazooka fire.[4]

With the 394th Infantry defenses penetrated and the regiment at risk of being cut off, at 1400 hours General Lauer ordered the regiment to withdraw out of the woods and reestablish its defense line around Mürringen. Foxholes and other defenses had already been dug in the Mürringen area earlier in December as part of a secondary defense line. In addition, Lt. Col. John Hightower's 1st Battalion, 23rd Infantry from the 2nd Infantry Division had been moved into the neighboring town of Hünningen.

The withdrawal of the 1st and 3rd Battalions of the 394th Infantry was complicated since there were numerous isolated pockets of resistance without good communications with the battalion command posts. The 3rd Battalion was in particularly rough shape and more isolated than the 1st Battalion. By nightfall, about 260 men of the 1/393rd Infantry reached Mürringen.

In the event, the defense of Mürringen was short-lived. Col. Riley was informed that half of Krinkelt was in German hands and that Büllingen was occupied by German tanks. It appeared that the 394th Infantry would soon be surrounded again, since these towns were the main connection to the rest of the 99th Division. By this time, the regiment could count only about 1,300 men of its original 3,050.[5]

Hightower's 1/23rd Infantry in Hünningen repulsed several attacks by Lemm's *Füsilier-Regiment.27* during the course of the day. Late on the evening of December 17, Hightower was instructed to withdraw his battalion into Krinkelt. He was reluctant to do this until Riley's battered 394th Infantry in neighboring Mürringen was ready to do so.

Col. Don Riley was mainly concerned about the severe shortage of ammunition among his troops. He believed that the regiment would have to fight its way back, and he radioed Lauer, asking for an emergency airdrop of ammunition. When it became clear that no resupply would be possible, Riley ordered the withdrawal from Hünningen around 0230 hours on December 18, starting with the regimental vehicles. He hoped that the darkness would shield his withdrawal. The regiment was instructed to move to Elsenborn by way of Krinkelt as part of a larger scheme to have the 99th Division defend Elsenborn Ridge while the 2nd Infantry Division took up a forward defense in Krinkelt-Rocherath. Riley's 394th Infantry gradually filtered back toward Elsenborn on December 18, and was back on line on December 19 after a harrowing and costly march across snow-covered fields in the dark.

Once the 394th Infantry began pulling out of Mürringen, Hightower's 1/23rd Infantry began its withdrawal northward. The 2/23rd Infantry had taken up positions on the high ground covering the junction of the roads to Wirtzfeld and Krinkelt, and the 1/23rd Infantry was assigned to new positions north of Wirtzfeld.

Osterhold's *Grenadier-Regiment.48* had failed to secure Mürringen during the course of the day. The division had formed a battle group called *Vorausabtelung Holz* (Holz Forward Detachment) under the commander of *Pz.Jg.Abt.1012*, *Major* Günther Holz. This formation was based on the divisional *Füsilier-Bataillon.12*, plus some Pionier (engineer) troops and the few surviving *StuG IV* assault guns. The formation advanced on Mürringen in the early morning hours of December 18, after Riley's 394th Infantry had withdrawn. Curiously enough, Engel's history of the *12.Volksgrenadier-Division* claims that Lemm's *Füsilier-Regiment.27* had captured Hünningen "by mid-day and mopping up lasted until evening."[6] This was not the case, and the village was not secured until after dark in the early morning hours of December 18, when the 1/23rd Infantry finally withdrew.

X+1: Break-In on Rollbahn A

By midnight on December 16–17, 1944, the situation in the Krinkelterwald was extremely confused for both sides. The German units in the woods, *Kampfgruppe Ott* and *Grenadier-Regiment.989*, had been in contact with one another along the Jans Brook, but they had no contact with divisional headquarters outside the woods. Outside the forest, the remainder of Siegfried Müller's *SS-Panzergrenadier-Regiment.25* had been ordered to push into the Krinkelterwald at first light, to join up with the other German troops in the woods and finally clear a path to the open fields facing Rocherath.

Müller assigned the mission to Richard Schulze's *II./SS- Panzergrenadier-Regiment.25*. The regiment's remaining unit, the *III.Bataillon*, remained in regimental reserve until the situation was clarified. Armored support was provided in the form of *Panzerjäger-Abteilung.12*, equipped with about twenty *Panzer IV lg.(V)* tank destroyers. However, the use of the tank destroyers would take time. Pioneers had created some ramps over the dragon's teeth at the Hollerath Knee, blocking access to Rollbahn A late on December 16. As a result, *Kampfgruppe Ott* had tried to move an assortment of trucks and other vehicles down the road that evening behind the main dismounted infantry attack. However, these vehicles became bogged down in the mud and now obstructed the road. Schulze's force was assigned a Pionier company in the hopes of extricating the vehicles, constructing small tactical bridges and otherwise making the road passable to vehicle traffic.

Lt. Col. Jack Allen's badly weakened 3/393rd Infantry had set up a defensive perimeter around the battalion command post. The 99th Division headquarters had assigned I Company, 394th Infantry as reinforcement and it was positioned on the battalion's flank. Allen was instructed by the division headquarters that he should conduct a counterattack on

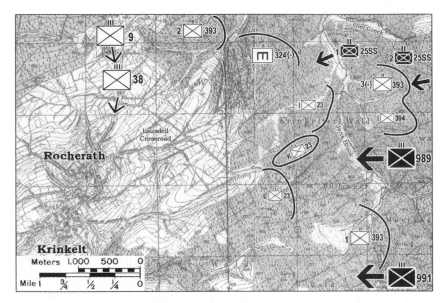

Battle in the Krinkelterwald, December 18, 1944
This map shows the attack by the *277.Volksgrenadier-Division* and elements
of the *12.SS-Panzer-Division* against the 393rd Infantry, 99th Division and a
blocking force of the 3rd Battalion, 23rd Infantry, 2nd Infantry Division. This
shielded the movement of the 9th Infantry and 38th Infantry from the Wahlerscheid area back to Krinkelt-Rocherath to set up a new defense line outside
the forest.

the morning of December 17 to retake the lost battalion positions, most
notably the area formerly held by K Company on the left flank. There
was still the presumption in Lauer's headquarters that the December 16
fighting was merely a diversionary attack intended to distract US forces
from the Wahlerscheid operation. This counterattack began around
0800 hours.

Allen's and Schulze's opposing forces collided with each other
around 0930 hours when *7.Kompanie, II./SS-Pz.Gren.Rgt. 25* crashed
into the understrength M Company (heavy weapons). During the fighting, M Company was pushed back about 100 yards. Allen ordered the
other companies to halt their attacks elsewhere, and I Company, 393rd
Infantry was instructed to move to the M Company positions and assist

in repelling the German attack. This succeeded in halting the German advance, at least temporarily.

The *7.Kompanie* commander, *Untersturmführer* Hirsch, and one of the platoon leaders had been wounded, and it took time for the Germans to reestablish the chain of command and proceed on their mission. The German battalion commander recalled the difficulties of leading his untrained troops into combat that day: "Since the men were largely without combat experience, only the deployment of the officers in the front lines could help. In the first hours, all the company commanders were casualties, either killed or wounded. That included the battalion adjutant, Unterstürmfuhrer Buchmann, and the technical officer. The NCOs took over the companies."[1]

The first *Panzer IV lg.(V)* from *Obersturmführer* Helmut Zeiner's *1.Kompanie, SS-Pz.Jg.Abt.12* appeared near the M Company positions and began firing its machine guns. One of the mortar platoons brought it under fire, but only managed to scatter the accompanying *Panzergrenadiers*. Artillery fire from the 370th Field Artillery Battalion was also directed against it, but the projectiles mostly exploded overhead in the trees without any effect on the *Jagdpanzer*. Four bazooka teams were sent to the area by Col. Allen and finally managed to disable it after hitting one of the tracks.

> About this time, two more German tanks appeared . . . They too were accompanied by infantry. When American artillery fire was brought to bear, they scattered. The bazooka-men turned their attention to these tanks and knocked one out. The other stopped behind it and continued to fire its MGs while standing in the main road. Then, two more enemy tanks appeared—making five in all—and these worked into the network of confused trails in the command post area. One of these was knocked out.[2]

Schulze's *II./SS-Pz.Gren.Rgt.25* continued its infantry attack through the woods, aided by the *Panzer IV lg.(V)* support. The specific composition of the German forces during this fighting is largely unrecorded. It is unclear whether Ott's *I./SS-Pz.Gren.Rgt.25* joined forces with Schulze's battalion, though this is likely. Whether the regiment's *III.Bataillon* was committed is not known, though it was likely to have been involved. The extent of participation by elements of the *277.Volksgrenadier-Division* is also very unclear.

Regardless of the precise composition of the German forces in the attack, the situation on the American side became untenable:

> All the time the enemy infantry had continued to press its attack along the M Company front, with the result that this position was becoming more and more endangered. The rest of the Battalion area was being swept with more and more intensity with machine gun fire. The situation was becoming desperate. Frequent reports to Regiment were made to this effect. The Battalion was running out of ammunition; the Germans were working through its positions in increasingly strong numbers; the men were becoming increasingly tired and hungry; casualties were piled up and there was no way to get them out. Altogether, it was not a happy situation. Finally, at about 1030 on this critical morning of the 17th, Regiment gave permission to the Battalion to withdraw to the old regimental reserve sector approximately 2,400 yards from Rocherath. Regiment also said that a unit of the 23rd Infantry [3rd Battalion] of the 2nd Division had gone into position about 1,600 yards to the west of the Battalion's present location and ordered them to withdraw to the assigned sector through this 23rd Infantry group.[3]

Lt. Col. Paul Tuttle's 3rd Battalion, 23rd Infantry had moved into the Krinkelterwald on the afternoon of December 16. Its original mission was to stage an immediate counterattack to help recover the positions of K Company, 393rd Infantry. The 23rd Infantry commander, Col. Jay Lovless, had resisted this order due to the small size of his force and the considerable uncertainties about the status of both friendly and hostile forces in the forest. Instead, 3/23rd Infantry was told to set up defensive positions in the woods. Tuttle placed Capt. Charles MacDonald's I Company in the ravine astride the main road where it crossed the Jans Brook. Little did they know that this was the main German

An evocative photo of a rifleman of the 18th Infantry, 1st Infantry Division in the forest west of Bütgenbach on December 17, 1944, when the division moved forward to block the *Hitlerjugend* attack.

objective, Rollbahn A. Companies K and L were placed farther south along two forest roads.

Tuttle's battalion had a hard time digging foxholes. The surface of the forest floor was covered with a few inches of slush and mud, but the ground itself was frozen solid. The riflemen spent the remainder of December 16 and the morning of December 17 chipping away at the frozen ground, trying to create fighting positions.

During a temporary lull in the fighting late on Sunday morning, the 3rd Battalion, 393rd Infantry began its withdrawal out of the Krinkelterwald. An initial effort was made to evacuate the wounded using available vehicles. There were still about a dozen severely wounded men that could not be carried nor was their room on the vehicles. As a result, the battalion surgeon, Capt. Frederick McIntyre, and a few of the aid station personnel agreed to remain behind with them when the battalion withdrew. All command post equipment that could not be moved, such as radios and switchboards, was destroyed in place. The withdrawal began around noon starting with the wounded and then in a column of companies, with L Company serving as the rear guard. L Company withdrew in stages, fighting and disengaging in careful steps.

The commander of I Company, 23rd Infantry, Capt. Charles Mac-Donald, recalled the scene as the first wave of troops from the 3/393rd Infantry withdrew through his unit along the Jans Brook ravine:

> A ragged column of troops appeared over the wooded ridge to the front of the 2nd and 3rd Platoons. There were not over two hundred men, the remnants of nine hundred who had fought gallantly to our front since they were hit by the German attack the preceding day. Another group the size of a platoon [forty men] withdrew along the highway, donating the few hand grenades and clips of ammunition they possessed to my 1st Platoon. Two men stayed to fight with my company. Two enlisted men, carrying a badly wounded lieutenant, stopped exhausted with my 3rd Platoon. I called for a litter squad.[4]

Moments later, the first German infantry appeared, in hot pursuit of the retreating 3/393rd Infantry. MacDonald called for an artillery barrage but got only three rounds. There was an ammunition short-age in the 99th Division artillery battalions due to their intense use the day before. Two M4 medium tanks from 741st Tank Battalion had been assigned to the defense, but after reaching the site, they decided to withdraw to "improve their positions" due to the claustrophobic con-ditions inside the forest. Tankers are not happy operating in forests, since visibility is poor and enemy infantry can sneak up on them unob-served unless they are vigorously protected by friendly infantry. There was no time to provide the tanks with an infantry security force, and they were unwilling to remain in a vulnerable location. The two tanks retreated back to the open farmland behind the Krinkelterwald after telling nearby riflemen that "it would be suicide for them to face the Tiger tanks."

Tuttle's 3/23rd Infantry was left to face a combined German infantry/armored force more than three times its size. MacDonald's I

Company bore the brunt of the attack since they sat astride the main road through the woods. As MacDonald recalled:

> Wave after wave of fanatically screaming German infantry stormed the slight tree-covered rise held by the three platoons. A continuous hail of fire exuded from their weapons, answered by volley after volley from the defenders. Germans fell left and right. The few rounds of artillery we did succeed in bringing down caught the attackers in the draw to our front, and we could hear their screams of pain when the small arms fire would slacken. But still they came![5]

By 1530 hours, I Company had withstood seven distinct attacks by German infantry. Around this time, Brockschmidt's *Panzer IV lg.(V)* tank destroyers appeared along the road and began shelling the company positions. MacDonald's one surviving bazooka had been damaged and was no longer functional. The machine-gun crews from M Company were out of ammunition and began to retreat without orders. The 1st Platoon, in the most exposed position nearest the road, began pulling back. MacDonald, unable to convince the retreating troops to stop, radioed to his other two platoons and instructed them to fall back to a firebreak running behind their positions. This reserve position was soon overrun by German infantry and tank destroyers.

As one of the *Panzer IV lg.(V)*s advanced along the firebreak with accompanying infantry, Pfc. Richard Cowan, a machine-gunner from M Company, fired on them with his .30-caliber machine gun. The *Panzer IV lg.(V)* fired a round that exploded in the tree above Cowan, temporarily stunning him. His later Medal of Honor citation described the engagement:

> [Company I] was attacked by a numerically superior force of German infantry and tanks. The first 6 waves of hostile infantrymen were repulsed with heavy casualties, but a seventh drive with tanks killed or wounded all but 3 of his section, leaving Pvt. Cowan to man his gun, supported by only 15 to 20 riflemen of Company I. He maintained his

position, holding off the Germans until the rest of the shattered force had set up a new line along a firebreak. Then, unaided, he moved his machinegun and ammunition to the second position. At the approach of a Royal Tiger tank, he held his fire until about 80 enemy infantrymen supporting the tank appeared at a distance of about 150 yards. His first burst killed or wounded about half of these infantrymen. His position was rocked by an 88mm shell when the tank opened fire, but he continued to man his gun, pouring deadly fire into the Germans when they again advanced. He was barely missed by another shell. Fire from three machineguns and innumerable small arms struck all about him; an enemy rocket shook him badly, but did not drive him from his gun. Infiltration by the enemy had by this time made the position untenable, and the order was given to withdraw. Pvt. Cowan was the last man to leave, voluntarily covering the withdrawal of his remaining comrades. His heroic actions were entirely responsible for allowing the remaining men to retire successfully from the scene of their last-ditch stand.

Aside from Cowan, the only other soldier remaining on the firebreak was Capt. MacDonald, frantically trying to contact the battalion command post. Company I was routed and forced to withdraw from the woods. The two companies farther south, also under intense pressure, soon followed. As they cleared the edge of the woods east of Rocherath, they could see German infantry exiting the forest at the same time.

The platoon of M4A1 tanks from Lt. Victor Miller's C Company, 741st Tank Battalion had taken up positions on the outskirts of the woods. Around 1450 hours, Miller reported that German tanks were emerging from the woods near his tank and one other from the platoon. The opposing armor consisted of a few *Panzer IV lg.(V)*s, most likely from *2./SS-Pz.Jg.Abt. 12*. The M4A1 medium tanks engaged the German tank destroyers, and in the process, two of the German vehicles were knocked out along with both American tanks. A few moments later, S/Sgt. Crisler's Sherman tank arrived on the scene and knocked out a third German vehicle. Crisler reported back on the fate of Miller and the two tanks. The tank battalion headquarters told him to take command of the remaining tanks in the platoon. Crisler's tanks accompanied the infantry back toward Rocherath.

About 500 yards from the edge of the woods was a small crossroads with a cluster of modest farm buildings. This is generally referred to as the Lausdell crossroads in most American accounts, though it is called *Lüsdell* in German. MacDonald's retreating platoons walked through the crossroads, heading back toward Rocherath. MacDonald later recalled the scene:

> We came upon a group of dirty infantrymen digging in along a hedgerow. What people are these? There was supposed to be nothing between the Germans and Paris but our thin line of riflemen in the woods. I did not know who they were or what had brought them here, but they looked to me like dirty, bedraggled gods who had suddenly descended from the heavens to set this ridiculous situation straight.[6]

The troops digging in at the Lausdell crossroads came from a reinforced battalion from the "Manchus," the 9th Infantry, 2nd Division. Like Tuttle's 23rd Infantry the day before, they had been hastily thrown into place in front of the onrushing German offensive in the hopes of buying some time while proper defenses were erected in the neighboring Twin Villages of Krinkelt-Rocherath.

Command Perspectives: Evening X+1

COMMAND PERSPECTIVE: V CORPS

Although Hodges's First US Army headquarters had adamantly refused Gerow's request to halt the V Corps' Roer dam offensive near Wahlerscheid through Saturday, December 16, by Sunday they had finally realized that they were facing a major German offensive and not simply a local diversion. Early on Sunday morning, Hodges told Gerow to do as he saw fit.

Gerow immediately called General Robertson at 2nd Division headquarters and gave him permission to withdraw from the Wahlerscheid attack. His new mission was to occupy defensive positions on the Elsenborn Ridge covering access to Eupen and Verviers, the main road junctions in this sector leading to the Meuse. Gerow left it up to Robertson how to carry out this mission.[1]

Robertson had been up all night planning the withdrawal and had already radioed his regimental commanders to prepare for movement. By late Sunday morning, the 23rd Infantry had already been reoriented to the new mission, with its three battalions committed in a scattered arc on either side of Krinkelt-Rocherath. The other two regiments were still in the Wahlerscheid area. Disengaging while in contact with the enemy is a risky business. Robertson decided to use a method called "skinning the cat." The forwardmost regiment, the 9th Infantry, would withdraw southward from "Heartbreak Crossroads" through the 38th Infantry. Then, the 38th Infantry would withdraw through the 9th Infantry. In this fashion, one regiment would secure the withdrawal route while the other leapfrogged back. Robertson's objective was to establish the 38th Infantry in Krinkelt-Rocherath to hold back the German tide until other units, including the 99th Division, could withdraw to Elsenborn Ridge, the ultimate defense position.

By the late afternoon of December 17, Robertson had managed to withdraw the 2nd Infantry Division out of its Wahlerscheid attack and reposition it in the Krinkelt-Rocherath sector.

In summarizing the action, General Robertson said that in about a 14 hour period from 0730 to 2200 on 17 December, the Division executed a daylight withdrawal from a position with five battalions in contact with the enemy, withdrew along a flank road in a light flank guard action some 6 miles to the south of its original positions, after which it occupied, organized, and defended a position to the flank while under attack "which is a pretty good day's work for any Division." General Robertson added "and the [Command and General Staff College at] Leavenworth would say it couldn't be done. I don't want to have to do it again."[2]

The troops of the 1st Battalion, 393rd Infantry, 99th Division are seen here digging trenches on Elsenborn Ridge on December 20, 1944, after the withdrawal from the Krinkelterwald.

The 38th Infantry was attempting to set up defenses inside Krinkelt-Rocherath because the Twin Villages controlled the road network leading to Elsenborn and the Meuse river. Four battalions of the 9th and 23rd Infantry Regiments had been deployed west of Krinkelt, shielding the division from the *KG Peiper* force that had passed through Büllingen. The other two battalions, the 1/9th Infantry and 3/23rd Infantry, were to the west of Krinkelt-Rocherath in an action described in more detail in the following chapter.

That evening, Robertson met with V Corps commander Gerow to discuss the situation. Robertson felt that the 2nd Infantry Division could hold Krinkelt-Rocherath long enough for the 99th Division to withdraw to Elsenborn. Both Robertson and Gerow felt that the Elsenborn Ridge was the ultimate defensive position for V Corps. Gerow agreed with Robertson's assessment and put him in charge of the 99th Division until it could be reestablished in good order on the Elsenborn Ridge; Lauer was assigned as his assistant divisional commander. This unusual action had been taken largely due to Robertson's exceptional leadership during the first two critical days of the German offensive; the disjointed state of the 99th Division, which was intermingled with 2nd Division troops; and Lauer's confused leadership in the first days of the battle.

The defense of the Twin Villages of Krinkelt-Rocherath had begun to gradually take shape on Sunday, December 17. This mission was assigned to Col. Francis Boos's 38th Infantry Regiment. The 3rd Battalion, 38th Infantry arrived in the village on the morning of December 17 and had set up its defense perimeter on the south side of Krinkelt, since the most immediate threat seemed to be a German advance from Büllingen or Mürringen.

Lt. Col. Frank Mildren's 1/38th Infantry arrived next at the eastern end of Rocherath on the evening of December 17. It deployed to the north of 3/38th Infantry in the fields on the southeastern outskirts of Krinkelt-Rocherath. Company C was badly hit by German artillery as it reached the outskirts of Rocherath, and the survivors were incorporated into the defenses in the town set up by the regimental Anti-Tank

Company. The 1/38th Infantry had not fully dug in when the first German attack started after dark, as described earlier.

The last of the regiment's battalions to arrive was Lt. Col. Jack Norris's 2nd Battalion late on the night of December 17, starting with Company E. This company was directed to assist the defenses centered around the AT Company, while Company G was assigned to the area around the regimental command post.

Besides the rifle companies, the defenses included some divisional attachments, including abut fifteen M4 tanks of Companies A and B of the 741st Tank Battalion, towed 3-inch anti-tank guns of the 801st Tank Destroyer Battalion, and M10 3-inch GMC tank destroyers of the 644th Tank Destroyer Battalion. The situation around Krinkelt-Rocherath was chaotic, with a steady flow of demoralized troops of the 99th Division retreating into and around the villages.

COMMAND PERSPECTIVE: *6. PANZER-ARMEE*

The penetration by *Kampfgruppe Peiper* in the early morning hours of December 17 seemed to offer hope that the *I. SS-Panzer-Korps* advance was finally on track. Radio reports continued to be received until noon, at which point *KG Peiper* had taken Ligneuville. Communications with *KG Peiper* and the follow-on waves started to fail by afternoon.[3]

Communications between Preiss's *I. SS-Panzer-Korps* headquarters and its subordinate divisions were confused, exacerbated in part by overly optimistic reports received from some of the division headquarters, which themselves had bad communication links with their subordinate regiments. This led to a serious misunderstanding of the progress, or lack of progress, during the Sunday fighting.

For example, at the end of December 17, the corps headquarters was under the impression that Krinkelt-Rocherath had fallen to the *12. SS-Panzer-Division* at 1800 hours. As a result, its instructions to the *277. Volksgrenadier-Division* were to march to Krinkelt-Rocherath to free up the *12. SS-Panzer-Division*. The right wing of the *Hitlerjugend* was instructed to advance on the Elsenborn Ridge. The left wing was instructed to advance to Büllingen, join with the *12. Volksgrenadier-Division*, and

A significant portion of the *Volksgrenadier* was intended to be equipped with the new *Sturmgewehr* StG 44 assault rifle. However, shortages of the weapon led to continued reliance on the 98k rifle in most units.

start a nighttime assault toward Bütgenbach at 0300 hours on Monday, December 18. When *I.SS-Panzer-Korps* headquarters forwarded these reports to Dietrich's *6-Panzer-Armee* headquarters, they in turn ordered the transfer of the *277.Volksgrenadier-Division* and *3.Fallschirmjager-Division* to the *67.Armee-Korps* as part of the swing north to the blocking line above the Hohes Venn. This followed the Autumn Mist plan, but it was extremely premature considering the actual situation around Krinkelt-Rocherath.

In point of fact, the situation of the divisions facing the Elsenborn Ridge was not so favorable. The *3.Fallschirmjäger-Division* had accomplished little on Sunday, after its embarrassing performance on the first day of the offensive. The battered *277.Volksgrenadier-Division* did not play a major role during the Sunday fighting due to the heavy casualties *GR.989* and *GR.990* suffered on December 16. Apparently, *GR.991* contributed to the push through the Krinkelterwald woods on Sunday, December 17. *SS-Panzergrenadier-Regiment.25* had finally managed to push through the Krinkelterwald by nightfall, a mission that the Autumn Mist plans had expected would have been accomplished in the first six hours of fighting on X-Day. Actions by *SS-Panzergrenadier-Regiment.26* are not well documented, but apparently the regiment pushed down the International Highway and cleared the opening to Rollbahn B, which had been abandoned when the 1/393rd Infantry withdrew during the afternoon. The main strike force of the *Hitler-jugend, I./SS-Panzer-Regiment.12*, had conducted a 15-kilometer road march during the day from the Blumenthal area to an assembly area near Udenbreth, but had not taken part in the fighting.

Reports continued to flow into German headquarters through the night, which began to clarify the situation. Krinkelt-Rocherath had in fact not been taken as previously reported, and the situation in Hünningen and Mürringen were not as secure as early reports had claimed. The plans for Monday, December 18, 1944, had to be changed. *SS-Panzergrenadier-Regiment.26* was instructed to advance up Rollbahn C through Losheimergraben, with the aim of capturing Bütgenbach. The infantry forces facing Krinkelt-Rocherath would be reinforced with tanks from *I./SS-Panzer-Regiment.12* to finally overcome American resistance in Krinkelt-Rocherath. The expectation was that the Monday X+2 attacks would finally open up the routes toward the Meuse.

The 2nd Division Stands Fast

GEN. WALTER ROBERTSON SPENT THE MORNING OF DECEMBER 17 TRAV-eling along the Wahlerscheid-Rocherath road, checking the progress of the withdrawal of the 2nd Division. The situation near Krinkelt-Rocherath was chaotic and disheartening: "Streams of men and vehicles were pouring down the forest roads through the junction in wild confusion and disorder. Control of the 99th Division had been irretrievably lost and the stragglers echoed each other with remarks that their units had been surrounded and annihilated. One of our own battalions from the 23rd Infantry had also been engulfed in what was actually a flight to the rear."[1]

In the late afternoon, Robertson visited the command post of the 395th Infantry, 99th Division and was warned that the Germans had pushed through the defenses of the 3/393rd Infantry and 3/23rd Infantry in the Krinkelterwald forest northeast of Rocherath. Realizing that the 38th Infantry was still not in place in Krinkelt-Rocherath, Robertson immediately understood he had to create a roadblock between the Krinkelterwald and Krinkelt-Rocherath to give Boos and the 38th Infantry enough time to set up their defenses in the Twin Villages.

When Robertson arrived at the Lausdell crossroads, the 9th Infantry Regiment was passing through in a column order of the 2nd, 3rd, and 1st Battalions. In the middle of the column, he instructed the A&P (Ammunition and Pioneer) platoon of the Headquarters Company, 3/9th Infantry along with K Company to immediately break off from the column and set up a hasty defense of the Lausdell crossroads 2,000 yards northeast of Rocherath. This was not enough to stop a German regimental attack, so he then ordered Lt. Col. William Dawes McKinley's 1st Battalion, 9th Infantry to pull out of the column and establish a defense of the Lausdell crossroads. McKinley was ordered to "hold the position at all costs" until ordered to withdraw. The 1/9th Infantry was authorized to take command of any units or stragglers withdrawing through the crossroads. The mission of the 1/9th Infantry was to temporarily shield the redeployment of the 2nd Infantry Division so that it could establish a firm defensive base in Krinkelt-Rocherath and Wirtzfeld behind the badly damaged 99th Division.[2]

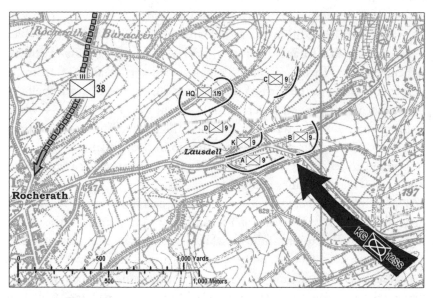

Defense of the Lausdell Crossroads
This map shows the defensive position of Lt. Col. William McKinley's 1st Battalion, 9th Infantry, which attempted to hold the Lausdell crossroads to permit the 38th Infantry enough time to set up defenses in Krinkelt-Rocherath from the evening of December 17 until the late morning of December 18, 1944.

1st Battalion, 9th Infantry Regiment, 2nd Division at Lausdell Crossroads

1st Battalion, 9th Infantry	Lt. Col. William Dawes McKinley
A Company	1Lt. Stephen Truppner
B Company	1Lt. John Milesnick
C Company	Capt. Arnold Alger
D Company	Capt. Louis Ernst
K Company (3/9th)	Capt. Jack Garvey
2/A/644th Tank Destroyer Battalion	1Lt Raymond Kilgallen

William Dawes McKinley was the great-nephew of William McKinley, president of the United States from 1898 to 1901, and son of Gen. James F. McKinley, adjutant general of the US Army in the mid-1930s. Although President McKinley is best known for his political career, he had been awarded the Medal of Honor for his actions at Antietam in the Civil War. William McKinley had followed in his family's footsteps and graduated from the US Army Military Academy at West Point in 1937; his brother graduated in the Class of 1941. He had served in the 9th Infantry before World War II and was its executive officer in 1943. This regiment was nicknamed the "Manchus" from its service in China at the turn of the century during the Boxer Rebellion. McKinley was wounded in action in Normandy on June 10, 1944, while leading an attack, and was later awarded the Silver Star for this action. After convalescing in England, he returned to the 9th Infantry and was appointed to lead the 1st Battalion. He was twenty-eight years old at the time of the Ardennes campaign.

McKinley's force consisted of his own battalion, the 1/9th Infantry, plus Company K of the 3/9th Infantry, thirty men of the 3/9th Infantry's A&P platoon, and four M10 3-inch GMC tank destroyers of 2nd Platoon, Company A, 644th Tank Destroyer Battalion. McKinley's battalion was significantly understrength after suffering heavy casualties in the fighting around Wahlerscheid on December 13–16. It had fallen from a strength of 713 men on December 13 to 409 men on the morning of December 17. "By this time, the Battalion was tired and had been continuously under fire for 96 hours. By this time too, the chain of command had been greatly weakened, the Battalion having lost two company commanders in A Company, one company commander in B Company, one company commander in C Company and numerous platoon leaders and platoon sergeants."[3]

Yet the battalion remained in fighting order. Platoon leaders became company commanders, squad leaders became platoon commanders, enlisted men became squad leaders. The men were exhausted and bitter. Having fought for nearly four days under appalling weather conditions, they had marched back to the Lausdell crossroads in the freezing rain.

As columns of disheartened soldiers of the 99th Division streamed to the rear, the "Manchus" were ordered to dig in at an exposed crossroad with little natural cover and hold the position "at all costs." This was the usual army euphemism for a mission that was likely to be very costly. "Col. McKinley told his staff that this was one of those tragic situations that history records. He may not have actually mentioned the Alamo, but it was in his mind."[4]

The conditions around the Lausdell crossroads were confused and chaotic. The battalion executive officer, Maj. William Hancock, later recounted: "Elements of the 99th Division were streaming toward the rear in a very disorganized state. Many of the men had thrown their weapons away and were inquiring of all they met 'Where is the escape gap?'"[5]

In combination with K Company and other subordinate units, McKinley had about 515 troops at the Lausdell crossroads late in the evening of December 17. The last of these troops arrived at the cross-roads at dusk around 1700 hours.[6] The executive officer of the 1/9th Infantry, Maj William Hancock, described the visibility that evening as "practically nil" with snow showers mixed with fog. S/Sgt. Norman Bernstein, the battalion operations sergeant, recalled, "The weather at this time was very foggy. There was snow on the ground and the visibility was limited to about 100 yards. Darkness fell at approximately 1800. The night was absolutely black."[7]

McKinley knew he would be facing enemy tanks. Since his battalion had been fighting against Westwall bunkers near Wahlerscheid, he had conducted a special bazooka training program for his battalion. In total, he had formed twenty-two bazooka teams. He had also stock-piled a further fifteen bazookas with the battalion's D Company (heavy weapons). McKinley's attention to bazookas was due to his disdain for the 57mm anti-tank gun issued to infantry anti-tank companies. He felt that this weapon, a US copy of the British 6-pounder anti-tank gun, was ineffective in facing German tanks and far too cumbersome for foot soldiers to maneuver in close combat. Even though the bazooka was largely ineffective in penetrating a German tank frontally, he recognized that in the hands of a brave infantryman, it could be maneuvered for a side or rear shot.

Besides the bazookas, McKinley depended on mines for anti-tank defense. The battalion had no anti-tank mines of its own, but the supporting platoon from the 644th Tank Destroyer Battalion was able to provide some. Each of the main roads had anti-tank mines laid on either side. The roads themselves were left clear to permit the withdrawal of elements of the 99th Division from the neighboring woods. Once German troops appeared, special mine teams were instructed to pull "necklaces" of mines across the road. McKinley had been warned that there might be American tanks from the 741st Tank Battalion still approaching the crossroad, so there was some reluctance to complete the anti-tank defenses by dragging the chains of mines across the roads.

Around 1830, troops of B Company, on the eastern (left) flank of the battalion nearest the Krinkelterwald, heard tracked vehicles moving toward them from the woods. They could not see whether they were friends or foes. The darkness, fog, and intermittent snow showers reduced visibility to less than a hundred yards. The formation emerging from the woods was a disorganized battle group of *Panzer IV lg.(V)* tank destroyers from the two companies of *SS-Panzerjäger-Abteilung.12*, accompanied by infantry from Richard Schulze's *II./SS-Panzergrenadier-Regiment.25*.

There was little coordination in the German attacks, judging from the few recollections of the survivors. *Obersturmführer* Wachter's *2.Kompanie, SS-Pz.Jg.Abt.12* apparently exited the woods along a road, now known as Zum Sasseven, directly into the Lausdell crossroads, while Helmut Zeiner's *1.Kompanie, SS-Pz.Jg.Abt.12* used a slightly more southerly route, the contemporary road Zur Hahnendall, which led to the southern approaches of Rocherath.

Wachter's *1.Kompanie* set out slightly later than Zeiner, around 1900 hours, heading straight for the Lausdell crossroads. Around 1930 hours, Company B, 1/9th Infantry reported that three tanks and some infantry had passed through their lines. The company's acting commander, Lt. John Milesnick, thought they were American. Some GIs nearer to the vehicles realized they were German. They had been close enough to hear them "talking and joking like the war was over."[8] McKinley ordered Company A to send a patrol to discover the identity of the tank-infantry force. On approaching them from the rear in the dark, the American patrol confirmed that they were Germans. They returned and reported this to McKinley.

McKinley requested an artillery strike against this German force, as well as fires against the opening in the woods where the mystery vehicles had first appeared. Fortunately, the artillery liaison officer, Lt. John Granville, had finally gotten his SCR-610 radio working after having had problems earlier in the evening. This minor technical repair would save the battalion later that evening, providing the 1/9th Infantry with an immediate link to divisional artillery. Without this functioning radio, the Lausdell crossroads would have been lost.

On Granville's radio instructions, supporting US artillery struck around the area between the Lausdell crossroads and Rocherath where the three German vehicles had disappeared. Lt. Stephen Truppner, commanding A Company, reported that the barrage set one "tank" on fire and that the German troops "were screaming and had dispersed in all directions." The burning armored vehicle also helped to provide some illumination of the battlefield.

Once it was realized that the armored vehicles were German, a necklace of anti-tank mines was pulled across the road when another column of German vehicles was approaching from about 400 yards in front of the American lines. Two *Panzer IV lg.(V)*s struck the mines and were disabled when their tracks were blown off. Two more *Panzer IV lg.(V)*s drove off the road around the disabled vehicles, but both were knocked out by roving bazooka teams from B Company. The combination of the ground fog and darkness made it possible for the American bazooka teams to approach the German vehicles very closely, especially if German infantry was not present.

2./SS-Pz.Jg.Abt.12 regrouped and launched another attack around 1840 hours. Granville directed fire against this column, reporting that four of the seven armored vehicles had been knocked out along with an undetermined number of infantry. Company B reported the approach of yet another column emerging from the woods that appeared to be almost a thousand yards in length:

> At 2036 hours, Lt. Granville, Liaison with the 1st Battalion, 9th Infantry, in position north-east of Rocherath, reported tanks at [the edge of woods] and along the road to the east. Continuous fire was placed on the tanks until 0540 hours on 18 December. Often this fire was in Lt. Granville's immediate vicinity but was reported effective and Lt. Granville accepted responsibility for the fires which did much to stem the attack and would not have been possible without his valiant direction.[9]

Granville called in artillery on the head of the column, walking the fire back and forth for ten minutes while the infantry's .50-caliber heavy machine guns raked the columns. Company B reported that "the night was filled with the screams of the wounded SS men." Among the casualties during the Lausdell crossroads fighting was the company commander of *2./SS-Pz.Jg.Abt.12*, *Obersturmführer* Wachter, and one of his platoon commanders.

In spite of the losses inflicted by artillery, the *Kampfgruppe* continued to push toward Rocherath, often infiltrating past the infantry company strongpoints in the dark. The Company B commander, Lt. Milesnick, hunted down one of the *Panzer IV lg.(V)*s with a bazooka around 2215 hours. One of the German tank destroyers that had been disabled with a broken track continued to fire at US positions with its main gun and a machine gun. Two GIs snuck up behind it with a 5-gallon jerrican of gasoline, placed it on the engine deck, and set it on fire with a thermite grenade, finally burning it out.

Another spasm of fighting broke out around 2230 when *Kampfgruppe Müller* attempted to coordinate the attack down all three forest roads. Lt. Granville had difficulty calling in artillery fire on his radio due to German radio interference. The Germans used captured American radios, broadcasting music on the frequencies being used. Granville changed the frequencies on his radio several times, trying to evade the

German jamming. He finally got through and shouted, "If you don't get it out right now, it will be too goddamn late!" He never received a reply due to renewed German radio interference, but three minutes later, the heaviest barrage of the night erupted all over the German lines. General Robertson considered the defense of the Lausdell crossroads so essential that he assigned all four divisional artillery battalions plus three corps 155mm howitzer battalions to provide support.

The 1/9th Infantry's executive officer considered the artillery support to have been the deciding factor in holding the Germans at bay that night:

> The vast amount of artillery support and the timely use thereof saved the battalion from complete decimation on the night of 17 December. It is my opinion that the continuous close concentration of artillery on the road leading into the battalion position from the heavily wooded area to the northeast, prevented the German armor from completely overrunning the battalion position on the night of 17 December. This is particularly true due to the fact that the armored column was canalized until it emerged from the woods, and partially canalized until it reached the crossroads. During the hours of 1930 17 December and 0600 18 December, over 8,000 rounds of artillery ammunition were fired in defense of the battalion position.[10]

After the fighting died down around midnight, McKinley had a field telephone line laid from the Lausdell crossroads to the northeastern outskirts of Rocherath, now defended by Col. Francis Boos's 38th Infantry. Boos informed McKinley that the 1/9th Infantry would be subordinated to his command and that he expected that his battalion would be ordered to withdraw from the crossroads at some point the next day. By this time, confused fighting had erupted on the southern fringes of Krinkelt-Rocherath.

THE FIRST FIGHTING IN KRINKELT-ROCHERATH

While Wachter's *2./SS-Pz.Jg.Abt.12* was heavily engaged around Lausdell crossroads, Zeiner's *1./SS-Pz.Jg.Abt.12* company avoided the main American defenses by heading down a road south of McKinley's 1/9th Infantry defenses. Zeiner's small force consisted of only three *Panzer IV lg.(V)*s, the others having been knocked out or disabled earlier in the day in the Krinkelterwald fighting. His vehicles were carrying a small number of *Panzergrenadiers* on their rear engine decks, with additional troops trudging behind in the dark. Moving through a snow squall and in complete darkness, Zeiner's force reached the southern outskirts of Rocherath. Although he didn't realize it, his column had been spotted by a lone Sherman tank commanded by Sgt. Ray Dickson of the 741st Tank Battalion stationed on the edge of Rocherath. Dickson recalled:

> Suddenly I saw the silhouette of a tank approaching at about a hundred yards. My gunner, Cpl. Kroeger, was traversing right, and Cpl. Scurry had a shell ready to load when a doughboy yelled: "Don't fire! That's our TDs and infantry withdrawing." We then held our fire. A few seconds later the tank reached the intersection. When we saw for sure it was a kraut tank, it was too late to fire.[11]

Due to the poor visibility and the confusion that night, the German column was able to pass unmolested. On reaching the southern side of Rocherath, Zeiner paused to assess the situation: "Silence! We strained our ears, listening into the night, the engines turned off. Nothing! I sent a few men from the infantry ahead as a scouting party . . . The result: the village was occupied by the enemy."[12]

Zeiner's small battle group reached the outskirts of Krinkelt-Rocherath after dark. Company A, 38th Infantry had been warned to expect an American M10 tank destroyer to retreat through their position. When Zeiner's vehicles approached in the dark and fog around 2130 hours, it was at first assumed to be American. However, when its identity became evident, it was brought under small-arms fire. The 1/38th Infantry lacked bazookas, which were mostly in the battalion's supply column that had not reached the town yet. The three *Panzer IV lg.(V)*s overran the Company A foxholes, heading into the town.

The accompanying *Panzergrenadiers* were engaged with small-arms fire, losing about fifteen men. Unprotected by trenches, the neighboring Company B was overwhelmed by the German attack. The Company B commander, his command group, two rifle platoons, and one machine-gun section were captured or killed. The German attack reached into as far as the village church, across the street from Mildren's 1/38th Infantry command post.

Zeiner's own tank destroyer surprised three M4 tanks from Company A, 741st Tank Battalion and quickly knocked them out. Zeiner's *Panzer IV lg.(V)* shot up Mildren's command post and its associated vehicles. Surviving elements of Company B retreated into the stone church. Close-range skirmishes with small arms continued in the dark streets. Capt. Edward Rollings's Company C was hit by a separate attack involving the two *Panzer IV lg.(V)*s and a platoon of infantry that had become separated from Zeiner's main group in the dark. Fighting engulfed this section of the town for about three hours. Due to the fog and dark, the conditions were extremely chaotic, with individual buildings changing hands repeatedly. The buildings were mainly of stone construction, making them ideal for defense.

The 1st Battalion, 38th Infantry had not had time to set up a proper command post, and the headquarters staff was soon engulfed by the fighting. The battalion communications officer, Lt. Jesse Murrow, attempted to knock out one of the German tank destroyers.

> 2nd Lt. Murrow, who had sustained a bullet wound in his wrist but could not be evacuated, made a single-handed attack against an enemy tank in the CP area. One of Lt. Murrow's favorite men, his wire sergeant, had been killed and Murrow was on the war-path. Bound on revenge, Lt. Murrow charged one of the German tanks with only a rifle grenade on the end of a M1 [rifle]. The tank fired at Murrow with its big gun. The shell missed him, but hit the wall beside him and seriously wounded him. For this action, Lt. Murrow has been awarded the DSC [Distinguished Service Cross].[13]

The ferocity of the fighting subsided in the early morning hours of December 18. Due to the confusion, Zeiner withdrew his *Panzer-jäger* company and the surviving forty grenadiers to the fields about 300 meters outside the town around 0600 hours in hopes of rejoining the rest of his battalion and obtaining fuel and ammunition. Isolated groups of German grenadiers remained in parts of Krinkelt-Rocherath through dawn. The fighting for the Twin Villages had just begun.

X+2: Dawn Attack on Lausdell Crossroads

BERLIN WAS FURIOUS ABOUT THE DELAYS IN THE VITAL *HITLERJUGEND* sector, and insisted that the American defenses be promptly crushed. The plan had been to launch the attack before midnight of December 17–18. This proved impossible due to the lingering delays moving *Hitlerjugend*'s *SS-Panzer-Regiment.12* forward from its staging area behind Hollerath. The tanks were intended to provide the spearhead of the attack, reinforcing *SS-Panzergrenadier Regiment.25*. The tank companies gradually arrived late in the evening of December 17 into the early morning hours of December 18, postponing the main attack until dawn on Monday, December 18.

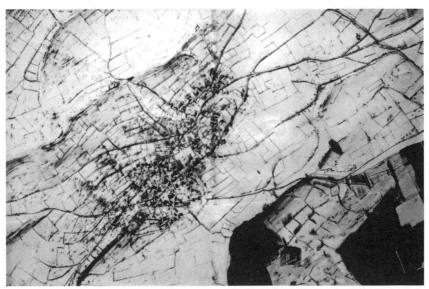

An overhead view of Krinkelt-Rocherath taken in early 1945 after the fighting. The Lausdell crossroads are at the upper right of the photo.

Arnold Jürgensen's *SS-Panzer-Abteilung.12* consisted of four tank companies: *1.* and *3.Kompanien* equipped with *Panther* tanks, and *5.* and *6.Kompanien* equipped with *PzKpfw IV Ausf J* tanks. The situation on Rollbahn B was still uncertain, so the tank battalion was instructed to use Rollbahn A's muddy forest road. The battalion spent most of the night moving into position through the woods from the Hollerath Knee to the forest clearing facing Rocherath.

One of the *Panther* tank commanders, *Untersturmführer* Wili Engel of *3.Kompanie, SS-Pz.Rgt.12*, recalled the night before the attacks while his tank was idle in the dark and dank Krinkelterwald:

How long will we wait here? Eternal waiting. Typical soldiering. Are we still attacking tonight or tomorrow morning? These questions eventually exhaust the monotonous conversation in our [tank's] fighting compartment. We doze off . . .

Misty weather—When you open the tank hatch, you get sleet in the face. The poor infantrymen over there in the woods. They are still battling with individual American squads, struggling tenaciously, and trying to withdraw to the foxholes in front of us in the dark. MG 42 machine guns scream, the light flak guns bark, tracer ammunition creates strings of lights in the night sky. Heavy projectiles fly overhead in close succession; they are ours. The American gunners shoot all the ammunition they have from their 105 and 155 mm field howitzers. For us, that is particularly alarming . . . The noise prevents any sleep. It's not easy anyway. Wherever you lean, the hard steel pushes back. It's also dog-cold. The heater can't work if you can't run the engine. Yes, comrade gunner, who sits there in front of me, and you comrade driver, radio operator and loader, I know you are reminiscing, just like me, of [our garrison town of] Frimmersdorf. Hard to believe that a few days ago we enjoyed such peaceful hours there. I am trying to capture the mood of the moment, to write something about it, in the certainty that it will be read by scribes of future sagas. I am certain that when they read my lines, they will be disappointed that we did not while away the time singing battle songs before the attack . . . A whistling sound in my headphones forces me back to reality. My boss, Hauptsturmführer Brödel, tells me to come. I get out of my tank with mixed feelings because the artillery fire has intensified considerably. The road is a swamp that almost sucks off my boots. The tank tracks have made a real mess here. To move forward, I can only jump forward from tank to tank. Shrapnel whistles by venomously, smacks against the tanks, splashes and smacks down somewhere in the earth. Once again, I get to know the usefulness of mud, if you have to hide in it purely for the sake of self-preservation. When I climb on [Brödel's] command tank, my uniform is filthy. Thank God, such vanities do not count here.[1]

Kurt Brödel was commander of *3.Kompanie, SS-Pz.Rgt.12*. His company was second in line for the morning's attack, with the mission to overrun the defenses in Krinkelt-Rocherath. The plan was conceived in haste with little firm knowledge of the battlefield. German intelligence was very confused about the situation in Krinkelt-Rocherath. As mentioned earlier, there had been reports that Krinkelt had fallen into German hands the night before. Although this report was later corrected, there was still the belief that Krinkelt-Rocherath was weakly defended and that with a good hard kick, it would fall into German hands. There was no real knowledge where the American 2nd Infantry Division might be. Most officers assumed that Krinkelt-Rocherath was held by the beaten units of the 99th Division that had been chased out of the Krinkelterwald. German doctrine did not favor the use of tanks in a defended town without ample infantry support. In view of the alarming delays in the plan to reach the Meuse, shortcuts and desperate gambles seemed unavoidable.

The spearhead of the attack consisted of the Hitlerjugend's two *Panther* companies, carrying *Panzergrenadier* troops on their engine decks. They were to be followed by the two *PzKpfw IV* companies and surviving elements of *II./SS-Pz.Gren.Rgt.25* on foot. The only fresh infantry reinforcements was *III./SS-Pz.Gren.Rgt.25*, which was instructed to stage an attack on the left flank directly toward Krinkelt once it made its way through the woods. The miserable weather before dawn was slightly above freezing, with a thick ground mist and the sleet changing to drizzling rain. As a result, visibility remained poor.

SS-Panzergrenadier-Regiment.25 had already taken significant casualties in the previous day's fighting, and it was clear that more infantry would be needed to clear the Twin Villages. The *277.Volksgrenadier-Division* had been shattered on the first day of the offensive, losing most of its small-unit commanders in the process. As a result, the division spent most of December 17 trying to reorganize. Two battle groups were assigned to the attack on Krinkelt-Rocherath. *Gruppe Johe* consisted of *Grenadier-Regiment.989* and a battalion from *Grenadier-Regiment.991*. It was commanded by *Major* August Johe, who replaced the injured *GR.989* commander. Josef Bremm, commander of *Grenadier-Regiment.990*, led the second battle group, which consisted of elements of his regiment and other bits of the division.[2]

McKinley at Lausdell Crossroads

In the early hours of December 18, McKinley's 1/9th Infantry at Lausdell crossroads was subordinate to Col. Boos's 38th Infantry Regiment in Krinkelt-Rocherath. The 38th Infantry was hastily creating defenses in the town, and Boos was not certain where the main German attack would fall. There had already been attacks from the southwest from Mürringen, as well as from the east and southeast, from the Krinkelterwald. As a result, his three battalions formed a thinly stretched, hemispherical defense line around the Twin Villages, with McKinley's defenses in an isolated clump to the east. Boos spoke to McKinley over the field telephone line and explained that his battalion would be ordered to withdraw into Krinkelt-Rocherath as soon as the 2/38th Infantry was firmly dug into its new defensive positions on the eastern side of Rocherath. This withdrawal did not take place as planned.

Although the early morning hours of December 18 passed without a major outbreak of fighting, the *1.Kompanie* of *SS-Pz.Rgt.12* began moving some of its *Panther* tanks out of the woods to positions where they could bring the Lausdell crossroads under fire. Around 0600 hours, the *Panther* tanks of *1.* and *3./SS-Pz.Abt.12* started up their engines and began moving forward from a clearing near Point 640. They carried *Panzergrenadiers* on their engine deck, with the remainder of

Lt. Col. William D. McKinley, commander of the 1st Battalion, 9th Infantry at Lausdell crossroads.

SS-Panzergrenadier-Regiment.25 following on foot. There are no German accounts of the attack on Lausdell crossroads, but an after-action report of the 9th Infantry described the initial fighting in the predawn darkness of December 18:

> At 0645, the full force of the German attack broke on the Battalion position. During the night, several tanks had infiltrated within direct fire distance and those began to fire to cover the movement of armored elements and infantry behind them. In the early morning hours before daylight, the men of the Battalion engaged the tanks and infantry with every means at hand. Conditions of visibility were almost nil, and communications with the 38th Infantry were spasmodic and difficult.[3]

The battalion executive officer, Major William Hancock, recalled the morning fighting in more detail:

Fog was extremely heavy and visibility limited to a few feet. The Germans attacked with tanks and infantry simultaneously. The real gallantry and tenacity of the front-line units proved to offset the superior force of the Germans. As the tanks and infantry attempted to roll over the positions, they were met with all means available. The tanks were permitted to pass into the lines while accompanying infantry was attacked from all sides with bayonets and trench knives. The battle raged spasmodically for the following two hours. The [American] defenders succeeded in defeating the [German] foot troops. Several tanks were destroyed by bazooka fire. At 0830 hours, the Germans attacked again along the whole front. Since the fog was lifting to some extent, three German tanks that had penetrated earlier in the morning came back to life. The tanks moved all along the front destroying the machine guns on the MLR [main line of resistance] . . . By this time, A and K Companies were desperate. The Germans had completely overrun their positions and the two front line platoons of A Company had been taken prisoner. The support platoon and company headquarters [of A Company] were still holding out. Company B was still holding the road crossing. C Company had succeeded in preventing the left flank of the battalion from being turned by a platoon of [enemy] infantry.[4]

The American infantry had few defenses against the attacking German tanks. Lacking the cover of night and fog, the American bazooka teams were more vulnerable to fire from accompanying *Panzergrenadier* troops than they had been the previous evening. Many bazooka teams were shot down before they could fire their rockets.

The *Panther* tank commanders were instructed to ignore the Lausdell crossroad defenses and to head directly for Rocherath. In the process, *1./SS-Pz.Rgt.12* overran the most exposed American unit, Company A, 9th Infantry. The *Panzergrenadier* troops following the tanks then tried to clear the trenches and foxholes of surviving American infantry. Around 0900, the Company A commander, Lt. Stephen Truppner, called McKinley and told him that they had been completely overrun. Truppner requested that artillery "be poured on his own position because the situation was hopeless anyway." He said his men "would duck in their foxholes and sweat it out."[5] Field artillery battalion laid down a thirty-minute fire mission on the Company A positions, disrupting the German attack and killing many *Panzergrenadiers*. Neither Truppner nor any of the men in the rifle squads escaped; less than a dozen men from Company A's machine-gun squad survived the dawn battle.[6]

The advancing tanks overwhelmed the neighboring K Company positions and soon reached the only buildings at the Lausdell crossroads, the Palm family farm. A bazooka-man from K Company, Pvt. William Soderman, attacked one of the *Panthers* from close range and knocked it out with a rocket hit on the side. Soderman's "private war" of hunting down German tanks later earned him the Medal of Honor. In spite of the occasional successes in knocking out a few German tanks, K Company was swamped. Capt. Garvey surrendered his headquarters in the Palm farmhouse when a German tank reached within a few feet of the front door and began to take aim. Only one officer and five men from K Company escaped the Lausdell crossroads fighting.

With Companies A and K largely gone, the flow of German tanks continued between the remnants of McKinley's defense at the Lausdell crossroads and the northeastern outskirts of Rocherath. Around 1000 hours, another *Panzergrenadier* attack was directed against Company B

Army artist Harrison Standley painted this scene of the Lausdell crossroads after the battle, with the Palm farmhouse in the foreground.

One of the bazooka-men of Company K, 9th Infantry, Pfc. William Soderman, was awarded the Medal of Honor after the war for his heroism at Lausdell crossroads. He is seen here being honored with the medal by President Harry S. Truman in a Rose Garden ceremony at the White House on October 12, 1945.

at the crossroads, leading to an intense small-arms battle. While this was going on, Col. Boos telephoned McKinley and told him that he could withdraw his forces at 1300, an impossible three hours later. A major artillery strike was promised to help defend the crossroads. McKinley warned Boos that he could not pull back to Rocherath since there were so many German tanks and troops between the Lausdell crossroads and Rocherath.

Shortly after this phone conversation, an officer of the battalion's anti-tank platoon spotted four M4 medium tanks of the 741st Tank Battalion operating on the northern side of Rocherath. Contact was made with the tank platoon commander, Lt. Gaetano Barcellona, who agreed to assist in the withdrawal.[7] McKinley pointed out a group of four German tanks that were blocking the retreat.

As the artillery barrage began around 1115, two of Barcellona's tanks maneuvered toward Rocherath, hoping to lure the four German tanks out of their blocking position. The other two Shermans remained near the crossroads in an over-watch position. The German tanks fell for the bait and maneuvered to intercept the two decoy Shermans. Barcellona knocked out two German tanks in quick succession, while the other two headed for the shelter of Rocherath.[8] One was disabled by a hit to the rear, and the last made it into the built-up area at the northern outskirts of Rocherath. With the path cleared for withdrawal, McKinley's men began to retreat north.

When the battalion reassembled near Elsenborn Ridge later in the day, there were only 20 officers and 197 men present of the approximately 515 men who had defended the Lausdell crossroads. Companies A and K had only 1 officer and 20 men from more than 200 at the start of the fight. McKinley's battalion had lost about three men out of every five in less than eighteen hours of fighting. Nevertheless, the sacrifice of this battalion had given the 2nd Infantry Division time to erect a credible defense in Krinkelt-Rocherath. They had stymied the advance of *SS-Panzergrenadier-Regiment.25* and the two battle groups of the *277. Volksgrenadier-Division*, lacerating the German infantry with prolonged artillery fire.

The crippling casualties suffered by the German infantry around the Lausdell crossroads would prove to be a critical ingredient in the failure of *12.SS-Panzer-Division*'s mission. Without infantry support, the

A pair of *Panther* tanks of *1.Kompanie, SS-Panzer-Regiment.12*, knocked out in the positions of Company A, 1/9th Infantry at Lausdell crossroads during the fighting in the early morning hours of December 18. The tank to the left is number 127, while the one on the right with the damaged track is 135, the platoon leader of the *3.Zug*.

panzers would prove to be very vulnerable inside Krinkelt-Rocherath. McKinley later estimated that his battalion had accounted for fifteen to seventeen German tanks and tank destroyers during the fighting around the crossroads, of which four were attributed to mines and the rest to bazookas. German infantry casualties were estimated at 200 killed and 500 wounded.

Capt. Charles MacDonald of the 393rd Infantry, who had witnessed the defense, later wrote:

> McKinley and the men of 1/9th and K Co., 3/9th had performed an incredible feat. By their stand, they had enabled two battalions of the 38th Infantry to reach the twin villages for a defense that otherwise probably could not have been mounted . . . They had left the ground around the cluster of roads and trails and the [Palm] farmhouse littered with German dead and the carcasses of 17 tanks and tank destroyers. For all the pertinacity and valor displayed by a number of other battalions of the 2nd Infantry Division during the fight for the twin villages, none performed with more fortitude and sacrifice than the men of McKinley's battalion and K Co. And for all the defenses of many another American unit during the German [Ardennes] counteroffensive, probably none exceeded and few equaled McKinley's battalion and K Co. in valor and sacrifice.[9]

The vital importance of the defense of the Lausdell crossroads was deeply appreciated by the other elements of the 2nd Infantry Division: "The immediate response of this stand prompted Col. Boos, commanding officer of the 38th Infantry and commander of all troops in the Krinkelt area to tell Lt. Col. William D. McKinley 'You have saved my regiment.' This prompted Maj. Daniel Webster, Division G-3 [Operations] to say 'You saved the Division.'"[10]

Krinkelt-Rocherath: Panzer Graveyard

AFTER HAVING CRUSHED THE RIGHT FLANK OF MCKINLEY'S DEFENSES, the tanks of *I./SS-Pz.Abt.12* charged toward Rocherath shortly after dawn. The *Panther* tanks of Helmut Gaede's *1.Kompanie* were in the lead, soon joined by the *Panthers* of Kurt Brödel's *3.Kompanie*. Aside from small numbers of German *Panzergrenadiers* riding on the engine decks of the tanks, most of the accompanying German infantry had been stripped away by the American artillery barrages and the infantry defenses at the Lausdell crossroads.

The panzer graveyard inside Rocherath. This is the scene opposite the village church and in front of the Kalpers house on the main street. *Panther* tank number 318 from *1.Zug, 3 Kompanie* has been burned out and its barrel ripped off. This tank is often misidentified as belonging to the company commander, Kurt Brödel, but his tank was numbered 305 and was knocked out farther down the road.

A tank attack into a town without enough infantry support was a recipe for disaster. German tactical doctrine insisted on the use of *Panzergrenadiers* to support the tanks in an urban battle with enemy infantry. Tanks were certainly not expected to operate alone in a defended town against enemy infantry that was equipped with anti-tank rocket launchers and supported by hostile tanks. However, two of the three battalions of *SS-Panzergrenadier-Regiment.25* had already been decimated in the two previous days of fighting in the Krinkelterwald, and the artillery barrages around the Lausdell crossroads shattered much of the remainder.

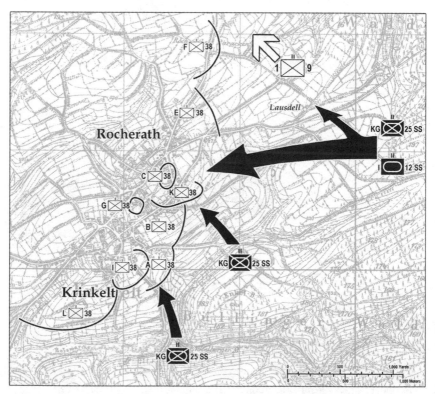

Defense of Krinkelt-Rocherath, Afternoon of December 18, 1944
This map shows the defensive layout of the 38th Infantry, 2nd Infantry Division in Krinkelt-Rocherath after the withdrawal of the 1st Battalion, 9th Infantry from the Lausdell crossroads.

The two battle groups of the *277.Volksgrenadier-Division* were so badly smashed by the American field artillery during the initial attacks that they played little role in the day's fighting inside the Twin Villages. The *Hitlerjugend* was under intense pressure to get the offensive rolling again, and a reckless tank attack seemed like the only solution.

THE KRINKELT-ROCHERATH DEFENSES

By the morning of December 18, Col. Francis Boos's 38th Infantry Regiment had set up its defenses inside Krinkelt-Rocherath. Lt. Col. Olinto Barsanti's 3rd Battalion, 38th Infantry had been the first to arrive on December 17, and it had set up its defense perimeter on the southwestern side of Krinkelt since at the time the main threat seemed to emanating from the Losheimergraben area.

The next to arrive was Lt. Col. Frank Mildren's 1st Battalion, 38th Infantry, which deployed in the fields in the eastern outskirts on the evening of December 17. This battalion was decimated in the initial fighting on the night of December 17–18, and Colonel Boos's report to the 2nd Division headquarters at 0200 hours on December 18 noted that "1st Bn. Badly disorganized, no dependable force . . . 1st Bn is of little help."[1] Company C had been badly hit by German artillery when

An aerial view of Krinkelt-Rocherath taken in 1947. The Lausdell crossroads and Krinkelterwald are out of view on this image, further to the right. The main German attacks emanated from the right side of this photo.

it reached the outskirts of Rocherath, and the survivors were incorporated into the defenses in the town set up by the regimental Anti-Tank Company. The 1/38th Infantry had not fully dug in when the first German attack started after dark, and both A Company and B Company had been mauled in the initial fighting with Zeiner's *Kampfgruppe* as described previously.

The final element of the 38th Infantry to arrive was Lt. Col. Jack Norris's 2nd Battalion late on the night of December 17. The reason that McKinley's 1/9th Infantry was left in its precarious position at Lausdell crossroads was specifically to allow the 2nd Battalion to establish its defenses in Rocherath. Besides the troops of the 38th Infantry were survivors of L Company, 23rd Infantry, who had retreated into Rocherath after the fighting in the Krinkelterwald the previous day. A number of units supported the 38th Infantry, including two medium tank companies of the 741st Tank Battalion; nine M10 3-inch GMCs of Company C, 644th Tank Destroyer Battalion; and several towed 3-inch anti-tank guns.[2]

38th Infantry Regiment, 2nd Infantry Division at Krinkelt-Rocherath	
38th Infantry	Col. Francis H. Boos
1st Battalion	Lt. Col. Frank Mildren
2nd Battalion	Lt. Col. Jack Norris
3rd Battalion	Lt. Col. Olinto Barsanti

Expecting a tank attack, the 38th Infantry had placed its 57mm anti-tank guns to cover various approaches to the town. However, the guns were useless when directly facing *Panther* tanks, since the 57mm gun could not penetrate the frontal armor of the *Panther* even at point-blank range. It had some capabilities in an ambush situation when firing at the *Panther* from the side and rear, but this depended on a certain amount of luck. As in the case of the fighting at the Lausdell crossroads, the principal infantry anti-tank weapon would be the "bazooka"

2.36-inch rocket launcher. Col. Boos later wrote that "the 57mm gun with normal AP [armor piercing] ammunition was found to be of such little value that I regard it as a practically useless weapon . . . Determined infantry armed with its organic weapons can and will stop German armor, principally by use of the rocket launcher [bazooka]."[3]

Company C, 644th Tank Destroyer Battalion deployed to Rocherath on December 16. In response to the German attacks, its 1st Platoon was detached and sent to Wirtzfeld for a short time on December 17, returning to Krinkelt later that day. On the morning of December 18, 1944, when the main German tank attack developed, there were nine M10 3-inch GMC tank destroyers in the town. Three of these were from the 2nd Platoon, Company A that had been attached to McKinley's force, and the remainder were from Company C. The three M10s from 2nd Platoon, Company C were located at the northeast corner of

Infantry bazooka teams played a critical role in the defense of Krinkelt-Rocherath. This is a team from Company D, 376th Infantry, 94th Division during the fighting at Butzdorf-Tettingen on January 18, 1945.

Rocherath; the three M10s from 2nd Platoon, Company A were mostly positioned along the streets on the northwest side of Rocherath; and the remaining three tank destroyers were on the southwest side of Krinkelt.[4] The tank destroyers were deployed in static positions, often between buildings, to cover major road junctions. In some cases they were camouflaged with structural debris.

Two companies from the 741st Tank Battalion moved from the Elsenborn Ridge to Krinkelt Rocherath on the morning of December 17. Three platoons were deployed on the south side of Rocherath overlooking Büllingen, and one platoon was deployed in Krinkelt overlooking the Krinkelt-Mürringen road. There was a total of about fifteen Sherman tanks in the immediate vicinity of Krinkelt-Rocherath.

Many of the M10 3-inch GMCs of the 644th Tank Destroyer Battalion were deployed in static ambush positions in Krinkelt-Rocherath, sometimes camouflaged with debris as seen here.

THE MAIN *HITLERJUGEND* ATTACK ARRIVES

Around 0730 hours, the first wave of eleven *Panther* tanks pushed past the Lausdell crossroads and raced into Rocherath along Wasserturm Strasse. This was a mixed bunch of tanks from both Gaede's *1.Kompanie* and Brödel's *3.Kompanie*. The 38th Infantry's regimental Anti-Tank Company, led by Capt. James Love, had its command post on Wahlerscheider Strasse, which intersected Wasserturm Strasse. Two bazooka teams in houses number 63 and 65 near the intersection on Wahlerscheider Strasse began sniping at the advancing German panzer column and scored numerous bazooka hits against the tanks without stopping any. Although the bazooka was capable of penetrating most tank armor, the erratic performance of its impact fuze often meant that its shaped charge warhead did not work as intended.[5]

Within a few minutes of entering Rocherath, the *Panther* company began to accordion together as it reached the debris-clogged streets. The column came to an abrupt halt. The *Panthers* had a small number of *Panzergrenadiers* still riding on their engine decks, and these surviving tank riders soon became casualties. The American riflemen from C and K Companies began spraying the tanks with small-arms fire and rifle grenades, killing or wounding most of the German grenadiers.

Without the *Panzergrenadiers*, the German tanks were isolated and nearly blind. The *Panther* tank commander could view the exterior through a ring of periscopes around his armored cupola. However, these had to be manually opened and closed, and so they offered very poor situational awareness in the confines of a town where enemy infantry might be lurking anywhere. The usual German practice was for the commander to ride with the cupola hatch opened slightly overhead, like a small armored umbrella. This provided better visibility than the periscopes, but it also left the tank commander vulnerable to enemy rifle fire. Several German tank commanders were killed or wounded in Krinkelt-Rocherath in this fashion.

The other two turret crewmen, the gunner and loader, were virtually blind. The gunner had a telescopic sight to aim the main gun and coaxial machine gun, but this had a very narrow field of view and was like looking at the world through a soda straw. The driver and radio operator / bow machine-gunner had periscopes, but these offered a very narrow field of view. To further complicate the situation, the *Panther* tank gun extended 14 feet from the turret, and so the turret could not be fully traversed in the narrow streets. Even though the *Panther* tank was powerfully armed and well protected with thick armor, in the tight confines of a town, it was very vulnerable to close attack by determined enemy infantry.

Capt. Love, on foot, tried to convince two M10 3-inch GMC tank destroyers to move closer to Wasserturm Strasse to deal with the *Panthers*. They refused to do so, telling Love that they had been ordered to maintain their defensive positions. The tank destroyer battalion was very leery of mixing it up on the streets of the Twin Villages, since their open turret tops made them quite vulnerable to close-range infantry attack by grenades or small-arms fire. Their thin armor was useless against any German anti-tank weapon, whether the infantry's *Panzerfaust* and *Panzerschreck* anti-tank rockets or the high-velocity tank guns of the panzers. As a result of these hypercautious tactics, the tank destroyers played a minimal role in the first day of fighting except for a few occasions when German tanks inadvertently exposed themselves to the hidden M10s.

Having been rebuffed by the tank destroyers, Love then found one of the M4 tanks of the 741st Tank Battalion and convinced the tank commander to move his Sherman down a side street so that it could engage one of the leading *Panther* tanks (number 327) against its weak side armor. The Sherman tank fired at the *Panther*, setting it on fire.

Another *Panther* behind it, number 154, attempted to move past the burning tank, but Pvt. Isabel Salazar from the AT Company positioned himself in a first-story window in house number 63 on Wahlerscheider Strasse overlooking the street, and struck the second *Panther* with a bazooka rocket from a range of 200 yards. The rocket warhead penetrated the tank armor, but the *Panther* continued to roll forward. It finally halted alongside the first *Panther*, where it burst into flames. It had taken a few seconds for the bazooka impact to ignite the ammunition propellant inside the *Panther*'s fighting compartment.

Panther 154 was engulfed in flames, and the two wrecked tanks blocked Wasserturm Strasse. Other tanks toward the rear of the column extricated themselves from the traffic jam and moved down other side streets, trying to reach Krinkelt. An hour later, Salazar scored another bazooka kill from his perch in the stone house when a *Panzer IV lg.(V)* came to a halt behind the two knocked-out *Panthers*.

As the *Panthers* slowly crawled forward toward Krinkelt, they were ambushed by tanks of the 741st Tank Battalion located down the side streets. Two broken-down M4 medium tanks, commanded by Sgt. Neidrich and Cpl. Hall, were located near the battalion's forward command post. As the *Panthers* passed by, the Shermans fired against their weak side armor. Five *Panthers* were knocked out in quick succession in a fury of gunfire.[6]

A pair of *Panther* tanks knocked out in front of the Kalpers house in Rocherath during the December 18 fighting. McCORMICK RESEARCH CENTER

A *Panther* tank of *1./SS-Panzer-Regiment.12*, probably number 125, knocked out in Krinkelt-Rocherath near the Mathais Jost store.

Willi Fischer, a *Panther* tank commander from *3.Kompanie*, recalled the horrifying scene inside Krinkelt-Rocherath in the wake of the initial attack:

> On 18 December 1944, we carried out the ill-fated attack on Krinkelt-Rocherath, a perfect "Panzer graveyard." The tanks of 1.Kompanie led the way, followed by our Kompanie under Brödel. I was lined up behind [Johann] Beutelhauser's tank, my platoon leader. When I got to the vicinity of the church, I saw a theater of horror. Beutelhauser's tank was hit in front of me. I could barely make out the position of the enemy anti-tank gun that hit him. Beutelhauser was able to jump off his tank and get to safety. I moved my tank to the protection of a house, unaware of what I would do next. Next to me was Brödel's burning tank; he was slumped lifeless in the turret. Along the road in front of me, all of the tanks had been knocked out and four of them were burning. Only one tank was still moving, I think Freier's, and it withdrew towards the battalion command post under my covering fire.

The surviving Panzer crews used this opportunity to withdraw under the protection of our tank, barely avoiding being taken prisoner by the encircling American riflemen. [Battalion commander] Jürgensen's tank showed up behind me. I was determined to get out of this hopeless situation and withdrew back beyond the cross-roads. But the cross-roads were targeted by the American anti-tank gun. The first round missed and the second struck the track and hull on the side. Luckily none of our crew was killed. The radio was wrecked and the track broken. I followed Jürgensen's instructions and backed up; the track slipped off and the tank bogged down once the road-wheels reached the mud.[7]

As the eastern roads into Rocherath became clogged, the German tanks began to probe for other access points. Lt. Robert Parker of the headquarters of Company C, 644th Tank Destroyer Battalion saw the German tanks passing through the center of Krinkelt near the church. Parker grabbed a bazooka and began a tank hunt. He was credited with destroying one *Panther* and disabling another, and was later decorated with the Distinguished Service Cross for his actions that morning. Another group of German tanks passed slightly south, through the positions held by the remnants of Mildren's 1st Battalion, 38th Infantry on the southern side of Krinkelt-Rocherath. One of the unit's officers recalled the attack:

At about 0800 on 18 December, 5 enemy [Panther] tanks came into town. The tanks reached the crossroad at the Battalion CP [at the junction of Wahlerscheider Strasse and Vierschilling Weg opposite the Krinkelt church] when they were fired on from every angle by automatic weapons. As a countermeasure, the tanks started to fire direct fire at close range into the CP building. All the light machine guns were posted upstairs and the enemy fired successively into the room occupied by the busy gunners. The doughboys managed to outguess him and dodged from one room to the next keeping the machine gun going all the time. The first two of the enemy tanks in line were put out of action by friendly tanks that were east of the Battalion CP. These tanks—the friendly ones—had been in town when the battalion arrived and remained there throughout the action up to that time. The third Panther was knocked out by a combination of several tank hunters' efforts. It was at the RJ [road junction] to the southwest of the CP when a bazooka team from the Battalion anti-tank platoon hit it in the track and immobilized it. The enemy crew was not damaged nor was its guns and it remained in place firing its guns. Both its heavy gun and its two machine guns were firing to the northeast up the [Vierschilling Weg] road past the Battalion CP. Lt Howard Emerich, the battalion motor officer, was coming to the CP from the northwest when he saw the tank firing. He retraced his steps, got a US Sherman from somewhere and put it in position about 200 yards due north of the CP. The American tank's 76mm gun finished off the enemy tank by a shot through the turret—the tankers had said it couldn't be done—that a 76mm wouldn't penetrate a Panther's turret. But there it was. The fourth tank got into position to the southwest of the CP and was knocked out by a combination of bazooka teams from A Company and the 81mm mortar Platoon from D Company [armed with bazookas].[8]

Panther 123 raced down the main street of Krinkelt-Rocherath, exiting down the Büllingen road toward Wirtzfeld. By this stage, it had eleven bazooka hits, several 57mm hits, and three 3-inch impacts. It was finally knocked out outside the villages by a M10 3-inch GMC of 2nd Platoon, Company C, 644th Tank Destroyer Battalion around 1100 hours by a penetration through the thinner rear armor.

A view of the other side of *Panther* 123 of *1.Kompanie, SS-Pz.Rgt.12* after it was knocked out south of Krinkelt. A surviving crewman is escorted away by a Signal Corps photographer from the team that took these photos.

The fifth *Panther* of the group, number 123, attempted to skirt around the wrecked and burning tanks. It was hit repeatedly by bazooka fire, but none of the rockets penetrated. Two soldiers from the 1st Battalion command post tried to prevent it from returning back into Rocherath and opened up the gates of a cattle pen, stampeding a group of cows toward the tank. The *Panther* machine-gunned some of the cows, but decided against moving in that direction.[9] Instead, it retreated back toward the company command post, crushing several jeeps on the way. A .50-caliber heavy machine gun team farther up the street kept it under a steady stream of fire, hoping to blind it by shattering the periscopes. The *Panther* crew was evidently afraid of being hit by the bazooka teams and finally managed to escape the area by driving down several alleys toward the western side of Krinkelt.

Panther 123 eventually returned to the main road, and moments later encountered a jeep from the neighboring 3/38th Infantry, which it ran over. A 57mm anti-tank gun from the 3/38th AT Platoon hit the

Panther in the turret. The turret began to rotate erratically, suggesting the traverse motor had been damaged or the crew injured. The turret eventually froze to one side, and the *Panther*'s gun barrel sideswiped two telephone poles. The damaged *Panther* raced past a M4 tank, which fired a single round but missed the fleeing tank. Several bazooka teams from M Company, 38th Infantry tried to engage the tank, but it was moving too quickly and their rockets missed.

The *Panther* finally managed to flee southward out of Krinkelt on the road toward Büllingen around 1100 hours. However, the M10 3-inch GMC tank destroyer number 4 commanded by Sgt. Stanley Kepinski from 3rd Platoon, Company C, 644th Tank Destroyer Battalion near the 3/38th Infantry command post saw it and fired three rounds through the thin rear armor, setting it on fire. A .50-caliber machine gun mounted on a jeep began firing at the *Panther*, killing one or more crewmen who were trying to escape out of the burning tank; two crewmen were later captured by an M Company bazooka team. When inspected later, *Panther* 123 had eleven partial bazooka penetrations and several scars from 57mm gun impacts.

Mildren's 1st Battalion was so understrength from the previous evening's casualties that at 0955 hours, Boos instructed the 2nd Battalion to set up a defense line behind the 1st Battalion to prevent the 38th Infantry defenses in the Twin Villages from being split in half. At the same time, L Company, 2/38th Infantry was sent to reinforce Love's regimental AT Company, which had been so instrumental in stopping the initial German tank attack on the eastern side of Rocherath.

Additional tank reinforcements from *SS-Panzer-Regiment.12* arrived later in the morning. At least two tanks decided to take an alternate approach via the northeast corner of town. However, they ran into an ambush by the 2nd Platoon, Company C, 644th Tank Destroyer Battalion, which claimed to have knocked out two of the *Panthers*.

Some of the late-arriving panzer reinforcements were tanks that were under repair and had not taken part in the initial attacks. For example, the *3.Kompanie* of *I./SS-Pz.Rgt.12* had at least three *Panther* tanks under repair, and once they were ready, they were sent as reinforcements

Col. Francis H. Boos, commander of the 38th Infantry, 2nd Infantry Division in December 1944.

Lt. Col. Frank Mildren, commander of the 1st Battalion, 38th Infantry, 2nd Infantry Division in the Ardennes in 1944.

in the early afternoon. *Untersturmführer* Wili Engel, the 3rd Platoon leader, did not take part in the initial morning attack because his tank had been damaged the previous evening while entering the Krinkelter-wald when it ran over a mine. He went back to the battalion repair yard, where he picked up another tank along with a second repaired tank commanded by *Hauptscharführer* Bellmer. Once both tanks were ready, they headed to Krinkelt. He recalled what he found there:

On the main street is Untersturmführer Jungbluth, the regimental ord-nance officer, who gives us the sign to maintain our direction. Some-how, I sense disaster, because this would violate a primary rule of tank combat: congested villages are to be avoided as far as possible without accompanying infantry. So in a fraction of a second, I cut to the left and tell [Bellmer's] accompanying tank to follow me. Less than half an hour later I get the proof that I acted correctly . . . We reached an open space near the church. We drive both tanks into "3 o'clock" posi-tion so that the bow is in the direction of the enemy and one side of each tank is protected by a house wall. Our exposed flanks are facing each other. Two streets leading directly into the American-occupied district are covered by our guns. Directly in front of us is the main road on which the company attacked and which we avoided . . . Our company's destroyed tanks present a shocking sight. At this moment, a single Panther, about 100 meters away, is approaching the battalion command post when it suddenly erupts into a burning torch. Shortly afterwards, the commander of this tank, Unterscharführer Freiberg, wearing a head bandage, appears at the command post and reports the following: "I saw a woman in a front door waving a white cloth. I turned my attention to her wondering what she wanted. It turned out that there was a disabled Sherman tank nearby, still with its crew and an operable gun that had scored this goal. Surely the same fate would have befallen me if I had followed the original instructions."[10]

Many of the *Panther* tanks knocked out during the day's fighting suffered hits on their weak side armor from Sherman tanks and M10 tank destroyers lurking on the side streets on the northern side of Roch-erath. For example, during the course of the December 18–19 fighting, the M10 tank destroyers fired eighty-two rounds. Only six of these were HVAP (hypervelocity, armor-piercing) projectiles, needed when attack-ing a *Panther* from the front. The rest were ordinary armor-piercing rounds, which were nearly useless against the thick frontal armor of the *Panther* but more than adequate in penetrating its thinner side armor.

FIGHTING IN KRINKELT

During the course of the day, Barsanti's 3rd Battalion, 38th Infantry on the southwestern side of Krinkelt saw very little fighting compared to the other two battalions since the main attacks emanated from the Krikelterwald. Around dawn at 0700 hours, a German soldier from the *Hitlerjugend* along with a captured American prisoner approached the 38th Infantry positions and demanded that American artillery stop shelling Hill 183 since a hundred American prisoners there might be hit. Barsanti asked if the prisoners were on the reverse slope of the hill, and when the German answered that this was the case, Barsanti called in an artillery strike of five field artillery battalions on the forward slope of the hill, preempting an expected German attack.

As the main German attacks hit Norris's 2nd Battalion, at 0800 hours Barsanti was ordered to transfer L Company to the 2nd Battalion to help reinforce this endangered front. Barsanti covered the gap in the 3rd Battalion defenses by creating Task Force Brakel under M Company commander Capt. Frank Brakel, made up of stragglers and other assorted troops with an especially heavy allotment of machine guns.

At 1100 hours, German troops attempted a "Trojan horse" maneuver against the 3rd Battalion. Using seven captured American 2.5 ton trucks, about 140 German infantry in partial US uniforms approached the 3rd Battalion positions a few minutes after a column from the retreating 99th Division had passed through. The I Company outposts thought the situation was suspicious, and a M10 tank destroyer fired a round over the first truck as a warning to halt. A patrol from I Company advanced forward about 500 yards to check out the occupants, but before they reached the trucks, they came under fire. The German troops, later identified as belonging to the *Hitlerjugend*, piled off the trucks and began running back to the woods. They were fired on by the 3rd Battalion, and Barsanti later estimated that about a hundred were killed.[11]

AFTERNOON ATTACKS

The attacks out of the Krinkelterwald resumed around 1300 hours, hitting the 2nd Battalion, 38th Infantry positions in Rocherath. By this time, the 1st Battalion had been so badly decimated that it was pulled out of line and sent to the west of the Twin Villages. Fighting was spasmodic as one wave of tanks and infantry was defeated, only to be followed by another attack. The second major afternoon attack began around 1405 hours, and this forced E Company and F Company to pull back. By 1500 hours, Boos instructed Norris's 2nd Battalion command post, located in the fields outside of Rocherath, to pull into the town to avoid being overrun once darkness fell.

The third afternoon attack out of the Krinkelterwald took place at 1520 hours and was broken up with artillery and mortar fire. The 2nd Battalion's G Company had been in regimental reserve for most of the day, but at 1630 hours it was returned to 2nd Battalion control to help reinforce the defenses in Rocherath. In conversations between Boos and General Robertson at 2nd Division headquarters, the issue of reinforcements was raised. Robertson agreed to transfer Companies A and C, 23rd Infantry from their current positions in Wirtzfeld to Krinkelt.

A pair of knocked out *Panthers*, numbers 327 and 154, on the main street in Rocherath with the village water tower evident behind. One of these tanks was knocked out when Capt. James Love of the regimental anti-tank company directed an M4 Sherman tank against it from one of the side street. The other was knocked out by a bazooka hit fired by Pvt. Isabel Salazar from a house overlooking the street.

This *Panther* belonged to the reconnaissance platoon of the *SS-Pz.Rgt.12* headquarters and was knocked out at the edge of the woods near Krinkelt-Rocherath during the fighting there on December 18. BILL AUERBACH

An essential element in the defense of the Twin Villages on December 18 was the critical artillery support provided both by the 2nd Division's four artillery battalions and by V Corps and 99th Division artillery. Many of the battalions were displaced on December 17, gradually congregating on the Elsenborn Ridge and ready for action on December 18. The most critical effect of the artillery support was in isolating the German tank companies inside Krinkelt-Rocherath from supporting German infantry. The field artillery battalions kept the access roads emanating out of the woods to the south and east of the Twin Villages under frequent bombardment, preventing the German infantry from reaching Krinkelt-Rocherath. For example, *III./SS-Panzergrenadier-Regiment 25*, which was supposed to attack from the woods south of Krinkelt, was held in place for most of the day by continual artillery fire.

American forward observers were instrumental in calling in accurate artillery fire whenever a German infantry advance seemed to be forming. By way of example, the 38th Field Artillery Battalion, 2nd Division fired about 4,500 rounds of 105mm ammunition on December 18 alone—nearly three units of fire, or about three times the expected rate of fire.[12] This was about 375 rounds per howitzer, more than four times the average daily expenditure for 105mm howitzers in the European Theater of Operations and considerably more than average use in offensive operations.[13] In forty-two hours of intense action from 1800 hours on December 17 until nightfall on December 19, this battalion alone fired 8,900 rounds of ammunition.[14]

US Field Artillery Fire Support during the Battle of Krinkelt-Rocherath[15]				
Battalion	Division	Weapon	Period	Rounds
12th FAB	2nd	155mm H	Dec. 17–19	3,359
15th FAB	2nd	105mm H	Dec. 17–19	4,746
37th FAB	2nd	105mm H	Dec. 17–19	7,286
38th FAB	2nd	105mm H	Dec. 16–D19	8,938
370th FAB	99th	105mm H	Dec. 17–18	4,000
776th FAB	V Corps	155mm H	Dec. 17–19	n/a
987th FAB	V Corps	155mm G	Dec. 18	65
Total				28,394

Lacking sufficient infantry, the German tanks had no way to overcome the many American nests of resistance in the sturdy Belgian stone houses. The German tanks attempted to blast the American infantry positions with their main guns and machine guns. While this inflicted numerous casualties on the American infantry, it could not take physical control of the buildings.

KRINKELT-ROCHERATH AT DAY'S END

As darkness fell, the situation in the Twin Villages remained chaotic, with neither side in firm control. German forces had occupied much of Rocherath and parts of Krinkelt. On some streets, German troops occupied some houses, with American infantry in the adjacent houses.

It was impossible to tell which side controlled many streets. The *Hit-lerjugend* used the cover of darkness to move more infantry into the town. Likewise, the American forces were reinforced during the course of the evening. About 300 soldiers from the 393rd and 394th Infantry Regiments, 99th Division straggled into Krinkelt-Rocherath during the night, part of the withdrawal toward Elsenborn.

The last major German attack of the day occurred at 1815 hours, when a small group of German armored vehicles from the *III./ SS-Panzergrenadier-Regiment.25* again tried pushing into Krinkelt. Around 2100 hours, another small attack by about seventy to eighty German infantry supported by three tanks attempted to push through the 3rd Battalion defenses on the southwest of Krinkelt but were beaten back. Around 2200 hours, a combat patrol of a few German tanks with accompanying *Panzergrenadiers* attempted to push into the American defenses near the Rocherath church. The 741st Tank Battalion had a few tanks under repair in the area. Cpl. Kelly Layman recalled the melee that ensued:

> Just about that time, we heard jerry tanks coming down the road with their doughs. That's when we started to sweat. My tank wouldn't go, so I climbed into A Company's dozer [tank]. I mean, I tried but he had a full crew and was moving out. I then decided to go over to the other tank. The sergeant was gone so I climbed into the turret and wound up in the bow gunner's seat. The A Company [dozer] tank had moved out and hadn't gone 50 yards when [the Germans] set him on fire, and the crew bailed out. In our tank we didn't know that there was a jerry tank only 30 yards to the right-rear of us. But we did know about the one right in front of us. It was the one on the right that hit us! We had only backed up about twenty feet when they let go with an HE [high explosive] and blew our right track off. We sat there for a couple of seconds trying to move, but it was no good. They hit us again with another HE in the turret and still we sat there. But when they put an armor-piercing through out motor compartment and set us on fire, it was time to bail out![16]

In the dark, both sides sent out anti-tank rocket launcher teams to hunt down enemy tanks. The 38th Infantry's I&R (Intelligence and Reconnaissance) platoon was used as an escort force to help protect American tanks and tank destroyers from roving German infantry armed with *Panzerfaust* and *Panzerschreck* anti-tank rocket launchers. German tanks continued to infiltrate into Krinkelt under the cover of darkness. Around 2230, a column of four German armored vehicles, led by a captured Sherman tank, passed by the C Company, 1/38th Infantry command post, heading toward the northern side of town. Although brought under small-arms fire, none were disabled.

Willi Fischer, leader of the 3rd Platoon of *3./SS-Pz.Rgt.12*, described the eerie scenes in the burning village from the vantage of his *Panther* tank. He was positioned near the village church alongside the *Panther* of *Hauptscharführer* Bellmer. Bellmer was a former infantry NCO who had transferred to the tanks only recently. This was the first time he commanded a tank in combat, and he found night-fighting from the claustrophobic confines of a tank to be particularly unsettling:

> The fighting in Krinkelt flickered on and on. Both sides fight with great determination. On the night of 18–19 December, the American artillery fire is thickening. The impacts are amazingly close to our tanks. As expected, Hauptscharführer Bellmer [in the neighboring tank] mistrusts his new surroundings. He feels trapped in his steel box. His view is limited. His peering infantry eyes, which are used to the darkness, no longer seem to work. In the reflection of the burning houses, shadows seem like moving tanks. Unknown sounds suddenly start to ring his ears. Suddenly the engine of his Panther howls, his tank rears up under the tension of the tracks and he starts racing backwards down the slope. I ask him over the radio where he expects to go and he replies that he had just been targeted by an American tank. I convince him that it was mirage. He returned his old position. Since he cannot see his own infantry, he decides to re-position the turret machine gun to the rear loader's hatch (for rear defense). He told me this later and we sometimes laughed at this "unique" idea.[17]

A *PzKpfw IV* of *I./SS-Panzer-Regiment.12* knocked out during the fighting in Krinkelt-Rocherath.

An M10 3-inch GMC of the 644th Tank Destroyer Battalion in Rocherath with a jeep to the left.

By the end of December 18, 1944, the fate of Krinkelt-Rocherath had not been decided on the battlefield. Neither side held firm control of the town. However, the dramatic defeat of the *I./SS-Panzer-Regiment.12* attack against Krinkelt-Rocherath had profound repercussions at higher levels of command, as will be described in more detail in a later chapter.

X+3: The Battle for Krinkelt-Rocherath Resumes

THE FAILURE OF THE *12.SS-PANZER-DIVISION* TO CAPTURE KRINKELT-Rocherath on Monday, December 18, led to a change of plans for both sides.

From the American perspective, the defense of Krinkelt-Rocherath was a delaying action, permitting the battered 99th Division to withdraw to a new defense line on Elsenborn Ridge. There were never any plans to hold on to the town indefinitely. With the delaying action successful, at 1700 hours on December 18, General Robertson told Col. Franklin Boos, the 38th Infantry commander, that a phased withdrawal from Krinkelt-Rocherath would take place the following day, Tuesday, December 19, to a new defense line stretching from Wirtzfeld to the Elsenborn Ridge.

From the German perspective, the defeat of the *Hitlerjugend* on December 18 forced a reconsideration of the focus of the *I.SS-Panzer-Korps* attack. The Autumn Mist plan had placed the focus of the *Hitlerjugend* attack along Rollbahn C on the Losheim-Bütgenbach axis. This had not taken place during the first three days of the offensive due to the traffic congestion leading to Losheim. Rather than continue to waste resources on a costly siege of the Twin Villages using the exhausted *SS-Panzergrenadier-Regiment.25*, the emphasis shifted to the fresh *SS-Panzergrenadier-Regiment.26*. The *3.Panzergrenadier-Division* was ordered to take over the occupation of Krinkelt-Rocherath. This would take at least a day to accomplish, so in the interim, the *Hitlerjugend* continued to tangle with the 38th Infantry in the ruins of Krinkelt-Rocherath on day X+3.

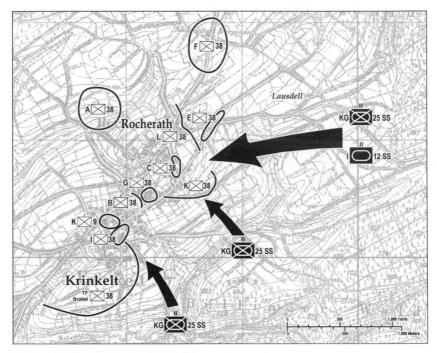

Defense of Krinkelt-Rocherath, December 19, 1944
This map shows the rearranged defenses of the 38th Infantry in the Twin Villages on the second day of the fighting due to the casualties in some of the rifle companies on December 18.

THE FIGHTING RESUMES

After an inconclusive night of raiding, the *Hitlerjugend* staged frontal attacks around dawn on December 19. Damaged tanks and tank destroyers were repaired in the Krinkelterwald and were used as the basis for the renewed attacks. There were two principal avenues of attack. One of these emanated out of the *III./SS-Panzergrenadier-Regiment* positions in the woods southwest of the Twin Villages, hitting the southwest side of the 3/38th Infantry positions in Krinkelt. The other attack came from the usual direction, against the 2/38th Infantry positions in Rocherath.

Much of the Twin Villages area was a no-man's-land, with German and American strongpoints near each other in the sturdy stone houses.

Since the 38th Infantry knew it would be withdrawing later in the day, a deliberate effort was made through the course of the day to send out teams to demolish damaged American and German tanks to prevent their recovery and repair. This generally involved various methods to set the damaged tanks on fire.[1]

The Germans made every effort to recover damaged tanks. Tanks that were immobile due to damage to their engines or suspension remained occupied to prevent their demolition. *Untersturmführer* Engel of *3.Kompanie, I./SS-Pz.Rgt.12* recalled his assignment that day:

> Under the threat of court-martial, [battalion commander *Sturmban-nführer* Arnold] Jürgensen had given me the responsibility to defend my tank, another tank of the 1.Kompanie and an unmanned PzKpfw IV. That was some pleasant feeling with the Americans in one half of the village and the eight of us on the other side in three inoperable tanks! Luckily, the Americans had no idea of our situation.[2]

The snow-covered firing position of a 105mm howitzer of the 38th Field Artillery Battalion, 2nd Infantry Division on Elsenborn Ridge in January 1945. This battalion was attached to the 38th Infantry during the defense of Krinkelt-Rocherath.

Much of the tank fighting took place on the eastern side of the Twin Villages. A *Panther* tank was firing on the company command post of C/38th Infantry, leading to a duel with an American bazooka team.

> Capt. Rollins yelled at [platoon leader Lt. George] Adams to get a bazooka and finish off the enemy tank that was harassing him. Adams grabbed a bazooka himself, climbed into what was left of the attic. Sgt. Rudolph Kraft, second in command of the squad that was manning the house, got the second bazooka and joined Adams in the attic. Wanting to get increased effectiveness from a volume of fire, the officer and sergeant decided to fire a volley at the tank. They loaded and aimed and at the count of three, attempting to fire. Kraft's weapon discharged, but Adams' misfired. The sergeant's round hit the bogie of the tank. Adams, discarding the useless weapon, took over as loader for Kraft. The second rocket entered the top of the turret and burst against the inside. Adams was bending over to load a third round which probably saved his life when a high velocity shell hit the wall of the house and was quickly followed by a second. Adams was slightly injured when the remains of the wall collapsed on him, and he and Kraft withdrew to the safety of the cellar.[3]

Tank-versus-infantry skirmishes were commonplace throughout the day. One of the odder skirmishes took place near the AT Company command post in Rocherath, the scene of considerable fighting the previous day:

> On the morning of the 19th, an individual [Panther] tank stopped immediately east of the CP and started shelling it with 75mm from its tank gun. This was only one of the many cases reported in which tanks fired HE [high explosive] against buildings ineffectively where AP [armor piercing] would have been deadly. The men from the C Company platoon down the street fired at the tank with small arms, distracting its attention. The tank traversed its gun and fired several rounds at the C Company position. When it did this, the men in the CP fired at the tank but did no damage. Again the tank traversed to

the CP and fired 4 to 5 rounds at the building. Then a thing happened that Captain Love [company commander] had never heard of being done before. The tank commander opened the hatch on the top of the tank. He took a Panzerfaust from inside the tank and fired it at the CP building, caving the whole top in. The tank withdrew. Only one man was injured in the collapse of the roof. The only reason that Captain Love could give for the German tank commander being able to put his whole body out of the top of the tank without being shot was that the people who saw it were so surprised that they didn't do anything.[4]

Besides the frequent encounters between infantry and German tanks, there were also a number of skirmishes between German and American armored vehicles, such as the following:

[Company C] found an enemy tank in a wooden barn about 60 yards north of the CP where it was apparently waiting in concealment for a likely target. It was well inside the barn, but unfortunately for its crew, its gun was too long to hide inside the building and someone saw it. One of the TD's [tank destroyers] in the vicinity could fire on it without moving from where it was. Several rounds brought the building crashing down on the tank and the TD finished it off.[5]

At 1345 hours, the American units in the town received detailed instructions about the withdrawal to take place after darkness fell. The bulk of the 38th Infantry and attached elements of the 23rd Infantry were instructed to withdraw to Wirtzfeld. Special engineer platoons were assigned to detonate various demolition charges before leaving to deny the Germans the use of any equipment or supplies. At 1500 hours, Colonel Boos held a meeting with the battalion commanders to go over the plan. Trucks and jeeps began moving out at dusk with the wounded.

Company C, 644th Tank Destroyer Battalion had not been particularly active in the previous day's fighting since they had tended to remain in static ambush positions for most of the day. Of the nineteen tanks and AFVs claimed to have been knocked out by the tank destroyers in the fighting, only six were claimed on December 18, and two of these were by dismounted bazooka teams. The company was prodded by the infantry commanders to take a more active role in attacking the remaining German tanks in town prior to the withdrawal. Of the nineteen German tanks and AFVs claimed by C Company during the fighting, thirteen were claimed from about 1400 to 1730 hours on December 19.

The last major German attack prior to the withdrawal took place after dark around 1600 hours by eleven to fifteen tanks and accompanying infantry out of the woods south of Krinkelt. The US artillery force on Elsenborn Ridge had been alerted to prepare for intensive fire around Krinkelt-Rocherath to prevent German interference in the withdrawal. The 1600 attack was broken up by a heavy artillery barrage, with three to eight tanks left burning in front of the 1/38th Battalion positions south of Krinkelt-Rocherath.[6]

The 38th Infantry began withdrawing on schedule, and the regimental command post was abandoned at 1930 hours and reestablished that night in Berg, a small town on the eastern side of Bütgenbach. The 3rd Battalion was the last to disengage around 2300 hours. The last infantry company to depart was M Company, 3rd Battalion.

> The company's move to Elsenborn Ridge soon became a race as the leading troops were moving as fast as possible to avoid the artillery and Nebelwerfer fire that was beginning to cover the only road leading to the new position. Each unit, frantically trying to keep contact to the front, soon multiplied the cadence by the time it reached the end of the column. With heavy overshoes and overcoats, the men began showing signs of exhaustion before going over a mile. A lot of men threw away their overcoats, making the going somewhat easier, an act which was regretted upon arrival at the new position.[7]

The withdrawing columns suffered some casualties from German artillery near the Wirtzeld area, but the artillery was not intense enough to halt the evacuation. Divisional engineers laid minefields behind the departing troops to discourage any German troops who might try to pursue them. During this process, T/4 Truman Kimbro was killed while

Troops of G Company, 2nd Battalion, 9th Infantry, 2nd Infantry Division on the march near Elsenborn Ridge on December 20, 1944. This battalion eventually deployed in the Camp Elsenborn area to the northwest of the town.

A 105mm howitzer battery of the 38th Field Artillery Battalion is seen here on Elsenborn Ridge on December 20, 1944. This battalion was attached to the 38th Infantry during the fighting for Krinkelt-Rocherath.

trying to complete a minefield under enemy fire. He was awarded the Medal of Honor posthumously, and his citation describes the action:

On 19 December 1944, as scout, he led a squad assigned to the mission of mining a vital crossroads near Rocherath, Belgium. At the first attempt to reach the objective, he discovered it was occupied by an enemy tank and at least 20 infantrymen. Driven back by withering fire, Technician 4th Grade Kimbro made 2 more attempts to lead his squad to the crossroads but all approaches were covered by intense enemy fire. Although warned by our own infantrymen of the great danger involved, he left his squad in a protected place and, laden with mines, crawled alone toward the crossroads. When nearing his objective he was severely wounded, but he continued to drag himself forward and laid his mines across the road. As he tried to crawl from the objective his body was riddled with rifle and machinegun fire. The mines laid by his act of indomitable courage delayed the advance of enemy armor and prevented the rear of our withdrawing columns from being attacked by the enemy.

Rear guards from the 741st Tank Battalion and 644th Tank Destroyer Battalion were the last to withdraw, accompanied by teams from the regimental I&R platoon who had been assigned last-minute demolition assignments. The after-action report of the 741st Tank Battalion noted:

The first tanks left Rocherath at 2015 and at 2030 the commanding officer of Company B, Capt. Vincent Cinquina, reported that the last tank had cleared, and the Engineers who had laid mines were coming out on the tanks. The withdrawal action was completed in a very satisfactory manner, and there was no evidence of pursuit by the enemy. The only difficulty encountered was when two Company A tanks became hopelessly bogged in attempting to get around a road block. They were destroyed by the crews.

By dawn on X+4, December 20, 1944, Krinkelt-Rocherath was finally in German hands. This was a sterile victory considering that the

Autumn Mist plan had expected that the spearheads of the *Hitlerjugend* would have been beyond the Meuse by this date. Instead, the division remained trapped, barely 7 kilometers (4 miles) from its starting point.

BATTLE CASUALTIES

Data on German losses in the Krinkelt-Rocherath fighting are lacking. The appendix in this book provides a more detailed look at the issue of German tank losses. From these sources, the author estimates that the total German tank and tank destroyer casualties in the December 16–21 fighting, including total losses and temporary combat losses, was about fifty to sixty AFVs.

Determining German personnel casualties during the battle for Krinkelt-Rocherath presents an even greater hurdle. Although personnel strength figures are available for December 8, 1944, and December 31, 1944, the vagaries of reporting and the complications presented by medical casualties versus combat casualties, plus the inflow of replacements, present a nearly insurmountable problem in estimating German personnel casualties in this battle. As mentioned above, the 38th Infantry estimated it had killed 300 to 400 Germans in the battle. Assuming the usual ratio of killed-to-wounded applied, total German casualties in the Krinkelt-Rocherath fighting were probably 1,400 to 1,800 men.[8] Total battle casualties for the *6.Panzer-Armee* in December 1944–January 1945 were at least 27,088, but there are considerable difficulties in breaking down these figures by time period and unit.[9]

US armored vehicles losses in the battle for Krinkelt-Rocherath totaled thirteen vehicles. This consisted of eight M4 medium tanks of the 741st Tank Battalion and three M4 medium tanks destroyed by their own crews after bogging down to prevent their capture. The 644th Tank Destroyer Battalion lost two M10 3-inch GMC tank destroyers knocked out in combat.[10] A total of eight towed 3-inch anti-tank guns of the 801st Tank Destroyer Battalion were destroyed by their own crews.

Casualties for the 99th Division during the peak fighting of December 16–23 totaled 1,997, of whom 198 were killed, 901 wounded, and 898 missing in action.[11] Casualties for the 2nd Infantry Division for the same period totaled 1,513, of which there were 63 killed, 664 wounded, and 786 missing in action. The overall casualties for the Battle of the Bulge from December 16, 1944, to January 14, 1945, were 2,137 for the 2nd Infantry Division and 2,536 for the 99th Division.[12]

ASSESSMENT

The battle for Krinkelt-Rocherath was a tactical defeat for the *12. SS-Panzer-Division "Hitlerjugend."* The division failed in its mission to promptly gain access to the road network to the Meuse and suffered especially heavy losses in the process. In contrast, the 2nd Infantry Division enjoyed a tactical victory at Krinkelt-Rocherath. Its mission was to delay the German advance long enough for the V Corps to erect a defense line in the Bütgenbach-Elsenborn-Monschau sector. The new defense line would be successfully defended for the remainder of the Ardennes campaign.

The failure of the German attack on Krinkelt-Rocherath was due to many factors, but several stand out. The first was the reckless tactics employed in the attack, in particular the tank attack on the morning of December 18. The use of a tank-heavy force in an urban environment against infantry violated German tactical doctrine. Without sufficient accompanying infantry, the tanks were especially vulnerable to American bazooka teams who could use the cover provided by the stone buildings in the town to hunt the tanks by stealthy approach. In addition, the German tanks were especially vulnerable to American tanks that were operating from prepared ambush positions.

The lack of German infantry support once the tanks reached the Twin Villages was due to the heavy casualties suffered by the infantry riding on the tanks, inflicted by American small-arms fire in the vicinity of Lausdell Crossroads and especially the heavy artillery support enjoyed by the 38th Infantry. US infantry commanders were lavish in their praise for the artillery support that they received, deeming it essential in the defense of Krinkelt-Rocherath.

An important factor in the rash decision to attack into Krinkelt-Rocherath using tanks was the pressure on senior *Hitlerjugend* commanders to speed up the pace of the offensive. When the main attack on Krinkelt-Rocherath took place on December 18 (X+2), the Autumn Mist plan had assumed that the *Hitlerjugend* would be well on its way to the Meuse and not trapped barely 5 kilometers from the start line. Neither the *6.Panzer-Armee* nor *I.SS-Panzer-Korps* had any real knowledge of the extent of US defenses in Krinkelt-Rocherath, and a bold tank attack seemed to offer better prospects for a quick success than another effort to rally enough infantry strength to undertake an infantry assault on Krinkelt-Rocherath. A combined-arms attack by tanks and *Panzergrenadiers* riding in armored half-tracks would have seemed to be the ideal solution, but only one battalion in the *Hitlerjugend* division was mounted on half-tracks and it belonged to *SS-Panzergrenadier-Regiment.26*, which had been assigned to the Losheim axis of advance.

German artillery played a minor role in the battle, but the reasons for this shortcoming have not been recorded in detail. To begin with, the divisional artillery of the *12.SS-Panzer-Division* appears to have played little or no role in the fighting since it was still stuck in traffic jams. Therefore, the attack depended on divisional artillery from the *277.Volksgrenadier-Division* and corps artillery. The scanty records available suggest myriad reasons including a shortage of available ammunition, the lack of forward observers with adequate means of communication, and the slow pace of moving the artillery forward due to the traffic congestion. Some American accounts of the German artillery preparation on the morning of December 18 indicate that some German artillery strikes fell on German infantry, suggesting significant fire control problems.

From the American perspective, the defense of Krinkelt-Rocherath was a model of combined-arms defense. The tenacious defense of the Twin Villages by the 38th Infantry was at the heart of the success, but the infantry was vigorously supported by divisional and corps artillery which kept the German infantry at bay. The 741st Tank Battalion provided close fire support within the town, and the unit was later awarded the Presidential Unit Citation for its actions.

We Fight and Die Here: Dom Bütgenbach

IN VIEW OF THE FAILURE TO PROMPTLY CAPTURE KRINKELT-Rocherath, the *6.Panzer-Armee* late on December 18 decided to shift the focus of the *Hitlerjugend* attack from the Krinkelt-Rocherath-Elsenborn axis to the original avenue suggested in the Autumn Mist plan, namely an advance to the Meuse via Bütgenbach. This sector contained better roads heading to the Meuse. The reason the *12.SS-Panzer-Division* was not already moving on this axis was the crowding of the approaches to Rollbahn C by the traffic around Losheim, followed by the use of this road network by the *1.SS-Panzer-Division* during the ill-fated attempt by *Kampfgruppe Peiper* to reach Rollbahn E. A contributory factor was the very slow approach to the battle zone by the remainder of the *12.SS-Panzer-Division*, notably *SS-Panzergrenadier-Regiment.26*, *Schwere-Panzerjägerabteilung.560*, and the divisional artillery.

The first element of the *12.SS-Panzer-Division* to reach the approaches to Bütgenbach was *Hauptsturmführer* Georg Urabl's *III./SS-Panzergrenadier-Regiment.26*. This was the only *Panzergrenadier* battalion in the division equipped with armored half-tracks, and so was used to spearhead the remainder of the regiment. This unit reached Büllingen around 0630 on December 19, which at the time was occupied by the *12.Volksgrenadier-Division*. The *12.Volksgrenadier-Division* was attempting to capture Wirtzfeld, which was being held by rear guards of the 2nd Infantry Division. In addition, its spearhead unit, *Vorausabtelung Holz* (Holz Forward Detachment), was probing toward Bütgenbach. This detachment was commanded by *Major* Günther Holz, leader of the division's *Panzerjäger-Abteilung.1012*, and was based on the divisional *Füsilier-Bataillon.12*, some Pionier troops, and the remaining *StuG IV* assault guns of Holz's battalion.

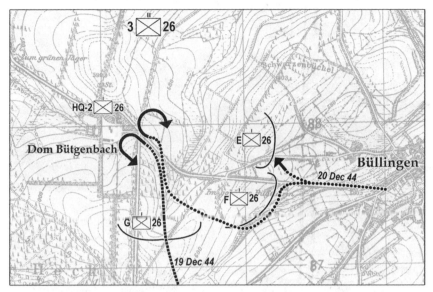

The Defense of Dom Bütgenbach, December 19–20, 1944
This map shows the initial positions of the 2nd Battalion, 26th Infantry, 1st Infantry Division around Dom Bütgenbach during the initial fighting on December 19–20, 1944.

On the American side, the importance of Bütgenbach was plainly evident to General Gerow and the V Corps. There was an enormous void in the Losheim Gap between V Corps and VIII Corps, which was gradually being filled by the newly arriving XVIII Airborne Corps under Maj. Gen. Matthew Ridgway. Gerow was able to get the 1st Infantry Division transferred to his command from the VII Corps reserve to cover the sector adjacent to the Losheim Gap. The 1st Infantry Division had been badly bloodied in the fighting in the Hürtgen forest and had been sent to the rear in early December for a month of recovery and rebuilding. The sudden commitment of the division to the V Corps put an end to this process, and so the 1st Infantry Division entered the Ardennes understrength.

The lead element of the division, Col. John Seitz's 26th Infantry, was alerted for movement at 1100 hours on December 16. Although Seitz was nominally in command, he had gone of leave shortly before the

A column from the 26th Infantry, 1st Division marches past Bütgenbach on their way to set up defenses south of the city to halt the *6.Panzer-Armee* attack. The damaged structure behind them is the Vennquerbahn viaduct that was constructed as part of the Venn Bahn railroad line by the Prussian state railway in the 1880s, when the province was still part of Germany.

deployment alert. The regiment's executive officer, Lt. Col. Edwin "Van" Sutherland, was in command, with Lt. Col. Frank Murdoch appointed as unofficial deputy for operations; Seitz returned on December 18. Lt. Col. John Corley's 3/26th Infantry arrived by truck at Camp Elsenborn at 0700 hours on December 17. It deployed between Bütgenbach and Büllingen shortly after midnight on December 17–18. Next in line was Lt. Col. Derrill Daniel's 2nd Battalion, 26th Infantry, which arrived around 1400 hours on December 17.

Although it was not apparent at the time, Daniel's 2nd Battalion, 26th Infantry would bear the brunt of the fighting in Dom Bütgenbach. This battalion had been decimated in early December 1944 during

Troops of the 26th Infantry, 1st Infantry Division march down the Bütgenbach-Büllingen road to establish defenses near Dom Bütgenbach on December 17, 1944.

fighting on the fringes of the Hürtgen forest near Merode and was in the process of reconstruction when the orders arrived to move to Bütgenbach.

> Companies E and F had been virtually annihilated, Company G shattered. Now the 2nd Battalion rifle companies were nine-tenths replacements and numbered not more than one hundred men each [instead of 193 authorized strength]. All told, there were seven officers in the battalion who had been on the roster at the beginning of December [out of a normal strength of thirty-five officers in the battalion].[1]

There was a certain degree of proud fatalism in the 26th Infantry. The regiment had fought encircled at Kasserine in February 1943 and again at Barrafranca on Sicily in July 1943. Daniel, who had fought in those previous battles, told his troops at Dom Bütgenbach: "We fight and die here."

Like many US Army officers in World War II, Daniel's path to the army was through the reserves. He was a graduate of Clemson University, becoming a 2nd lieutenant through the Reserve Officer Training Course (ROTC) in 1926. He went on to earn a doctorate in entomology from Cornell in 1933, serving with the New York State Agricultural Experiment Research Station as a specialist in insect pests. A bit older than most Regular Army officers, he was mobilized at the start of the war at age thirty-six and received battalion command in Tunisia.

A 57mm gun crew of the 1/26th Infantry manhandle their 57mm anti-tank gun into position near Bütgenbach on December 17. The anti-tank defense of Dom Bütgenbach centered around its 57mm anti-tank guns. These weapons were extremely unpopular in the infantry since they could not reliably penetrate the frontal armor of German tanks, only the side armor. As can be seen here, they were unwieldy for their crews to move. Each infantry regiment had eighteen 57mm anti-tank guns: nine in the regimental Anti-Tank Company and three each in the three battalion HQ companies.

A group portrait of the officers of the 2nd Battalion, 26th Infantry. Lt. Col. Derrill Daniel can be seen with the walking cane. On his right is his executive officer, Capt. John "Frank" Dulligan. McCORMICK RESEARCH CENTER

He subsequently served with "The Big Red One" on Sicily, during the Normandy landings, and the battle for Aachen as the 2/26th Infantry commander. By the time of the Ardennes campaign, he was one of the most highly decorated officers in the European Theater. By war's end he had been awarded the Distinguished Service Cross, the Silver Star with six Oak Leaf Clusters, and the Bronze Star with two Oak Leaf Clusters. He would later serve as an assistant division commander in Korea, and a divisional and corps commander in the late 1950s.

Daniel's battalion was deployed astride the main road from Büllingen to Bütgenbach near a large manor farm called the *Dömane Bütgenbach* (Bütgenbach Estate). This farm had a core of stone buildings at the center of the estate and was on a slight elevation overlooking the road from Büllingen. It is usually called "Dom Bütgenbach" in most American accounts due to the use of that abbreviation on US tactical maps.

This aerial photo taken in 1947 shows the ruins of the village of Büllingen. Dom Bütgenbach is slightly outside of this view to the far left.

26th Infantry Regiment at Dom Bütgenbach

26th Infantry Regiment	Col. John Seitz
2nd Battalion, 26th Infantry	Lt. Col. Derrill Daniel
E Company	Capt. Pierre Stepanian
F Company	1Lt. James Rea
G Company	1Lt. August McColgan

The 26th Infantry in the Bütgenbach area was designated as CT26 (Combat Team 26th Infantry) since it included more than the infantry regiment. It also had the 33rd Field Artillery Battalion from the division and later received other attachments including C Company, 703rd Tank Destroyer Battalion (four M10 3-inch GMCs and four M36 90mm GMCs), a platoon from the 734th Tank Destroyer Battalion, and two tanks from C Company, 745th Tank Battalion.

On December 17 the 26th Infantry temporary commander, Van Sutherland, met with Major General Lauer of the 99th Division, to which his unit was temporarily attached. Sutherland was left very uneasy by the meeting. Lauer "had no idea where his battalions were. He told us to move through Bütgenbach until we met the Germans."[2]

Sutherland and Murdoch established the CT26 defenses as a triangle, with the 1st Battalion holding the town of Bütgenbach itself, the 2nd Battalion at Dom Bütgenbach, and the 3rd Battalion on a hill between Büllingen and Bütgenbach.

First contact was made with German forces at 1240 hours on December 18 when a German scout car approached the defenses of the 2/26th Infantry near Dom Bütgenbach. The vehicle was knocked out, and a captured prisoner indicated it was from the *1.SS-Panzer-Division*. This was from *Kampfgruppe Peiper*'s assorted small detachments that were probing along the roads after the battle group had seized Büllingen.[3] Later in the day, K Company reported spotting German armored vehicles milling around in Büllingen, and they were brought under fire by the 33rd Field Artillery Battalion. These were from the advance guard of Urabl's *III./SS-Panzergrenadier-Regiment.26*. The *Panzergrenadiers* soon found that Büllingen was a dangerous location for billeting, since it was under continual US artillery fire. The fire was intense enough that the armored half-tracks were moved behind various buildings to shield them from the artillery barrages. Eventually, the *Hitlerjugend* were forced out of Büllingen due to the heavy shelling and took up new positions in the forested area farther south.

On the night of December 18–19, *Vorausabteilung Holz* of the *12.Volksgrenadier-Division* attempted to capture Dom Bütgenbach. The attack started around 0225, and American accounts estimated the strength as about twelve tanks and two companies of truck-borne infantry. The tank strength was probably wrong, as by this time *Pz.Jg.Abt.1012* had only about a half-dozen *StuG IV* assault guns still operational. However, it is also possible that the attack force received armored reinforcements from the recently arrived *Hitlerjugend* contingent, most likely gun-armed armored half-tracks. An account by the 26th Infantry described the attack:

> A total of 7 tanks came almost to the Battalion's position. They were hit by bazooka, 57mm anti-tank guns and AT grenades . . . Direct artillery fire broke up the attack. Three tanks finally got through and ran up and down the road going into Dom Bütgenbach, putting direct

fire on the Battalion. Five or six men in Dom Bütgenbach were hit by enemy tank fire. The tanks, driven back by artillery and infantry, stopped at the line of departure. Patrols later found 100 enemy dead. It was believed that two of the three tanks were hit [two were found disabled later].[4]

An account by the *12.Volksgrenadier-Division* recalled that "the attack bogged down directly in from of Domäne Bütgenbach because the area had been fortified as a strongpoint by the Americans."[5]

After reaching Büllingen in the predawn hours of December 19, *III./Panzergrenadier-Regiment.26* began sending out scouting patrols to the Schwarzenbüchel, Dom Bütgenbach, Morscheck, and Richelsbusch. The scouting patrol sent toward the Schwarzenbüchel hill found the area occupied by the 3/26th Infantry, but returned unscathed with a report that the hill was heavily defended.

The patrol sent to Dom Bütgenbach was hit by gunfire and two armored half-tracks were destroyed. Capt. Pierre Stepanien, the commander of E Company, described the engagement:

At 1010 on 19 December, 2 tanks and a company of infantry of the 12th SS Panzer Division came in from the south, ran through our positions and blasted them. Several of the E Company men were wounded. Artillery and TD [tank destroyer] fire from near Dom Bütgenbach was brought in while the men stayed in their foxholes. One of their tanks was knocked out and their infantry stopped cold by this fire. It is probable that all of their infantry in this attack were killed.[6]

One of the German armored vehicles was hit by a 90mm antiaircraft gun deployed in a direct-fire anti-tank role. In the course of this engagement, one of the 90mm guns was knocked out by German anti-tank rocket fire.

The *Hitlerjugend* patrols sent to the Morscheck and Richelsbusch woods southwest of Büllingen found the area occupied by the *3.Fallschirmjäger-Division*, which could offer little information on American dispositions in the sector.[7]

While Urabl's *III.Bataillon* was conducting its scouting patrols, the trailing elements of the *Hitlerjugend* began arriving in Büllingen on December 19. This included the headquarters staff of *SS-Panzer-Regiment.12*, *Hauptsturmführer* Gerd Hein's *I./Panzergrenadier-Regiment.26*, Major Streger's *Schwere-Panzerjägerabteilung.560*, and *II./SS-Artillerie-Regiment.12*.

Although additional *Hitlerjugend* units were still on the road heading to Büllingen, there was considerable pressure from the *6.Panzer-Armee* to press ahead to capture Bütgenbach as quickly as possible. As a result, the available units in the Büllingen area were subordinated to *Sturmbannführer* Herbert Kuhlmann, the commander of *SS-Panzer-Regiment.12*, as *Kampfgruppe Kuhlmann*. The intention was to stage a combined attack by *KG Kuhlmann* toward Bütgenbach and the *3.Fallschirmjager-Division* toward Weywertz. The earlier scouting concluded that Dom Bütgenbach was heavily defended, so the decision was made to conduct the attack in the dark.

THE DECEMBER 20 ATTACK

Kampfgruppe Kuhlmann started the attack around 2200 on the night of December 19–20 and first hit F Company. The commander of F Company, 1Lt. James Rea, recalled the attack:

> At 0130, 20 December, an attack developed from Büllingen. They came up the east–west road [N632]. About six tanks and about two companies of infantry. They hit the roadblock of mines across the road. The rest of the tanks then went off the road and came cross-country to the north–south road [N658] into Dom Bütgenbach. It was dark, so it was impossible for the battalion to see how to shoot. The Germans fired into F Company, knocking out three bazooka teams. Company H lost a machine gun section and 4 or 5 men. The Germans had no artillery preparation for the attack.[8]

According to German accounts, the attack encountered problems from the start. The commander in the lead *Jagdpanther* heading up the road was hit in the head and killed. The driver tried to back up off the road, but in the dark, rammed the following *Jagdpanther*.[9] "The 33rd Field Artillery turned loose a barrage in front of the positions and by 0145 hours, all was quiet. It was to prove to be the lull before the main attempt."[10]

The fighting resumed a few hours later against the 2nd Battalion positions. The German attack force consisted of *I./SS-Panzergrenadier-Regiment.26*, led by a group of tank destroyers from *s.Pz.Jg.Abt.560*. A later 26th Infantry report described the attack:

> Coming out of the mist which cloaked movements but seventy-five to a hundred yards away, the enemy tanks loomed up in front of the riflemen, who fought back with anti-tank guns, grenades, and rocket-guns. The massed tanks broke through the curtain of fire from the infantrymen and the immediate supporting fires laid down by the artillery and tank and tank destroyer elements, and overran the company main lines of resistance. Machine gunning the foxholes, the tanks sought to open a wedge for the following German infantry. Overrun and out-gunned, many riflemen died at their posts. Mortar crews left their weapons and joined the riflemen in repelling the German infantry. Machine gunners directed heavy and accurate streams of fire at the enemy. The smashing of machine-gun emplacements by the tanks that rode over the positions failed to halt the fire of the remaining machine gunners. Assistant gunners took over the positions of the "E" and "F" Company machine guns when the gunners became casualties. Ammunition bearers manned the weapons or fought as riflemen against the German tanks. The hostile armor rode back and forth across the gap, but failed to silence the riflemen who still fought off the German infantry. In the close fighting that followed, German tanks confidently made for the group of buildings housing the battalion CP, and two company CPs. Locked in combat, the opposing infantry forces hurled every available man into the struggle.[11]

The 33rd Field Artillery Battalion, realizing the scale of the German attack, called on other divisional and corps artillery for assistance. Eventually, the fire from the 5th and 955th Field Artillery Battalions was added to the fray, along with the 90mm anti-aircraft guns of the 414th Anti-Aircraft Battalion. When a large formation of German infantry was seen advancing up the north–south road into Dom Bütgenbach, the

Jagdpanther number 134 of *s.Pz.Jg.Abt.560* was knocked out along the Büllingen-Bütgenbach road, probably by artillery fire. Its 88mm gun barrel has been shattered and blown off.

A close-up of the destroyed *Jagdpanther* number 134 on the Büllingen road. A close examination of the glacis plate below the gun mantlet shows that it has been shattered and caved in, probably as the result of the impact of a heavy artillery projectile. The clump of wire running over the vehicle is US Army communication wire. The wrecked vehicle was used as a convenient way to hold the wire off the ground.

contemporary route N658, the attack was decimated by a heavy, multi-battalion barrage starting at 0342 hours. The after-action report of the 26th Infantry provides more details about the attack:

> At 0330 hours, about twenty tanks and a battalion of infantry hit the 2nd Battalion positions, placing greatest pressure on Company E and Company F. Maximum artillery fire was called for by Lt. Colonel Daniel and the 33rd Field Artillery tied in the efforts of all of its batteries as well as the batteries of the 955th Field Artillery and the 15th Field Artillery Battalions.
>
> The enemy artillery and mortar barrage upon the 2nd Battalion position proved intense as the enemy tank and infantry drove into the 2nd Battalion. Tanks succeeded in overrunning the lines between Companies E and F, but the infantry remained in their places, trusting to the tank-destroyers and anti-tank guns behind them to dispose of this threat to their rear. The enemy infantry seeking to follow through was unable to penetrate the lines that held under the most intense pressure ever experienced by the companies. The mist and smoke of the early morning made the fighting a matter of close range firing. Anti-Tank guns waited until the tanks were within pointblank range before letting go their rounds, and the enemy rocket-gun teams following the tanks were able to subject the anti-tank crews to rocket-gun fire. The reserve force of the 2nd Battalion, a platoon of G Company, was quickly committed, and a company of the 1st Battalion requested. C Company was pulled out of the 1st Battalion line and swung over into the 2nd Battalion sector. Two platoons were committed to back up F Company and two platoons were placed in battalion reserve.[12]

During the defense of F Company, Corp. Henry Warner, a gunner on one of the 57mm anti-tank guns from the regimental anti-tank company, particularly distinguished himself, eventually being awarded the Medal of Honor. His later citation described the action:

> Serving as 57-mm. antitank gunner with the 2d Battalion, he was a major factor in stopping enemy tanks during heavy attacks against the battalion position near Dom Bütgenbach, Belgium, on 20–21 December 1944. In the first attack, launched in the early morning

of the 20th, enemy tanks succeeded in penetrating parts of the line. Cpl. Warner, disregarding the concentrated cannon and machinegun fire from 2 tanks bearing down on him, and ignoring the imminent danger of being overrun by the infantry moving under tank cover, destroyed the first tank and scored a direct and deadly hit upon the second. A third tank approached to within 5 yards of his position while he was attempting to clear a jammed breach lock. Jumping from his gun pit, he engaged in a pistol duel with the tank commander standing in the turret, killing him and forcing the tank to withdraw.[13]

The main tank support for the Dom Bütgenbach defenses came from Lt. Leonard Novak's 2nd Platoon, C Company, 745th Tank Battalion. Lt. Col. Daniel positioned the tanks behind the infantry defenses to deal with any German tanks leaking through. On December 20, Novak's platoon was credited with hitting six German tanks, destroying three. One of the platoon's tanks was knocked out by a German anti-tank rocket.[14]

Although most of the attack took place in the 2nd Battalion sector, the German advance spilled over to the neighboring 3rd Battalion defenses to the northeast in the vicinity of Schwarzenbüchel hill: "I Company positions were placed under intense cannon and machine-gun fire as the German tanks sought to rejoin the enemy infantry forces. Not a squad budged from position. The firepower of the entire company leveled at the German armored vehicles forced these to sheer off . . . Next to be subjected to pressure was L Company's platoons. Repulsed in this sector, the tanks turned back."[15]

During the course of the early morning fighting, a company of German *Jagdpanzers* had broken through the infantry lines and headed for the Domäne Bütgenbach manor farm, where the 2nd Battalion command posts were located. The 26th Infantry had placed its supporting tanks and tank destroyers in rear positions with an aim to giving them wide fields of fire. However, in the darkness and fog, they were unable to engage the German armored vehicles. When the German armored vehicles advanced forward, the supporting American armor was finally able to engage them at point-blank range. This was later described in a 26th Infantry HQ report:

In back of the main line, a fight as bitter as that between the infantry forces was being decided. Eight German tanks had pierced the lines, and these had ranged in back of the lines until the German infantry had closed in and locked in hand-to-hand [combat] with our infantry. [The German armored vehicles] had then struck at the group of houses in which two company CP's and the battalion CP were located. Under direct tank fire that leveled the walls of several buildings, the CP personnel organized rocket-gun teams and by daring use of these weapons forced the tanks to take cover behind some brick buildings. [American] tank destroyers and tanks then combined efforts, and in intense fighting drove the [German] tanks from cover to cover until supporting tanks from other sectors of the regiment arrived to close with the enemy armor. Under intense fire . . . the German tanks withdrew . . . Two of our tanks were lost, and five of the enemy's left blazing wrecks as the two survivors raced from the gap in "F" Company's positions and moved towards the protection of Büllingen . . . The remnants of the battered panzer battalion made two more attempts. Under our accurate artillery fire, and up against the stonewall defense of the entire regimental line, the enemy was forced to abandon the field with his mission unaccomplished.[16]

The fighting died down around 0530 hours, and some of the German armored vehicles and troops returned to Büllingen. There were recriminations over some of the actions by companies of the *s.Pz. Jg.Abt.560*. The *Jagdpanzer* company commander who had broken into the 2/26th Infantry lines complained to Herbert Kuhlmann, the battle-group commander, that "in his judgement, the withdrawal of the Jagdpanzer company on the right had not been necessary and that otherwise the attack could have continued successfully."[17] He was referring to the *Jagdpanzer* company that had attacked the 3rd Battalion around Schwarzenbüchel hill. It is not clear from surviving German accounts whether this withdrawal was sanctioned by Kuhlmann or was taken on the company commander's initiative.

The December 20 attack had been especially costly for *s.Pz. Jg.Abt.560*. From its starting strength of seventeen *Jagdpanther*s and twenty-six *Panzer IV lg.(V)*s, it had been reduced to only three *Jagdpanthers* and ten *Panzer IV lg.(V)*s.[18] Not all of these vehicles were combat casualties. A significant number of *Jagdpanthers* had become bogged down in the muddy fields southeast of Dom Bütgenbach. The *Jagdpanzer* company commander also excused the costly and ineffective performance of *s.Pz.Jg.Abt.560* during the attack. Offensive missions were difficult to achieve using Jagdpanzers. Without rotating turrets, they were less versatile in fire fights, especially at close-range, compared to Panzers. The Abteilung had not been trained for action as assault guns.

The numerous damaged vehicles could not be repaired in the chaos of Büllingen, so much of the battalion was sent back to Tiefenbach for repair. The surviving thirteen tank destroyers were consolidated into a single company and put under the command of one of the few surviving officers, *Hauptmann* Heinz Wewers.

A view of a farm field near the road between Bütgenbach and Büllingen with three knocked-out *Jagdpanther* tank destroyers of *s.Pz.Jg.Abt.560*; the village of Büllingen is visible in the background. A number of these vehicles bogged down in the mud, while others were hit by US artillery fire while trying to attack Dom Bütgenbach.

A view down the Bütgenbach-Büllingen road after the fighting. Many German vehicles were knocked out along this road by US artillery but were pushed off the road after the battle to clear it for traffic. In the left foreground is a *PzKpfw IV* with *Jagdpanther* number 134 behind it. On the opposite side of the road are some overturned trucks and a *Panzer IV lg.(V)*.

During the lull in the fighting in the morning, Lt. Col. Daniel attempted to restore order in the 2nd Battalion sector:

> Mines and tank destroyers were requested by the 2nd Battalion commander, three more AT guns were sent up at 10:00 hours. An engineer platoon was also requested to help lay about 1,000 anti-tank mines in front of the battalion positions, but these did not arrive until late in the afternoon. Heavy enemy fire still pounded the 2nd Battalion positions after the enemy tank and infantry withdrew.[19]

Anticipating further attacks on Dom Bütgenbach, the 1st Division began to scrape up units to reinforce the battered 26th Infantry. The

18th Infantry sent its E Company, which was assigned as the reserve of the 26th Infantry. C Company of the 1st Battalion, 26th Infantry was moved from the town of Bütgenbach and took up positions to the southwest of the manor farm to shield the western flank of the 2/26th Infantry. An anti-tank gun platoon in the 3/26th Infantry positions was moved over to Dom Bütgenbach to make up for the many 57mm guns lost in the 2/26th Infantry sector.

Command Perspectives:
The First Turning Point

By the evening of December 18, 1944, the outcome of Hitler's Ardennes offensive had largely been decided. The failure of the *6.Panzer-Armee* to conduct a timely breakthrough in its sector meant that the tactical objective of the operation, the capture of Antwerp, was no longer likely. Armaments minister Albert Speer, a close confident of Hitler's, called December 18, 1944, "the first turning point."[1] The recognition of this failure took about two days to sink in among the senior German leaders, but crucial tactical decisions were made that evening that would affect the course of the Ardennes campaign.

The German Perspective at the End of X+2

By the end of the day of December 18, it had become apparent that the *6.Panzer-Armee* had failed to make a speedy penetration of the American defenses. The attack by the *67.Armee-Korps* in the Monschau area had faltered from the very start. This was not of any deep concern since this corps had very modest resources and very modest objectives. The greater concern was the poor performance of Priess's *I.SS-Panzer-Korps*. The attack on the first day of the offensive had failed to make a break-in of the American main line of resistance.

This was slightly redeemed early on the morning of December 17 when *Kampfgruppe Peiper* had finally pushed into the Losheim Gap. However, radio contact with Peiper's battle group was lost almost immediately, and the whereabouts and progress of this spearhead remained a mystery for more than a day. On December 18, German signals intelligence units picked up short-range American tactical radio transmissions that indicated Peiper had reached Stavelot. In spite of its progress toward the Meuse, Peiper's battle group was now cut off from the remainder of the *1.SS-Panzer Division*. Attempts were under way to forge a link between Peiper and the follow-on battle groups.

Progress had been far poorer in the *12.SS-Panzer-Division* sector. The attempt by *SS-Panzergrenadier-Regiment.25* to secure Krinkelt-Rocherath with the support of *I./SS-Panzer-Regiment.12* had failed on December 17 and 18, although parts of the Twin Villages were now in German hands. By the evening of December 18, there were few details in Berlin or in Rundstedt's OB West headquarters regarding the casualties suffered that day in this engagement. The second mission for the *12.SS-Panzer-Division* on December 18, a push by *SS-Panzergrenadier-Regiment* to Bütgenbach, had never materialized due to continuing problems to push units into the field through the traffic congestion in the Eifel region. As a result of these two failures, a brisk advance to the Meuse on December 19 seemed exceedingly unlikely.

The two special operations planned in this sector had also failed. Operation Greif, the Skorzeny-led spearhead, never really started due to the failure of the infantry divisions to secure any firm break-ins on X-Day. Operation Stösser, the airborne landings on the roads toward Antwerp, had turned into a fiasco. Although some paratroopers had indeed been dropped, they had lost touch with higher commands and there was little reason to expect any favorable consequences for this mission.

In spite of the growing evidence that Autumn Mist had become derailed due to the failures in the Elsenborn sector, Berlin remained guardedly optimistic due to the successes in Manteuffel's *5.Panzer-Armee*. *General* Walter Warlimont, the deputy chief of operations at Jodl's OKW headquarters, noted that Hitler's high command "was carried away by these partial successes and was completely the prisoner of its own wishful thinking. It therefore entirely failed to realize that with every day the enemy was allowed for the movement of his considerable reserves, the prospects of a major victory, getting anywhere near the planned objectives, were becoming more improbable.[2]

OPTIONS NOT TAKEN

Had Autumn Mist proceeded as planned, two critical decisions would have taken place on X+2. The *II.SS-Panzer-Korps* would have been committed behind Priess's *I.SS-Panzer-Korps* somewhere near the Meuse, either to take over the spearhead mission if *I.SS-Panzer-Korps* was exhausted or to advance to Antwerp in parallel if Priess's command retained enough strength after the break-in battles. Secondly, it was anticipated that the *15.Armee* in the Aachen area would join the Autumn Mist contingent, launching its attack north of Dietrich's *6.Panzer-Armee*.

In the event, neither of these two decisions were made as planned. Of the two contingencies, the activation of the *15.Armee* was the more crucial. By December 17, Rundstedt's OB West headquarters had realized that the US Army had no reserves in the immediate area beyond those already committed, and therefore would be obliged to move them into the Ardennes from other sectors.[3] The most likely sector to provide reinforcements to the Ardennes was the Aachen area, containing elements of the First US Army and the Ninth US Army. Activation of the *15.Armee*, as planned by Hitler under Watch on the Rhine, would accomplish two goals. At a minimum, it would tie down US Army forces in the Aachen area, preventing them from being shifted into the Ardennes. Under the best of circumstances, the *15.Armee* could be used to encircle several US divisions in the Aachen area, fulfilling the operational objectives of Watch on the Rhine's Small Solution.

This became all the more attractive by the evening of December 18, since it was becoming painfully apparent to Rundstedt and other senior commanders that the opportunity for reaching the Big Solution at Antwerp was becoming impossible. In Model's Army Group B headquarters, more-limited objectives became the new focus.[4] In a telephone conversation with Rundstedt and Jodl on the evening of December 18, Model expressed his view that the offensive had failed.[5]

Rundstedt had already started preparations for the start of the *15.Armee* offensive on December 17. His headquarters was deeply distressed when on the evening of December 18 they were informed that Hitler had unilaterally cancelled the planned commitment of the *15.Armee* in the Ardennes offensive. Hitler explained that he "anticipated strong Allied resistance [in the Aachen sector] together with the intention of using all and every available unit to widen the breaches made in the attack front proper."[6] Hitler proposed that the best units in the *15.Armee*, including the *9.Panzer-Division* and *15.Panzergrenadier-Division*, be shifted to the *6.Panzer-Armee* sector for commitment. In view of the fact that the *6.Panzer-Armee* could not even commit existing allotments, including the panzer divisions of *II.SS-Panzer-Korps*, the addition of two more divisions, many miles away from the Ardennes, was little compensation for the cancellation of the *15.Armee* attack.

The OB West war diary concluded that Hitler and the OKW "had passed up the good chance of encircling Allied forces in the Aachen salient. The German units remaining in the [*15.Armee*] sector would not even suffice for a containing attack. Developments would have to show whether this renunciation of all previous planning would lead to the attainment of the far-flung objective of the OKW any quicker."[7]

By December 19, X+3, it had become widely accepted among senior German commanders that the Big Solution was impossible. The situation in the Elsenborn sector was so alarming that on December 18–19, Jodl's headquarters sent a general staff officer to the sector to determine the reasons for the bogging down of the *6.Panzer-Armee*. Another officer was sent from Model's Army Group B headquarters as well. They promptly reported back that the delays were caused by bad roads, poor training of the troops, and the unsuitability of the terrain to the deployment of tanks.[8] None of these factors could be ameliorated with the resources on hand.

Dismay over the poor performance of the *6.Panzer-Armee* was becoming prevalent among senior German commanders. *SS-Obergruppenführer* Wilhelm Bittrich, commander of *II.SS-Panzer-Korps*, had been given temporary command of the *67.Armee-Korps* in the Monschau area after Hitzfeld's command post had been bombed. He quickly became aware of the situation in the neighboring *I.Panzer-Korps* sector to the south and concluded that it would be useless to continue the efforts to capture Elsenborn Ridge. He informed Dietrich's *6-Panzer-Armee* headquarters of his assessment, as well as Model's Army Group B headquarters.[9]

The growing recognition that the *I.SS-Panzer-Korps* had failed in its mission was recognized by Dietrich's *6.Panzer-Armee* headquarters by December 19. The army's chief of staff, *Generalmajor* Fritz Krämer, proposed to halt any further offensive actions and create a defense line including the *1.SS-Panzer-Division*, *3.Fallschirmjäger-Division*, and *12.Volksgrenadier-Division* running from Stoumont to Büllingen. At the same time, the *12.SS-Panzer-Division* would disengage and be reassigned to the *II.SS-Panzer-Korps*. Since there was no penetration likely in the *6.Panzer-Armee* sector, Bittrich's *II.SS-Panzer-Korps* would be committed in Manteuffel's *5.Panzer-Armee* sector.[10] This plan tacitly accepted the loss of *Kampfgruppe Peiper*. The original hope had been that the *12.SS-Panzer-Division* advance to Bütgenbach and beyond would

Some US troops inspect a German airborne supply canister containing ammunition near Kornelimünster, south of Aachen, that had been dropped by German transport aircraft on the night of December 17–18 as part of the badly bungled Operation Stösser airborne landing. These containers landed about 30 kilometers (20 miles) from their intended drop-zone.

continue to the east of *KG Peiper*, freeing it from its trap. Dietrich himself admitted after the war that he had recognized that the *6.Panzer-Armee* attack had failed on "the third or fourth day" (December 18–19).[11] A postwar assessment by US Army historians based on German records was that "all echelons from [Rundstedt's] OB West on down had realized the failure of the 6.Panzer-Armee by 19 December."[12]

As days went by, the war diary of Rundstedt's OB West headquarters offered gloomier and gloomier assessments of the Elsenborn sector. The assessment on the morning of December 20 noted that "the Elsenborn attack is gaining only quite insignificant ground," a euphemism for an abject failure. The entries the following day concluded that "by the evening of 20 December . . . the stubborn resistance of the enemy opposite 6.Panzer-Armee in the sectors of Elsenborn and Stavelot could not be overcome," acknowledging the defeat of the main attack force in the Ardennes.

As mentioned earlier, Model had made clear his belief that the offensive had failed as early as December 19. Acknowledging this to Hitler was another matter. Model's Army Group B headquarters made a calculated attempt to offer a less pessimistic viewpoint, knowing full well that Hitler abhorred any signs of defeatism. In a report to Rundstedt on December 20, Model admitted that "operations so far had made slower progress than anticipated" but that the offensive could prove successful under certain conditions. The conditions were the destruction of US forces in the Elsenborn-Malmedy area, the release of all OB West and OKW reserves, the supply of sufficient fuel, and the delivery of adequate replacements. Model fully realized that these preconditions were impossible; the attack in the Elsenborn sector could not be redeemed.

SHIFTING THE *SCHWERPUNKT*

By Wednesday, December 20, there was widespread recognition that the focal point of the Ardennes offensive in the *6.Panzer-Armee* sector had failed. Something had to be done without raising Hitler's ire. Hitler would not countenance negative assessments, so the change in plans was couched in more-neutral phrases. As a result, Rundstedt's OB

West headquarters shifted the *Schwerpunkt* from Dietrich's *6.Panzer-Armee* to Manteuffel's *5.Panzer-Armee*. The *5.Panzer-Armee* had broken through the 28th Division on the approaches to Bastogne and had destroyed much of the 106th Division. As a result, its panzer spearheads were advancing much more quickly than those in the Elsenborn sector. The most immediate consequence of this decision was to shift the second wave of the *6.Panzer-Armee*, Bittrich's *II.SS-Panzer-Korps*, from Dietrich's control to Manteuffel's *5.Panzer-Armee*.

From a purely tactical standpoint, this made perfectly good sense. Battlefield success was being reinforced. From a strategic and operational standpoint, it was a tacit admission of failure. Unless the *Schwerpunkt* had reached the Meuse within the first few days of the offensive, the chance for winning Hitler's Big Solution had vanished. The Big Solution goals were only feasible from the Elsenborn sector because the distances from the *5.Panzer-Armee* sector to the Meuse were significantly longer. The essence of the Big Solution was to reach the Meuse and begin the advance on Antwerp before the US Army could respond. Every day of delay made it more and more likely that the US Army would mobilize its considerable forces and block any further German advance. By December 20, the race to the Meuse was lost, and with it, any chance for the Big Solution.

Nor was there much hope for attaining the Small Solution that was favored by Rundstedt and Model. The objective of this version of the Ardennes plan was not simply to reach the Meuse, but to trap a significant number of US Army divisions on the eastern side of the river. Since Hitler had opted for the Big Solution, the focus of both the *5.Panzer-Armee* and *6.Panzer-Armee* was the race to the Meuse, and not the envelopment of US forces in the Ardennes. If Hitler had authorized the activation of the *15.Armee* attack in the Aachen sector, it is conceivable that this could have formed the northern point of a pincer action to trap large chunks of the First US Army. But he had no interest in the Small Solution, rightly deriding its insignificant operational or strategic opportunities. He wanted to gamble for big stakes.

A Junkers Ju 52/3m transport aircraft downed near Asselborn, Luxembourg. This aircraft was part of *Transport-Geschwader.3*, which delivered von der Heydte's *Fallschirmjäger* troops during the ill-fated Operation Stösser airborne landing on the night of December 17 18.

With the failure of the Big Solution by December 20, the Ardennes offensive had lost its mission. There were no longer any realistic prospects for winning either the Big Solution or the Small Solution. Hitler's vision by this stage of the war was so delusional that he would not recognize that his Big Solution had failed. By any rational standards, the Ardennes offensive had to be called off, or some mission of operational significance had to be substituted for the Big Solution. Hitler failed to conceive of such an alternative mission, and after December 20 he seemed content to grasp for some minor tactical victory. His goal eventually became the capture of Bastogne, a prestige victory that no longer mattered. Heinz Guderian, the chief of the general staff, begged Hitler to transfer the Ardennes panzer divisions east in anticipation of an imminent Red Army winter offensive out of central Poland toward Berlin. Hitler dithered, coveting the chump prize of Bastogne.

For Rundstedt and Model, their consolation prize was to reach the Meuse river. As a matter of professional pride, this seemed a plausible objective since it would offer a partial vindication of their earlier promotion of the Small Solution. But without the envelopment and destruction of significant US Army forces east of the Meuse, reaching the river would be an entirely sterile victory.

By this stage, the *Wehrmacht* had become a zombie army. Lacking any plausible operational mission, it was fighting for the sake of fighting.

X+5: Another Attack on Dom Bütgenbach

ALTHOUGH RUNDSTEDT HAD LARGELY GIVEN UP ANY HOPE THAT THE *6.Panzer-Armee* could reinvigorate its offensive, there was still the chance that modest tactical advantages could be gained by opening the road network beyond Bütgenbach. The *1.SS-Panzer-Division* had been stymied in its attempts to reach *Kampfgruppe Peiper* via Stavelot, but there was still the possibility that a *12.SS-Panzer-Division* advance beyond Bütgenbach could relieve Peiper or create new opportunities in conjunction with the actions of the *5.Panzer-Armee* around St. Vith.

By December 20, 1944, the elements of *Hitlerjugend* that had been involved in the battle for Krinkelt-Rocherath had finally disentangled themselves and joined up with the rest of the division in the Büllingen-Hünningen area. More importantly, *SS-Artillerie-Regiment.12* had finally extracted itself from the traffic jams and had begun to deploy its field guns to support future attacks toward Bütgenbach.

In view of the failure of the Dom Bütgenbach attack on December 20, Hugo Kraas, the *Hitlerjugend* commander, decided to try a different approach to secure the road junctions at Bütgenbach. Since Büllingen was under continual American artillery fire, he decided to move his remaining *Panzergrenadier* battalions to the wooded areas south of Bütgenbach. Two of these, *II./SS-Panzergrenadier-Regiment.26* and *III./Panzergrenadier-Regiment.25*, were instructed to move to the Richelsbusch woods near the Morschreck road junction, southwest of Büllingen. They were assigned two armored elements for support, *SS-Panzerjäger-Abteilung.12* on the right flank and the remnants of *I./ SS-Panzer-Regiment.12* on the left. The half-track-mounted *III./SS-Panzergrenadier-Regiment.26* was moved slightly west of these battalions in the Bütgenbacher Heck woods. *I./SS-Panzergrenadier-Regiment.26*,

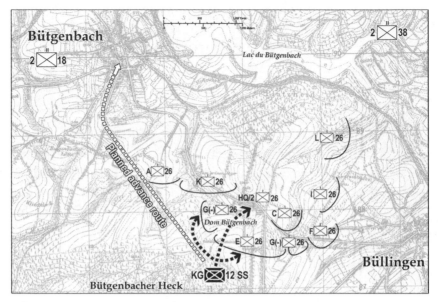

The Defense of Dom Bütgenbach, December 21, 1944

The *12.SS-Panzer-Division* was planning to launch a predawn attack on Bütgenbach in the early hours of December 21, trying to skirt around the stubborn
resistance in the Dom Bütgenbach area. Due to the delays in the arrival of a
Panzergrenadier battalion, the attack was reoriented to another direct assault
into Dom Bütgenbach.

along with the surviving tank destroyers of *s.Pz.Jg.Abt.560*, were put
into divisional reserve to be committed as necessary. *SS-Artillerie-
Regiment.12* had two 105mm battalions near Büllingen and Hünningen, its 150mm battery south of Honsfeld and its *Nebelwerfer* multiple
rocket launcher battalion near Hünningen.

Tank support for the attack was substantially less than the December 20 attack due to the heavy casualties suffered by *s.Pz.Jg.Abt.560*,
now reduced to a single company of thirteen vehicles under *Hauptmann*
Wevers. These were reinforced by *I./Panzer-Regiment.12* tanks that had
survived the Krinkelt-Rocherath massacre. The two *Panther* companies had been reduced to five operational *Panther* tanks, four of these
commanded by experienced platoon or company commanders. The two

PzKpfw IV companies were somewhat stronger, about ten tanks. The survivors from *SS-Pz.Jg.Abt.12* were also present for the attack, with maybe a half-dozen *Panzer IV lg.(V)* tank destroyers. In total, there were probably about three-dozen tanks and tank destroyers available for the December 21 attack.

Kraas's plan was to avoid moving his panzer force up along the Morschreck-Bütgenbach road. This was due to concerns that any German movement along this road attracted heavy concentrations of American artillery fire. In addition, there had been complaints from *s.Pz.Jg.Abt.560* about the muddy conditions of the road, which had caused many vehicles to become bogged down in the attack that morning. Instead, Kraas planned to skirt west of the Dom Bütgenbach defenses, push up along a secondary road via Hill 575 that paralleled the Büllingen Bütgenbach road, and then capture Bütgenbach from the western side. The plan presumed that 1st Infantry Division defenses around Dom Bütgenbach would retreat once Bütgenbach was captured behind them.

A view of the Domäne Bütgenbach manor farm taken in July 1906 when it was called the Königich Eifel–Domäne Bütgenbach (Royal Eifel–Bütgenbach Estate). McCORMICK RESEARCH CENTER

A painting by US Army artist Harrison Standley depicts the Domäne Bütgen-bach manor farm after the battle there in December 1944.

The Lost Battalion

Kraas's plan was undermined by the inevitable friction of war. Karl Hauschild's *II./SS-Panzergrenadier-Regiment.26* became caught up in a traffic jam in Honsfeld on the evening of December 20, with vehicles crammed three abreast on the narrow roads. This was a truck-mobile battalion equipped with about sixty-five trucks and other vehicles. With time running out, the battalion disembarked and set off on foot, leaving their assorted transport vehicles to make their own way out of the traffic mess. They marched to their planned start point in the Richelsbusch woods on a circuitous path from Hünningen via Hill 596 starting at 2300 hours. This was a distance of about 4 kilometers (2.5 miles), which seemed manageable in four hours. However, the route through the rural countryside was not well marked, and the march took place on a dark, overcast night. The other two *Panzergrenadier* battalions assigned to the first wave of the attack reported to Kraas that they had arrived at their starting points by early morning of December 21, in time for the start of the attack at 0330 hours. Hauschild's battalion was nowhere to be found.

On schedule, *SS-Artillerie-Regiment.12* began pounding the American positions. Kraas, stationed near the Morschreck crossroads, realized that Hauschild's battalion had still not reported being ready. With the radio net failing, Kraas dispatched members of the headquarters staff to find the missing battalion. This took time in the dark, and as a result, Kraas postponed the attack until 0530 hours. The divisional artillery halted their fire for the time being. Eventually two of the missing companies were located, but the third was absent. Kraas postponed the attack again to 0630 hours. The last company had become lost in the trackless and muddy farmland and was about a kilometer west of its intended location. Kraas reset the start time to 0645 hours.

These delays wrecked the original plans. Instead of taking place in the dark, Kraas realized that by the time the attack actually got under way, it would already be dawn. As the attack force emerged from the woods, it would be visible to the American troops in Dom Bütgenbach. Instead of the advance being unobserved in the dark, and therefore unmolested by American artillery fire, the attack force would be spotted and subjected to flanking fire from Dom Bütgenbach and the deadly American artillery batteries. A surprise attack in the dark against the town of Bütgenbach no longer seemed possible. It would require a daytime advance as much as 6 kilometers (4 miles), all the while pummeled by American artillery fire.

Kraas was forced to change the plan. Rather than skirting the 2/26th Infantry positions in Dom Bütgenbach, he decided to push his entire force against the manor farm once and for all, and after overrunning those positions, push into Bütgenbach from the south instead of from the west. Instead of a two-pronged panzer attack, the available tanks and tank destroyers would conduct a steamroller attack directly into the 2/26th Infantry defenses, capture the manor farm, and then push up the road to the town of Bütgenbach. Kraas hoped that the greater volume of German artillery firepower available that morning would make a crucial difference compared to the previous day's attack.

THE ATTACK BEGINS

At 0645 hours, the German artillery resumed its fire, concentrating on Daniel's battered 2/26th Infantry defenses at Dom Bütgenbach. Even before the start of the artillery barrage, the American defenses had been warned about the impending attack from outposts embedded at the edge of the Bütgenbacher Wald: "The outposts on the east were pretty far out; they also were placed on the west side of the woods. They heard the enemy moving [in the dark] when the Germans didn't suspect they were being observed. The command posts picked up this information immediately and brought down direct fire. [German] tank-infantry coordination was perfect until they were hit by artillery fire."[1]

The panzer force of *Kampfgruppe Kuhlmann* had departed Büllingen a short time earlier, drove down the road southwest to the edge of the Bütgenbacher Heck forest, and then set off cross-country with the forest about a hundred meters (110 yards) to their left and the American defenses along a hedgerow 150 meters (165 yards) to their right. The first casualty occurred when the *Panther* tank of *Untersturmführer* Jansen ran over a mine, disabling it for the time being. The panzer formation continued to advance, parallel to the American defense line, in order to spread out enough to provide the space necessary to deploy the three-dozen vehicles from march order to attack formation. The *Panther* tanks of *3.Kompanie, SS-Panzer-Regiment.12* were in the head of the column, and their unit history recalled the initial phase of the attack:

> To the right of us, about 100 to 150 meters away, stood a line of tall spruce trees. They were on the high ground at the edge of a pasture that lay hidden behind them. The manor house, the objective of our attack, must have been in a dead zone, invisible behind them. Fog still enveloped the pasture, but it was dissolving quickly. Instinctively, as if by order, all the tank turrets swung toward the row of trees on our right flank. No shots had yet been fired, but the overwhelming silence was oppressive and threatening. As we advanced, we fired a few bursts from our turret machine guns through those trees, starting the battle against an imagined enemy, in the knowledge that he was hiding somewhere, well camouflaged, his eye pressed to the sight of his anti-tank gun . . . The spearhead Panzer was commanded by Untersturmführer Schittenhelm, followed by Hauptmann Hils, Untersturmführer Engel, an Unterscharführer of the staff company, and behind him the PzKpfw IVs of the 5. and 6. Kompanien, then Jagdpanzers and self-propelled infantry guns.

Untersturmführer Schittenhelm had just reached an outcropping of the forest, when a flash of flame, as if ignited by the hand of a ghost, shot up from the rear of his [Panther]. A thick, heavy mushroom cloud of smoke covered the vehicle, two men bailed out. Hauptmann Hils issued orders to shift position toward 3 o'clock. He stood in the turret of his [Panther], studying the map once again, to make sure of his exact location. Then he fired his signal flare pistol to mark the final direction of the march. It flickered out over the downward sloping terrain leading to the estate. We awaited the "March, march!" order [over the radio] for the attack. Since nothing happened, I looked again toward his Panzer. The turret was burning! Hauptmann Hils could no longer be seen. The hull crew was abandoning the [Panther] I assumed the turret crew [including] . . . Hauptmann Hils had been killed.

Suddenly, an indescribable, devastating American artillery salvo struck us. The pasture turned into a plowed field; a number of Panzers took direct hits. Well-aimed anti-tank gun fire resumed, directed at Untersturmführer Engel's [Panther]. He pulled back about 20 meters so that the rear of the Panzer faced the woods. From there, he was hoping to have a better field of observation. At the same time, he reported on the situation by radio. In the line of trees, as we anticipated from the start of the attack, he assumed that there were at least two American anti-tank guns. Since he could not score any direct hits, he fired high explosive rounds into the tree tops in quick sequence to neutralize the American gun crews with shrapnel. He was successful, and several Americans fled into the nearby forest. Immediately, he ordered his [Panther] forward to the tree-line. For the first time, there was a clear view of the manor farm and he quickly opened fire on it. The unrelenting [American] artillery fire continued. Eventually, Untersturmführer Engel's [Panther] was also knocked out; his crew was able to bail out.[2]

During the initial stages of the German attack, fire support for the 26th Infantry was limited to the 33rd Field Artillery Battalion, which had been attached to CT26 since the start of the operation. As the scale of the German attacks became clear, the other three field artillery battalions of the 1st Infantry Division began to engage the German staging areas near the Bütgenbacher Heck and the Richelsbusch woods. The four field artillery battalions of the 2nd Infantry Division were added around 0930 hours and the 155mm battalion of the 99th Division around 1000 hours. While it was not apparent at the time, the US artillery would fire over 12,000 rounds that day, a 1st Division record.

While the American artillery began striking the forward panzers, the German artillery barrage wreaked havoc on the forward infantry defenses of the 2/26th Infantry, causing substantial casualties to the infantrymen in the forward foxholes. The first large German attack emerged around 0715 hours. The 2nd Battalion had laid several fields containing 2,500 mines after the December 20 attack, but the Germans had apparently seen the mine-laying, as their attack was directed through one of the few gaps in the minefields, as later described by Colonel Daniel:

> At 0715, a large force of about 12 tanks and a reinforced infantry battalion attacked. The outposts saw them coming out of the woods and called for artillery and 57mm anti-tank gun fire which drove them back for a few minutes but they came back again. The 2nd Battalion had about 4 battalions of artillery [firing in support]. Their tanks got through the fire and the infantry outposts. The three tanks came through a gap in the hedgerow and two of them went up and down the south side [of the hedgerow] firing into the foxholes, seeking automatic weapons in particular. They knocked out some machine guns and 2 BAR's [Browning automatic rifles] and also put direct fire on the two AT guns. The Battalion directed artillery and bazooka fire, knocking out one tank with a bazooka. The bazooka-man's assistant was wounded so he loaded and fired the bazooka himself.
>
> During the fight, one tank came through a gap in the 500 yard hedgerow. The tank commander stopped at one foxhole, got out, waved his pistol, and one American came out and got into the tank as a prisoner . . . [The tanks] got eight Company E men on the right flank and about 24 men were reported missing from Company G. The Battalion counted 8 of their tanks burning—knocked out by bazookas and AT guns. An 81mm mortar got one of them.[3]

The regimental after-action report offers another perspective on the start of the December 21 battle:

> Following another heavy artillery barrage, the enemy tanks and infantry attacked the 2nd Battalion positions once more in an effort to force the main road running through Bütgenbach. Six German tanks were destroyed by artillery fire which fell close to the forward positions, and the flames of these lit the area of fighting. Enemy tanks succeeded in penetrating the lines this time through G Company positions. When anti-tank fire was placed on these, the German tanks took refuge behind some buildings near the battalion CP, and fired upon the battalion rocket-gun teams that tried to get within range. In an effort to drive the enemy tanks out, mortar fire was called down upon the battalion positions; when these tanks left the shelter of the buildings, the anti-tank crews fired upon them. It was slow work, for the tanks moved from building to building, and then had to be systematically mortared out.[4]

The tanks that entered the grounds of the manor farm were mostly from the *PzKpfw IV* companies of *I./SS-Panzer-Regiment.12*. One of the tankers from *5.Kompanie*, *Sturmmann* Heinz Müller, later recalled this fighting:

> We staged the attack to the left of the road and approached the first houses of the estate. However, the Grenadiers were stalled and unable to keep pace with us because of the heavy artillery fire. During that attack, one of the tracks was blown off Oberscharführer Kretzschmar's tank. We took one of his crew into our vehicle, and continued the attack with six men in our Panzer. We were knocked out close to the first houses of the estate. Then, we tried to reach our own lines along the road, without success. After moving back toward the spot at the estate where we had been knocked out, we managed to be spotted by our company, and [our crew] split up into the remaining tanks. Since we were in front of the manor farm without Grenadiers, the order came to pull back.[5]

Oberscharführer Willy Kretzschmar, mentioned in Müller's account, also penned a recollection of the fighting near the manor farm from his perspective:

> Half of the right drive sprocket of our Panzer was blown away and the track rolled off. We were stuck. A row of trees and hedges located approximately 150 meters away was still occupied by American infantry. Using our turret and hull machine guns, as well as high explosive projectiles, we were able to keep them at bay for the time being. For two hours, we played "dead" because of the intense artillery fire. The snow-covered pasture previously white, had turned black [from the artillery blasts]. When there was a break in the barrage, I ran over to the closest PzKpfw IV, to ask that they pull my tank back on its track. Regrettably, it had been knocked out. The other PzKpfw IVs and Panzerjäger had suffered the same fate; most were knocked out by artillery and heavy mortar hits. At about 14.00 hours, a Panzer from the neighboring company came back. I waved, it came over, and pulled us back onto the track. We then fixed it in a makeshift manner and climbed back aboard it, under constant American artillery attacks. Then we drove in the direction of the main road at walking speed using half of the remaining drive sprocket. On the way, I picked up the crew of Otto Knoof's knocked-out tank.[6]

The German tank attack against the command posts in the manor farm was later recalled by the E Company commander, Capt. Pierre Stepanian:

> Company E was confronted with 3 tanks which pushed around and exposed the E Company flank. The tanks hit a half platoon of E Company men on the right flank, hitting one of the 57mm anti-tank guns on the right and a squad of men around 0800 or 0900. The left half of the line on the east stood firm for 2 hours. When they saw tanks in Dom Bütgenbach near the E Company CP, they started firing in that direction. The three [German] tanks were firing into the CP. After a time, an American tank located north of Dom Bütgenbach destroyed one of the tanks in front of the command post. Another tank firing

into the CP was knocked out at 1600. The remaining tank taking cover behind the two knocked out tanks, blew two holes in the CP, hitting about 9 CP personnel. The men could not move about the road at this time because any movement drew fire from the [German] tanks . . . No enemy infantry got through the artillery screen. The effectiveness of this screen may be seen in patrol reports which indicated that there were 500 enemy dead in front of the battalion line.[7]

The chaotic melee around the Domäne manor house involved German tanks and armored vehicles, but the *Panzergrenadiers* were nearly all stopped in front of the 2nd Battalion defenses, mainly by concentrated artillery fire. An American patrol was later sent into the Bütgenbacher Heck, where they found more than 300 dead German infantry. *Oberscharführer* Karl Leitner, a platoon leader in the *6.Kompanie* of *II./SS-Panzergrenadier-Regiment.26*, recalled the heavy toll inflicted on the German infantry:

[December 21] was our first day of combat since re-organization. Only the NCOs had any front experience. During the advance, we crossed through a very sparsely wooded area, the terrain slowly rising upward. Suddenly, a barrage began. We heard the incessant detonations and sought cover immediately. My assistant leader and I jumped into a ditch, a good meter deep . . . We were lying next to each other. Shells exploded on the forest floor and in the trees. Just the spearhead of our platoon had been caught by the barrage which was very concentrated and lasted for about one hour. After approximately ten minutes, a shell hit to the right of us, probably the trunk of a tree. We were hit by shrapnel in our ditch. My assistant leader must have been badly wounded in the lung, he only gasped and died a short time later. I had taken a piece of shrapnel in my right hip. Then, a shell exploded in a tree behind me. A piece of shrapnel hit me in the left ankle. Other fragments slashed my right foot and ankle. I pushed myself half under my dead comrade. Soon after, fragments from another shell hit me in the left upper arm. That was at about 0900. In the afternoon, an armored half-track ambulance vehicle arrived and collected us, while the barrage was still going on. All three assistant platoon leaders and I were casualties.[8]

The German tank attacks continued to focus on the substantial walled enclosure of the Domäne, with its many stone farm buildings. The battalion and company command posts were all located in this area. The situation in the manor farm area was chaotic through the morning and afternoon as German tanks milled around the farm compound while American infantry bazooka teams and armored vehicles hunted them down. The sturdy farm buildings withstood multiple hits from both American and German artillery. No *Panzergrenadiers* had made it through the 2/26th forward defenses, and the German tank crews were not at all inclined to try to dismount and enter the buildings. So the work of the various command post staffs continued in spite of the threat posed by the tanks.

The regimental commander, Lt. Col. Derrill Daniel, was operating from the basement of the farm's main stone house. In the early afternoon, Daniel's command post reported to the divisional headquarters that they still had three German tanks in front of the post and asked for two companies of the 635th Tank Destroyer Battalion to deal with them. On the opposite side of the square from the main farmhouse were two stone barn buildings that two German tanks were using for shelter. They would occasionally move forward, fire a round or two at the main farmhouse, and then withdraw behind the barn buildings. One of the C Company soldiers was in the farmhouse at the time and recalled the situation in the battalion command post:

> Colonel Daniel was personally directing artillery fire over the radio . . . He was even asking for corps artillery and at one point he yelled over the radio, "Get me all the damned artillery you can get." There is no doubt in my mind that Colonel Daniel almost singlehandedly slowed the German advance until reinforcements slowly began to arrive and started to build on our positions. Thanks to Colonel Daniel, and fortunately for us, the German infantry had taken all sorts of casualties from the artillery fire and were unable to penetrate our defenses in any number.

Lt. Col. Derrill Daniel, commander of the
2nd Battalion, 26th Infantry, 1st Infantry
Division that defended Dom Bütgenbach.
McCORMICK RESEARCH CENTER

When Colonel Daniel was informed that tanks had penetrated
to within twenty yards of the building, he asked to be kept advised of
their movement. I would inch up the cellar stairs and when the tank
crews spotted me, they would turn the 88s and fire a round. But before
they did, I would come flying down those cellar steps.

The situation remained that way for what seemed an eternity.
Colonel Daniel continued with the artillery fire and then called for
fire directly on our positions in an effort to knock the enemy off us.
He then called for volunteers to knock out the tanks with a bazooka.
One young soldier somehow, with help, managed to get on the roof of
the farmhouse and miraculously disabled one tank. It seemed like an
impossible task but somehow that kid got the job done. The remaining tank stayed for awhile and then turned tail, probably realizing
that he was stuck out like a sore thumb without support. It was for-
tunate for us that our artillery inflicted so much damage to German
infantry—otherwise we would have surely been outflanked.[9]

A view inside the Domäne Bütgenbach manor farm with a M36 90mm GMC of the 644th Tank Destroyer Battalion to the left and the knocked-out *PzKpfw IV* of *Sturmmann* Heinz Müller of *5.Kompanie, SS-Pz.Rgt.12* to the right.

Around 1500 hours in the afternoon, a 90mm anti-aircraft gun in a defensive position overlooking the manor farm finally drove away the last German tank from the command post area: "The gun fired at the long building and with three shots, chased the tank away from it. The Battalion kept the buildings. It is known that the Battalion got 11 of the 12 tanks and may have disabled the other one."[10]

Lt. Leonard Novak's 2nd Platoon, C Company, 745th Tank Battalion was also active in the Dom Bütgenbach defense that day. The battalion was credited with eight German tanks during the fighting on December 21, but had two of its remaining tanks disabled by German fire.[11]

Medics evacuate a wounded *Panzergrenadier* during the Ardennes fighting, with a *Sd.Kfz.251/3* command half-track behind them.

By the afternoon, the 2/26th Infantry had suffered such heavy casualties that Lt. Col. Daniel considered a contingency plan for withdrawing the battalion to a more defensible position. He was dissuaded from doing so, knowing full well how difficult it would be to conduct such an exposed withdrawal while still in contact with an enemy force. He reconsidered after being promised substantial reinforcements from elsewhere in the 1st Infantry Division. The first to arrive was the 2nd Battalion, 18th Infantry, which relieved Company B, 1/26th Infantry, which then moved down to Hill 598, closer to Dom Bütgenbach, to reinforce K Company.

The German attack began to subside around 1600 hours. The unit hardest hit was G Company. It had started the day with 77 men: 68 riflemen and a machine-gun section of 9 men. At full strength it would have been about 190 men. The company lost 13 killed, 10 wounded, and 12 missing, or about half its men. E Company suffered 3 dead, 15 wounded, and 12 missing. The ranks of the small-unit leaders were especially grave, with the weapons platoon leader, 4 squad leaders, and 3 assistant squad leaders casualties.

As mentioned earlier, the artillery support on that day set a unit daily record of 12,000 rounds. This consisted of 291 fire missions consisting of 3 counter-battery fires, 44 against enemy troops, 48 against enemy tanks, 18 against vehicles, 17 against enemy counterattacks, 56 interdiction missions against enemy staging areas, 2 against German observation posts, 85 harassing missions against road junctions and known German operating areas around Büllingen and Hünningen, and 18 miscellaneous targets. The 26th Infantry commander, Col. Seitz, said later in the day: "The artillery did a great job. I don't know where they got the ammo or when they took time out to flush the guns but we wouldn't be here now if it wasn't for them . . . A hundred [Germans] . . . came at one platoon and not one of them got through."

X+6: The Final Battle for Dom Bütgenbach

THE FAILURE OF THE DECEMBER 21 ATTACK LED ARMY GROUP B TO instruct Kraas that the *Hitlerjugend* would be pulled out of the Bütgenbach sector and sent farther west in hopes of exploiting penetrations made in the neighboring *5.Panzer-Armee* sector. It would take a day or more to extract the *Hitlerjugend* from this sector. In the meantime, Army Group B ordered a pincer attack against Bütgenbach the next day. The *12.Volksgrenadier-Division* formed the eastern side of the pincer, attacking Bütgenbach from the Wirtzfeld area. An armored battle group from the *Hitlerjugend* formed the western pincer.

The *12.Volksgrenadier-Division* attack was far enough east that it largely missed the 1st Infantry Division, running up against the western edge of the 2nd Infantry Division defenses held by the 38th Infantry Regiment. The *Volksgrenadier* commander, Gerhard Engel, later described his division's portion of the attack:

> In the morning hours of 22 December, both regimental groups prepared for the attack in accordance with orders. During the morning, Grenadier-Regiment.89 was already stopped on the heights west of Wirtzfeld by concentrated artillery fire from an American artillery group near Elsenborn. The divisions had been told that the elimination of this group was planned before the attack. This did not occur, and could not succeed because we lacked artillery observation units and the necessary artillery observation aircraft. Füsilier-Regiment.27 advanced, tracking south of the railway line Büllingen–Bütgenbach and it reached the difficult scrub forest area south of the reservoir [Lac du Bütgenbach] around noon, though with casualties. The attacking forces here were insufficient. [American] flanking movements from south of Bütgenbach and concentrated artillery fire from the west from

Bütgenbach itself forced the regimental groups to dig in. In the early afternoon hours, the divisional commander decided to withdraw both regimental groups back to the initial line of departure, and Grenadier-Regiment.89 was ordered to defend the heights west of Wirtzfeld. The attack collapsed because of the shortage of infantry striking power, the shortage of essential assault guns for support, and finally the enemy artillery fire from the Elsenborn area. With this attack, activities in the 12.Volksgrenadier-Division came to an end. The collapse of the offensive in the northern sector began to make itself felt.[1]

While the *12.Volksgrenadier-Division* struck to the east of the 26th Infantry defenses, the *Hitlerjugend* battle group switched its attack from Dom Bütgenbach to the 26th Infantry defenses on the western

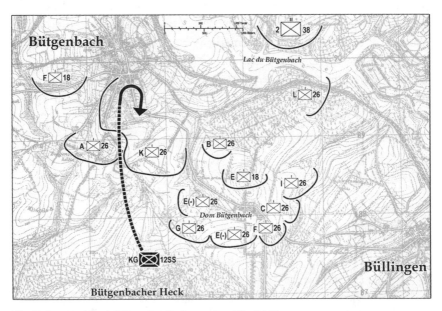

The Defense of Dom Bütgenbach, December 22, 1944
This map shows the final attempt by the *12.SS-Panzer-Division* to reach Büt-genbach from the southwest, again avoiding the defenses around Dom Bütgenbach. This attack also failed, ending the major attacks by the *Hitlerjugend* in this sector.

side of Bütgenbach. The *Kampfgruppe* consisted of Urabl's half-track-mounted *III./SS-Panzgrenadier-Regiment.26*, surviving elements of *SS-Panzergrenadier-Regiment.25*, and the few remaining tanks and tank destroyers of *SS-Panzer-Regiment.12*. Of the six grenadier battalions in the *Hitlerjugend*, Urabl's *III./SS-Panzergrenadier-Regiment.26* had retained the most strength. It had been kept in reserve for most of the December 21 attack based on the plan to use it as the rapid exploitation force once the Dom Bütgenbach defenses were finally cracked open.

Although all three of its grenadier companies were equipped with *Sd.Kfz.251* armored half-tracks, two of its companies, the *9.Kompanie* and *11.Kompanie*, attacked on foot on December 22 due to a lack of fuel for their vehicles. Only one grenadier company, *10.Kompanie*, attacked using their half-tracks. The *Sd.Kfz.251/9* gun-armed half-tracks from the dismounted companies, armed with short 75mm guns, were transferred to the battalion's heavy weapons company, *12.Kompanie*. As a result, *12.Kompanie* had formidable firepower for such a small unit, totaling ten armed half-tracks: four *Sd.Kfz.251/22*s with the long 75mm PaK 40 anti-tank gun and six *Sd.Kfz.251/22*s with the short 75mm gun.[2] Due to the fog and snow, these gun-armed half-tracks were frequently mistaken for tanks by the US infantry, which accounts for the large number of German "tanks" claimed to have been destroyed in the day's fighting.

The 26th Infantry Regiment after-action report described the initial fighting:

> A Company was attacked at 0630 hours with six enemy tanks and several hundred infantry, hitting the left platoon of the company. Again, the enemy tanks were able to penetrate the line, but the infantry was stopped by the courageous stand put up by the overrun infantry and the platoon on the right side of the company line. In a daring move, Company B was swung out of the battalion line, and working south from the town, it worked through one platoon of Company A that had held its position and then swung east to drive the enemy back.[3]

While the attack against A Company was eventually halted, the attack against K Company to the south was initially successful. This attack hit K Company about 0830 hours and created a gap about 800 yards wide between A and K Companies. The regimental history described the initial action: "The first sign of the attack for K Company had been the appearance of a huge Panther tank loaded with grenadiers. The tank destroyer backing the company had taken the tank in its sights and blasted both the tank and its supporting infantry."[4]

The *Panther* tank knocked out in this early fighting was probably the command tank of the *I./SS-Panzer-Regiment.12* commander, Arnold Jürgensen. Accompanying him in the tank was the *III./SS-Panzergrenadier-Regiment.26* commander, Georg Urabl, who was coordinating the attack of his half-track *Panzergrenadiers*. Jürgensen died in the hospital the following day, while Urabl was seriously wounded and taken back to the rear for treatment. In spite of the destruction of the lead tank, the attack by Urabl's *III./SS-Panzergrenadier-Regiment.26* succeeded in overrunning the K Company positions using their armored half-tracks.

The 26th Infantry reported that the "attack swarmed over the K Company positions, and the line withdrew only to re-form immediately in a slight draw . . . The bitterest fighting ensued: men stabbed and slashed each other with bayonets, hurled grenades at close range, and the enemy tanks lumbered their way to the front and sides of the hard-pressed companies."[5]

The 26th Infantry's main reserve had been B Company in Bütgenbach, but it had already been committed to help reinforce the beleaguered A Company. The 1st Division sent the 1st Battalion, 18th Infantry to Weywertz with plans to eventually use it to recover the ground lost by A and K Companies. The neighboring 2nd Infantry Division was also contacted, and they began to move G Company, 38th Infantry to the Lac du Bütgenbach area behind the town of Bütgenbach to prevent the Germans from reaching beyond the town.

The 745th Tank Battalion also began shifting more of its C Company into the Dom Bütgenbach area to assist in the defense. Lt. Novak's 2nd Platoon, C Company had born the brunt of the fighting but had

The Ammunition and Pioneer Platoon, 1st Battalion, 26th Infantry, 1st Division reinforce the defenses in the Bütgenbach sector in early January 1945 by planting another anti-tank minefield.

one tank knocked out and two damaged in the previous two days of fighting. The 1st and 3rd Platoons were moved forward on December 22 and took part in the day's fighting. The 1st Platoon was credited with knocking out one German tank and one tank destroyer while at the same time losing an M4A3 (76mm) tank and M4 (105mm) assault gun to enemy fire. The 3rd Platoon, C Company was crediting with knocking out two German tanks.[6]

In the meantime, the *Panzergrenadier* troops riding on their *Sd.Kfz. 251* armored half-tracks penetrated the town of Bütgenbach. *Unterscharführer* Günther Burdak of *9.Kompanie, III./SS-Panzergrenadier-Regiment.26* recalled the morning attack: "Taking advantage of the heavy snowfall, the attack moved ahead at a good pace, but it stalled just outside of Bütgenbach. Several armored personnel carriers penetrated into the village, but had to retreat again since the [supporting *12.Volksgrenadier-Division*] were unable to advance. The battalion was pulled back to the starting position and given a blocking mission."[7]

By early afternoon, the situation had begun to stabilize for the American defenders as the German attack began to recoil. At 1400 hours, the 26th Infantry reported to division HQ that their positions "will be all right. The enemy just started up this area with a mixed column. Our artillery is doing a job on them right now. Tanks, infantry, artillery, and AA are in the column. We still have this gap. [We] have three strong points which seal the gap so there is no place they can pull through. Company B is counterattacking right now."[8]

The artillery fire devastated the German column and halted the early afternoon attack. Closing the gap created in the K Company sector took longer than expected. By late afternoon, B Company had created a defensive "goose egg" in the creek bed immediately south of Bütgenbach, while A Company had been pulled back and put in 1st Battalion reserve. At dusk the 18th Infantry did not expect they would arrive in the sector until the following day, but around 2130 hours they reported that they had managed to reach the area and placed their three companies in line to defend Bütgenbach to the southwest. The 33rd Artillery kept up a steady stream of illumination rounds in front of the defenses and the star shells lit up the darkness, discouraging the German troops from trying to infiltrate the area.

Divisional artillery had been instrumental in defeating the German attacks, and a 26th Infantry after-action report noted that "the repulse of the German attack, like the day before, was due largely to the fire of the division guns." General Engel specifically mentioned the American artillery as one of the principal causes for the failure of the *12. Volksgrenadier-Division* attack. Divisional and supporting artillery on December 22 actually exceeded the number of missions from the day before, 334 versus 291. The 334 fire missions included 2 counterbattery, 48 against enemy troops, 77 against enemy tanks, 13 against vehicles, 17 against enemy counterattacks, 56 interdiction missions against enemy staging areas, 4 against German observation posts, 73 harassing missions against road junctions and known German operating areas around Büllingen and the Bütgenbacher Heck forest, and 19 miscellaneous targets.

The December 22 attack on Bütgenbach was the last major action by the *12. SS-Panzer-Division* in the Elsenborn sector. The division was ordered to pull out of the *6. Panzer-Armee* sector and shift to the *5. Panzer. Armee* to the west. On December 23, *SS-Panzergrenadier-Regiment.25*, *SS-Aufklärungs-Abteilung.12*, and *SS-Panzerjäger-Abteilung.12* were already under way to the new sector. Most of the rest of the division followed on December 24. There was still some *Hitlerjugend* presence in the Krinkelt-Bütgenbach area for a few days as repair crews tried to extract as many damaged tanks and tank destroyers as possible. Many of the vehicles lost around Dom Bütgenbach had to be left behind since they were still within view of American defenses.

German casualties in the four-day battle for Bütgenbach are not known. The 26th Infantry estimated that it had inflicted 1,200 casualties. Patrols sent out on December 23 counted forty-four "tanks," though this probably consisted of a mixture of panzers, *Jagdpanzers*, and *Sd.Kfz.251* armored half-tracks.[9] US casualties are better documented, and the accompanying chart on page 306 shows 26th Infantry Regiment casualties during this period.

26th Infantry Strength and Casualties, December 16–23, 1944								
Date	Strength			Gains*			Losses		
	Officers	EM**	Total	Officers	EM**	Total	Officers	EM**	Total
Dec. 16	141	2,582	**2,723**	7	18	**25**	2	15	**17**
Dec. 17	142	2,586	**2,728**	1	12	**13**		6	**6**
Dec. 18	142	2,562	**2,704**		9	**9**		33	**33**
Dec. 19	144	2,544	**2,688**	2	9	**11**		27	**27**
Dec. 20	142	2,477	**2,619**		2	**2**	2	69	**71**
Dec. 21	139	2,386	**2,525**		7	**7**	3	98	**101**
Dec. 22	135	2,673	**2,808**		376	**376**	4	89	**93**
Dec. 23	145	2,730	**2,875**	11	113	**124**	1	56	**57**

*Gains = hospital returns + replacements
**EM = enlisted men

The Defeat of Autumn Mist

On Christmas Day 1944, X+9, *Generalfeldmarschall* Gerd von Rundstedt formally asked permission from the OKW headquarters in Berlin to halt the Autumn Mist offensive and to switch to the defensive. Rundstedt argued that even the Small Solution was now out of reach.

By Christmas, the new *Schwerpunkt* in Manteuffel's *5.Panzer-Armee* sector had failed to gain sufficient traction or speed. Its two main drives had been stopped. The *II.SS-Panzer-Korps'* attempt to reach the Meuse had been stopped in a series of vicious tank battles with the 3rd Armored Division around Manhay. Even if the panzers had reached their intermediate objective of Érezée, it was still another 50 kilometers (30 miles) to the Meuse. The other *5.Panzer-Armee* spearhead in the Bastogne sector, the *2.Panzer-Division*, had come closer than any other German unit to the Meuse near Dinant. By Christmas, it was trapped and crushed in a pocket near Celles by the 2nd Armored Division. Its chances for crossing the Meuse at Dinant were highly improbable since the British had sent sizable reinforcements to the opposite side of the river in this sector. More importantly, the Dinant crossing led nowhere of operational significance. Crossing the Meuse at Dinant would have been a nice consolation prize for Rundstedt and Model, but it held no tactical value. By late December 1944, the German panzer force was exhausted.

Whether Hitler was willing to admit it or not, the *Wehrmacht* in the Ardennes was now on the defensive in the face of a relentless American counterattack. Hitler, of course, refused Rundstedt's Christmas request to withdraw from the Ardennes. Hitler sought a face-saving victory, no matter how paltry. He craved the crossroad town of Bastogne as his consolation prize.

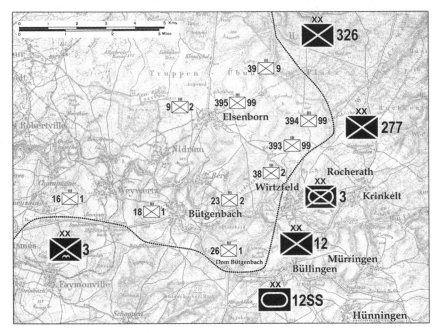

Elsenborn Sector, December 23, 1944
This map shows the Elsenborn sector in the wake of the failed *Hitlerjugend* attacks on Dom Bütgenbach. At this point, the *12.SS-Panzer-Division* was ordered to the *5.Panzer-Armee* sector, which it reached in the days after Christmas.

The *12.SS-Panzer-Division*, crippled from the fighting in the Elsenborn sector, was ordered to take part in this futile venture. The *Hitlerjugend* were committed to the Bastogne sector in late December near Sazdot, but the division's campaign near Bastogne was short-lived. On January 12, 1945, the Red Army launched its long-anticipated Vistula-Oder offensive toward Berlin. Dietrich's command, renamed as the *6.SS-Panzer-Armee*, was sent to the Russian Front, the *Hitlerjugend* along with it.

THE SIGNIFICANCE OF THE BATTLES FOR ELSENBORN RIDGE

The defeat of the *6.Panzer-Armee* in the Elsenborn sector derailed the Autumn Mist plan. When the *12.SS-Panzer-Division* failed to secure a route to the Meuse via Elsenborn or Bütgenbach in the first days of the campaign, the attainment of Autumn Mist's operational goals became exceedingly unlikely. The rapid advance of *Kampfgruppe Peiper* into the Losheim Gap on X+2 seemed to offer salvation for the offensive, but this spearhead was quickly trapped and withered on the vine. Without the success of one or both of these panzer spearheads, the chances of quickly reaching the Meuse evaporated.

As Speer and other senior German leaders had realized, December 19–20 was the first turning point in the Battle of the Bulge. At this point, its chances for operational success had ended. All that could be attained was a minor tactical success, perhaps defeating a few American divisions. But Hitler's dream of a decisive strategic turning point for Germany in the war had failed within the first few days, largely due to the forgotten battles near Elsenborn Ridge.

There are two principal reasons the Battles for Elsenborn Ridge are not better known. To begin with, most accounts of the Battle of the Bulge are from the American perspective. The German perspective, especially the operational goals of the Autumn Mist plan, are not widely appreciated. German historical literature on the Ardennes offensive is not especially extensive, and German historical records were mostly lost during the war. There are substantial gaps in the historical record for these battles on the German side, especially at the tactical level. The Battle of the Bulge dragged on for several more weeks after the defeat of the *Hitlerjugend* near the Elsenborn Ridge, and this has disguised the fact the *Wehrmacht* had already lost the battle in any meaningful sense before Christmas 1944.

The Battles for Elsenborn Ridge have been forgotten for other reasons. The little-known political context of later American military memories of the Battle of the Bulge is one of those reasons.

On the evening of December 19, Eisenhower's headquarters told Gen. Omar Bradley that his 12th Army Group headquarters would turn over the northern sector of the Ardennes to the control of his British rival, Field Marshal Bernard Montgomery. Eisenhower felt obliged to do so because the German offensive had severed key communication links between the 12th Army Group and the corps headquarters in the northern sector, namely Gerow's V Corps and Ridgway's newly arrived XVIII Airborne Corps. Montgomery was better placed to manage this sector until communications could be restored. Bradley was deeply embittered by this decision. After the battle, Montgomery took undue credit for the Allied victory in the Ardennes, and his claims largely rested on the actions in the Elsenborn and Losheim sectors. This only served to further inflame the rivalry between Montgomery and Bradley. In the years after the war, the animosity between Bradley and Montgomery remained at a simmer, eventually flaring up when both commanders penned their war memoirs.

Historians on both sides of the Atlantic took sides. Not surprisingly, most American military historians favored Bradley's perspective. The first substantial account of the Battle of the Bulge was Robert E. Merriam's *Dark December*, published in 1947. Merriam was a young army historian during the war and had interrogated many of the senior German commanders in 1945 as part of the US Army's efforts to record the history of the war. Hugh Cole, author of the official US Army history of the Battle of the Bulge that appeared in 1965, was an army historian who served with Patton's Third US Army in the ETO and initiated the US Army's valuable "Combat Interviews" program.[1] Neither of these accounts ignored the Battles for Elsenborn Ridge. However, the memorialization of the Ardennes campaign tended to share Bradley's focus on the battles under his command, especially the battle for Bastogne. Bradley became chief of staff of the army after the war, and many of his senior commanders went on to major leadership positions. "Lightning Joe" Collins, the VII Corps commander who helped save Bastogne, succeeded Bradley as army chief of staff.

In the American popular memory, Bastogne has become the Battle of the Bulge. If the Battles for Elsenborn Ridge are remembered at all, it is usually for the massacre at Malmedy perpetrated by *Kampfgruppe Peiper*. Not only Krinkelt-Rocherath and Bütgenbach but other critical battles in the northern sector such as St. Vith have largely been forgotten. Visitors to the Ardennes today will find several fine museums

This simple memorial stands today near the forest entrance to Rollbahn A at the Hollerath Knee. The stone memorial commemorates the men of the *277.Volksgrenadier-Division*, while the wooden memorial notes the site of the battle between the American 99th Infantry Division and the German *277.Volksgrenadier-Division*. STEPHEN ANDREW

devoted to the Battle of the Bulge in the Bastogne area. Aside from a few small memorials, there is hardly anything commemorating the battles in the Krinkelterwald, Krinkelt-Rocherath, or Dom Bütgenbach.

WHY DID AUTUMN MIST FAIL?

The previous discussion in this chapter has argued that the Battles for Elsenborn Ridge were at the heart of the failure of Operation Autumn Mist. This question can be further illuminated by examining the tactical roots of the failure.

The Autumn Mist plan was inherently flawed and had poor prospects for success due to terrain and weather. The Elsenborn sector had a very poor road network for east–west movement. This was due to its location along the Belgian-German frontier and the added complications of the Westwall barriers. The lack of an adequate road network on the German side of the border led to massive traffic jams that slowed the deployment of German mechanized forces in the first critical days of the offensive. Speed and surprise were the two ingredients essential to the success of Autumn Mist. The mobility problems in this sector were the source of friction that sapped the speed of the German offensive.

The thaw in the winter weather in the third week of December further complicated the mobility of German forces. The non-paved roads through the forest became quagmires and severely degraded their value for rapid access to the better road network beyond the Belgian frontier. In addition, the muddy ground conditions made it dangerous for German vehicles to move away from the main roads, since it frequently led to the vehicles becoming bogged down in the muddy farm fields. As a result, the small villages astride the main roads such as Krinkelt-Rocherath and Dom Bütgenbach became essential tactical objectives. They could not be easily bypassed. The stone construction of most of the buildings made them well suited to defense by infantry.

Some senior German commanders have also faulted Krämer's attack plan in the *6.Panzer-Armee* sector. *Generalmajor* Carl Wagener, chief of staff of the neighboring *5.Panzer-Armee*, later argued that the initial attack should have taken place on a wider front, and that once the infantry found a weak point, these should have been exploited.[2] Wagener wrote:

> It would have been possible, on a wide front, to attack many enemy positions, and to find a soft spot somewhere to penetrate, even if tactically, every attack must have a focal point as well as depth. In spite of the strong artillery preparation, the SS could not succeed in breaking through the first enemy lines. The bulk of the army was crowded behind one another, on a few bad roads, and never deployed.[3]

The validity of this criticism can be questioned. Wagener admitted that the *5.Panzer-Armee* and *6.Panzer-Armee* viewed each other as rivals, and his criticism may have reflected that tension. Wagener also suggested that the plan should have had the *Kampfgruppen* attack alongside one another, rather than being deployed in echelon. This criticism is somewhat more valid, but still runs into difficulties over the issue of traffic jams and the shortage of adequate traffic access points along the border.

The *Wehrmacht* was suffering from a steep decline in quality, even compared to the summer of 1944. This included not only the regular army, the *Heer*, but so-called elite units such as the *Waffen-SS* and *Luftwaffe Fallschirmjäger* units. Most of the units taking part in the Ardennes offensive were rebuilt in October–November 1944 after having been decimated in the summer of 1944. There was not sufficient time for adequate training, nor was there sufficient fuel or ammunition

After being withdrawn from the Ardennes, the *6.Panzer-Armee*, renamed *6.SS-Panzer-Armee*, was sent to the Russian Front and served during the campaign in Hungary. This photo was taken in the Gran bridgehead, where the *Hitlerjugend* took part in Operation Südwind.

for training. There was also a severe shortage of combat-experienced small-unit leaders such as NCOs and junior officers, and a widespread shortage of critical matériel including key combat vehicles, artillery ammunition, tactical radios, and a host of other equipment. As a result, none of the infantry divisions used in the initial break-in phase were assessed at combat values of 1 or 2, and were only rated at combat values of 3 or less, meaning suitable for defensive operations, not offense.

Although many military histories of World War II treat the *Waffen-SS* as an elite force, it had profound flaws, some of which came to the fore in the Ardennes. The *Waffen-SS* saw its greatest expansion in 1943 at a time when the *Wehrmacht* was being forced into the strategic defensive. It developed its reputation as a dogged defensive force in the harsh battles on the Russian Front. Its panzer divisions did not learn offensive skills in the great *Blitzkrieg* battles of 1939–41. This was evident in two critical offensive tasks: reconnaissance and combat engineering. *Generalmajor* Wagener later complained "the SS could not reconnoiter."[4] It is fairly astonishing that neither *Kampfgruppe Peiper* from *1.SS-Panzer-Division* nor the lead *Kampfgruppen* of the *Hitlerjugend* used their reconnaissance battalions in the traditional scouting roles. Instead of using them up front to find weak points in the American lines, they were typically employed as one more battle group. Likewise, the combat engineer (Pionier) units were often left farther back in the columns rather than to the front to deal with the perennial problems of enemy obstacles and terrain obstructions. This was particularly evident in the *KG Peiper* attack.

The Autumn Mist plan overestimated *Wehrmacht* capabilities and underestimated the US Army. Assessments of the combat capabilities of the US Army were still wedded to stereotypes developed after the battle of Kasserine Pass in Tunisia in early 1943. The chief of staff of the *5.Panzer-Armee* later noted that "the German high command completely underestimated the superiority of the enemy in all fields."[5]

Perhaps the most dangerous assumption in the Autumn Mist plan was that the Allies would take three days before mobilizing their reserves, giving the *Wehrmacht* a narrow window of opportunity to plunge toward the Meuse.[6] In fact, the US Army response was much faster than that. At the operational level, Eisenhower's SHAEF headquarters began committing reserves on the first day. On the tactical level, Gerow's V Corps began to shift its forces within the constraints of the higher commands. The most sluggish American responses were in the intermediate levels of command: Bradley's 12th Army Group and Hodge's First US Army. In the event, the 2nd Infantry Division was moved in a timely fashion to block Rollbahn A, and the 1st Infantry Division was moved in a timely fashion to block Rollbahn C, thereby bottling up the *Hitlerjugend* attack.

On January 4, 1945, Lt. Gen. Leonard Gerow, commander of V Corps, awards Maj. Gen. Walter Robertson the Bronze Star for his actions in halting the German Ardennes offensive.

There was an attitude inherent in the Autumn Mist plan that the US infantry divisions would crumple during the initial attack as easily as they had done in 1943. Facing three-to-one odds, the green 99th Division held back the *I.SS-Panzer-Korps* attack for thirty-six hours. This delay proved essential since it gave Gerow and Robertson the time to move the 2nd Division into place in the foreground of Elsenborn Ridge. The defense of the Lausdell crossroads by McKinley's 1/9th Infantry showed the formidable combination of an American infantry-artillery defense. The actions of the 38th Infantry in Krinkelt-Rocherath and the 2/26th Infantry at Dom Bütgenbach was further evidence of the hardening of the US Army since 1943. The US Army in the Ardennes in 1944 was not the US Army of Tunisia in 1943.

Büllingen was recaptured by the 1st Infantry Division in January 1945, by which time the village was heavily damaged by the incessant artillery barrages of the previous fighting.

The successful defense of the Elsenborn Ridge denied the *Wehrmacht* a decisive victory in the Ardennes and diverted the German forces into a prolonged, attritional struggle toward Bastogne that offered no prospects for German operational success. Given the weakened state of the *Wehrmacht* at the end of 1944, an attritional campaign inevitably favored the US Army, which could bring its superior mobility and firepower to bear. The Battles for the Elsenborn Ridge did not end the German Ardennes offensive, but it prevented the *Wehrmacht* from attaining its operational objectives.

Appendix: *Hitlerjugend* Tank Casualties in the Ardennes

How many tanks did the *12.SS-Panzer-Division* lose in the battles of the Krinkelterwald, Krinkelt-Rocherath, and Dom Bütgenbach? This question is not as simple to answer as it may seem. The main problem is the lack of consistent archival data on *Hitlerjugend* tank strength and tanks losses in December 1944. A secondary problem is the very definition of "tank loss." Here, the term "tank" is used loosely to also include tank substitutes, namely the *PzKpfw IV lg.(V)*s and *Jagdpanthers* serving with the *Hitlerjugend* in the Ardennes.

Starting with the second problem, what is a "tank loss"? When an airplane is shot down in combat, it is almost invariably a total loss. This is not the case in tank combat. In many cases, tanks are temporarily put out of action. For example, a track is damaged after running over a mine, stopping the tank. Or a bazooka rocket penetrates the tank, killing or injuring several crewman but leaving the rest of the tank unharmed. In these cases, the tank can be recovered and put back into action. Sometimes, a tank is put out of action by non-combat causes. For example, a poorly trained driver maneuvers the tank carelessly and it slips into an irrigation ditch alongside a road, immobilizing the tank. The German *Panther* had an especially troublesome final drive system, and it was not unusual for an inexperienced driver to immobilize the tank by poor handling of the clutch and transmission.

There are situations in which tanks are so severely damaged that they are irredeemable. Tanks are usually not written often as total losses unless they suffer a catastrophic fire that is intense enough to damage the armor. This most often resulted from an ammunition fire. The other cause of irredeemable loss occurred when the tank fell into enemy hands.

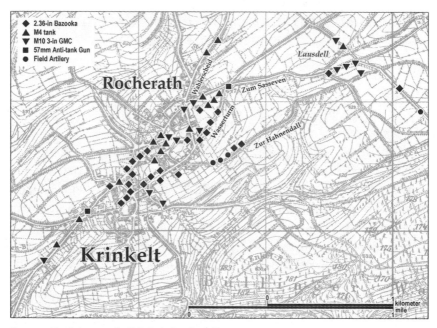

German Tank Losses in Krinkelt-Rocherath
This map is a transcription of a map prepared by the S-3 (Operations) of the 38th Infantry identifying where its units had claimed to have knocked out German tanks and armored fighting vehicles during the two-day battle inside the Twin Villages. The symbols identify the type of weapon credited with knocking out the tank.

As this discussion suggests, it is worthwhile to distinguish two types of combat losses for tanks: temporary combat losses and total losses. German reporting on tank strength and losses differed depending on the type of document. Most often, the reporting included four basic categories: total strength, operational strength, tanks under repair, and total losses. The most problematic of these categories is the "under repair" quantity. This nominally referred to tanks that were under short-term repair, but by 1944 it became a grab-bag category including lightly damaged tanks as well as severely damaged tanks that had little or no chance for rebuilding. The clearest example of this comes from the Normandy campaign. German records indicate that the units in Normandy lost only 913

AFVs in June–August 1944 but "lost" an unbelievable 1,998 in September 1944 when there was very little tank fighting.[1] The reason for this anomaly was that units kept many heavily damaged tanks in the "repair" category through the summer, regardless of whether there was any chance for their eventual repair, and only wrote them off after the end of the campaign when they were abandoned in France.[2] In other words, the "repair" category hid many combat casualties alongside tanks with minor damage, and it is very difficult to distinguish the two.

The vagaries of the reporting system led to changes in the autumn of 1944, when units were told by corps headquarters to report only the operational strength figure since the other categories were essentially meaningless during combat operations.

GERMAN TANK CASUALTIES

The scale of casualties in the Battles for Elsenborn Ridge are unrecorded and controversial. Meyer's divisional history notes that "there is only sketchy information regarding the German losses of personnel and material."[3] There are no surviving records from the *12.SS-Panzer-Division*; German tank losses were heavy, but their full extent is poorly recorded.

Maj. Gen. Michael Reynolds in his account of the *I.SS-Panzer-Korps* puts the total at eighteen tanks and tank destroyers lost at Krinkelt-Rocherath.[4] This seems to be based on the research of German military historian Timm Haasler, who has made a detailed study of available photographic evidence of the battlefield.[5] However, the figure of eighteen tanks and AFVs represents the absolute minimum of tank combat losses of the *Hitlerjugend* in the Twin Villages. There were very few photos taken inside Krinkelt-Rocherath during the fighting. Most of the photos were taken in February 1945 when the Twin Villages were retaken by the 2nd Division, or were taken after the war by Belgians living in the area. From these photos, seventeen or eighteen knocked-out German tanks and tank destroyers can be identified. Many damaged tanks and tank destroyers were probably recovered by the *Hitlerjugend* after December 20, of which many if not most were repaired.

The seventeen or eighteen tanks and tank destroyers left behind were presumably those that had suffered internal fires serious enough to compromise the integrity of the tank's armor and so were not worth recovering. The similar minimum figures for Dom Bütgenbach are twelve tanks and AFVs.[6]

Another potential source of data comes from a later Ardennes study done for the US Army by Data Memory Systems Inc.[7] This study was intended to provide extremely detailed, day-by-day statistics for the Battle of the Bulge that could be used to test a major US Army war-game simulation system operated by the US Army Concepts Analysis Agency.[8] I compiled the following chart showing operational strength based on this data. However, I am not very confident about these numbers, since they appear to be heavily based on estimates rather than day-to-day German data and they have some obvious problems. For example, the data lists inventory for both the *Panzerjager IV* and *StuG III* in the division when in fact it did not operate the *StuG III* at this time.[9] I have combined these two categories as *Panzer IV lg.(V)* in this chart.

Hitlerjugend AFV Strength Data from ACSDB					
	PzKpfw IV	Panther	Panzer IV lg.(V)	Jagdpanther	Total
Operational Dec. 16, 1944	38	41	47	14	140
Operational Dec. 22, 1944	28	13	40	11	92
Operational Jan. 8, 1945	5	4	34	11	54

US assessments of the German tank casualties in Krinkelt-Rocherath represent the opposite extreme from the Reynolds estimate. The S-3 (Operations) of the 38th Infantry Regiment prepared a map after the fighting that showed the locations of claimed tank kills; no distinction was made between *Panther* tanks, *PzKpfw IV* tanks, and *Panzer IV lg.(V)* tank destroyers. This map shows seventy-seven "tanks" knocked out, consisting of twenty-one by US tanks, twenty-four by bazookas, nineteen by tank destroyers, seven by artillery, three by 57mm anti-tank guns, and three unknown or mines. A version of this map is presented on page 320.

Col. Franklin Boos, the 38th Infantry commander, estimated on January 4, 1945, that the defenders in Krinkelt-Rocherath had knocked out sixty-seven German tanks and that German casualties were three to four hundred dead.[10] The after-action report of the 741st Tank Battalion claimed twenty-seven tanks knocked out, but another memorandum prepared later put the total at twenty-nine. The 644th Tank Destroyer Battalion claimed eighteen tanks knocked out.[11] The American kill claims are probably overstated due to double-counting, with tanks and tank destroyers firing on German tanks that had been knocked out in previous engagements.

ORIGINAL GERMAN RECORDS

Comprehensive statistics from German army records on German AFV strength, such as the very useful General Inspector of the Panzer Troop tank status series, largely petered out after November 1944 or were simply lost.

There are a few surviving records for the *12.SS-Panzer-Division*, mainly the monthly *Zustandbericht* reports and periodic *Kriegsgliederung* reports.[12] A few sporadic reports were also compiled by higher commands tracking the progress of the preparations for Autumn Mist.[13] Another source were the maps prepared for the OB West on a daily basis, which sometimes include tank strength figures.[14] These have not been cited here, as they appear to be extremely unreliable.[15]

An additional problem with the data concerns the issue of what vehicles were actually being counted.[16] Some of the divisional data includes only the tanks and tank destroyers organic to the *12.SS-Panzer-Division*, namely *I./SS-Panzer-Regiment.12* and *SS-Panzerjäger.Abteilung.12*. Others seem to include data from attached units, namely *Panzerjäger.*

Abteilung.560. So, for example, the December 15, 1944, report seems to include the broader array of units subordinate to the *Hitlerjugend* division, but it has its own oddities.[17] For example, it seems to lump the *PzKpfw IV* tanks and *Panzer IV lg.(V)* tank destroyers together, and the *Jagdpanther* tanks are lumped into a category labeled *Sfl.*, which may include other miscellaneous vehicles.[18] The most detailed set of data is for January 8, 1945, since it clearly notes that it includes the *s.Pz. Jg.Abt. 560* and also includes data on replacements being sent to the division.[19]

The raw data from these various sources is listed in the chart below. Other types of tank-related vehicles, such as the various flak anti-aircraft vehicles on the *PzKpfw IV* chassis, are not included in any of these tables.

Strength Data for the *12.SS-Panzer Division*				
	PzKpfw IV	**Panther**	**Pz. IV lg.(V)**	**Jagdpanther**
Total Dec. 8, 1944	42	42	22	
Total Dec. 10, 1944	42	41	22	
Total Dec. 15, 1944	54	37		
Total Dec. 31, 1944	27	17	18	
Total Jan. 8, 1945	20	28	29	6
Total Feb. 1, 1945	14	28	13	
Operational Dec. 10, 1944	39	38	22	
Operational Dec. 15, 1944	39	22		
Operational Dec. 31, 1944	13	7	15	
Operational Jan. 8, 1945	12	20	12	3
Operational Feb. 1, 1945	12	21	7	
In repair Dec. 10, 1944	3	3		
In repair Dec. 15, 1944	15	15		
In repair Dec. 31, 1944	14	10	3	
In repair Jan. 8, 1945	8	8	17	3
In repair Feb. 1, 1945	2	7	6	
Replacements Jan. 5–15, 1945	5	13	2	12

Due to the many complications in the divergent data sources, I have compiled a more pertinent chart that lists the total divisional strength of tanks and AFVs at the start of the campaign and the total divisional strength on January 8, 1945, when the division was being pulled out of action. I then calculated total losses by subtracting the January 8, 1945, totals from the starting strength. I indicated the "repair" data for January 8 as "temporary losses," since most of these vehicles were probably derelict at this stage of the campaign. I made this assumption based on a comparison between the January and February figures, which do not show a sudden return of large numbers of vehicles to operational status, especially in light of the replacements that were received in mid-January.

I calculated "combined losses" by adding the temporary and total losses. The "total losses" represent the minimum number of tanks and AFVs lost by the *Hitlerjugend* in the campaign; the "combined losses" represents the maximum and is probably the more relevant of the two numbers.

Summary Tank and AFV Data for the *12.SS-Panzer-Division* in the Ardennes

	PzKpfw IV	Panther	Pz. IV lg.(V)	Jagdpanther	Total
Total Dec. 16, 1944	42	42	50	17	151
Total Jan. 8, 1945	20	28	29	6	83
Operational Jan. 8, 1945	12	20	12	3	47
Temporary losses	8	8	17	3	36
Total losses	22	14	21	11	68
Combined losses	30	22	38	14	104

NOTES

INTRODUCTION

1. Eisenhower, *Bitter Woods*, p. 224.

HITLER'S PLAN

1. General der Panzertruppen Hasso von Manteuffel, Fifth Panzer Army: 12 Sep-12 Oct 1944, FMS B-037, 1945, p. 14.
2. Bauer, *Idea for the German Ardennes Offensive in 1944*.
3. Zaloga, *Patton vs. the Panzers*.
4. Jodl's formal role was as the head of the *Wehrmachtführungsstab* (Wfst) of the OKW. This type of outline plan is called an *Aufmarschanweisung* and includes the basic elements of the plan, the guiding principles, and general instructions, with the subordinate headquarters assigned to flesh out the details.
5. Jung, *Die Ardennen Offensive 1944/45*, pp. 106–7.
6. In German, Operation Liège-Aachen is *Lüttich-Aachen*, while the Big and Small Solutions are *Grosse Lösung* and *Kleine Lösung*.
7. von Luettichau, *Ardennes Offensive, Chapter II*, p. 2.
8. Ibid., p. 7.
9. OB West was the Western Front command. Army Group B (*Heeresgruppe B*) in northern Germany/Netherlands and Army Group G in Alsace and central/southern Germany were under its command.
10. von Luettichau, *Ardennes Offensive, Chapter II*, pp. 30–31.
11. Zimmermann et al., *OB West, Part 2*, Appendix 16, "Remarks on Part 2 by GFM Rundstedt," p. 11.
12. These instructions, titled "Richtlinien für das Angriffsverfahren der Operation 'Wacht am Rhein,'" can be found reproduced in their entirety in the classic German account of the Ardennes offensive: Jung, *Die Ardennen Offensive 1944/45*, pp. 311–16.
13. von Luettichau, *Ardennes Offensive, Chapter III*, pp. 20–21.

SCHWERPUNKT

1. "Operation S" refers to Operation Stösser, an airborne operation intended to capture key Meuse river bridges in advance of the panzer advance. von Luettichau, *Ardennes Offensive, Chapter II*, p. 9.
2. von Luettichau, *Ardennes Offensive, Chapter II*, p. 5.

3. MacDonald, *Time for Trumpets*, p. 160.
4. Rundstedt made this demand in his response to Jodl on November 3, 1944. von Luettichau, *Ardennes Offensive, Chapter II*, pp. 28–29.
5. Krämer had formerly served as Dietrich's chief of staff in the *I. SS-Panzer-Korps* during the summer of 1944 and was commander of the *12. SS-Panzer-Division* in the autumn of 1944 when transferred back to the *6. Panzer-Armee* post. Krämer was a former *Heer* officer, not admitted to the *Waffen-SS* until August 1944.
6. Dietrich, *Interview with Obstgrf "Sepp" Dietrich*, ETHINT 16, p. i.
7. These remarks were made by 1Lt. Robert E. Merriam from a conversation with Dietrich on August 8–9, 1945. Merriam would go on to write the first comprehensive history of the Battle of the Bulge. Dietrich, *Interview with Obstgrf "Sepp" Dietrich*, ETHINT 15, p. i.
8. Krämer, *Commitment of the 6th Panzer Army*, p. 14.
9. Ibid., p. 13.
10. Ibid., pp. 24, 31.
11. Krämer, Ibid., pp. 17–18.
12. Interview with Manteuffel in Hart, *Other Side*, p. 459.
13. Lehmann, *I. SS-Panzer-Korps during the Ardennes Offensive*, p. 2.
14. Preiss, *Commitment of the I. SS-Panzer-Korps*, p. 6.
15. Lager Elsenborn was a military base established by the German army in the 1880s when the Elsenborn area was still part of Germany. It was gradually modernized after World War I by the Belgian army as Camp d'Elsenborn and consisted of barracks and training grounds. It was located on the northwest side of the town of Elsenborn.
16. The US 1st Infantry Division captured a copy of the *12. SS-Panzer-Division* pre-attack intelligence summary, which was translated and distributed as Annex No. 5 to G-2 Periodic Report No. 190 on December 26, 1944, as "Enemy Pre-Breakthrough G-2 Estimate." NARA, RG 407, Entry 427.
17. Priess, (FMS A-877), pp. 8–9.
18. Accounts by the *1. SS-Panzer-Korps* frequently refer to the US Army 1st Armored Division, which had been deployed in the Italian theater, rather than the 9th Armored Division that was actually in the Ardennes. The threat from Elsenborn is mentioned in Meyer, *History of 12. SS-Panzerdivision Hitlerjugend*, p. 234.
19. von der Heydte, *Battle-Group von der Heydte*.
20. Schadewitz, *Meuse First*.

THE *HITLERJUGEND* DIVISION

1. Milner, *Stopping the Panzers*.
2. Sullivan, "Combat Motivation."
3. Casualties totaled 8,532 men, but several units did not report their casualties. The casualty breakdown was 1,858 killed, 4,425 wounded, and 2,249 missing. Bernage and Meyer, *12. SS-Panzer-Division "Hitlerjugend,"* p. 414.

4. Gen. Walter Robertson of the 2nd Division was fifty-six, while Gen. Walter Lauer of the 99th Division was fifty-one years old. The youngest American divisional commander of the war, Gen. James Gavin, was thirty-seven years old.

5. A list of the small-unit commanders in the division can be found in Meyer, *History of 12.SS-Panzerdivision Hitlerjugend*, Appendix 6, "Officer Positions and Names of Occupants in 12.SS-Panzer-Division Hitlerjugend," pp. 352–57.

6. Kraas, *Die 12.SS-Panzerdivision "Hitlerjugend,"* p. 6.

7. This instruction was described during a prisoner-of-war interrogation of a tanker, *Sturmmann* Max Denisch of *1.Kompanie, I./SS-Panzer-Regiment.12*, captured on December 18, 1944, during the Krinkelt-Rocherath fighting. He stated that the instruction came from the new divisional commander, who he misidentified as "*Brigadeführer* Kurt Wise or Pietsch," who was decorated with the *Ritterkreuz mit Eichenlaub* (Knight's Cross with Oak Leaves). This presumably refers to Hugo Kraas. First Army PWI Report, No. 1, 21/22 Dec 44, NARA, RG 407, Entry 427, p. 2.

8. *Die 3.Kompanie*, pp. 61–62.

9. *Maschinenfabrik Augsberg-Nurnberg, Nurnberg Germany*, Munitions Division, US Strategic Bombing Survey, 1945, p. 19.

10. There is some confusion about sub-unit designations in this formation. The battalion itself identified its three companies in the usual sequential style as *1., 2.,* and *3.Kompanien*. However, the *Hitlerjugend* sometimes identified the battalion as *III./SS-Panzer-Regiment.12* and so identified the companies as *9., 10.,* and *11.Kompanien* as if they followed the usual divisional sequence.

11. This type of vehicle was originally called the *Jagdpanzer IV*. The type was improved by switching from the original L/48 gun, as used on the *PzKpfw IV* tank, to the longer L/70 gun, the same type used on the *Panther* tank. The improved version was renamed by Hitler on July 18, 1944, as the *Panzer IV lang (V)*, with *lang* (long) indicating the later and longer L/70 gun, and *(V)* indicating its production by Vomag. In practice it was called the *Panzer IV L/70 (V)* or *Panzer IV lg.(V)*, and the latter designation is used here for convenience. For technical details, see Baschin and Block, *Jagdpanzer IV*. Regarding unit strength, see Dugdale, *Panzer Divisions*, pp. 73–79.

12. Meyer, *History of 12.SS-Panzerdivision Hitlerjugend*, p. 238.

13. Kraas, *Die 12.SS-Panzerdivision "Hitlerjugend,"* pp. 5–6.

14. Kraas, *Die 12.SS-Panzerdivision "Hitlerjugend,"* pp. 5–6.

15. The only available armored engineer vehicle was the *Sd.Kfz.251/7* Pionier armored half-track that carried a set of ramps to assist the *Panzergrenadier* half-tracks in crossing ditches or obstructions. Seven of these were supposed to be in the armored engineer company of the half-track battalion, but in fact there were only a handful in December 1944.

16. Kraas, *Die 12.SS-Panzerdivision "Hitlerjugend,"* p. 6.

17. *(gep.)* indicated *gepanzerte* (armored). Dugdale, *Panzer Divisions*, p. 85.

18. Dugdale, *Panzer Divisions*, p. 76.

19. Reichhelm, *Commentary on Kraemer's Report*, p. 7.
20. Krämer, *Commitment of the 6th Panzer Army*, p. 19.
21. Priess, (FMS A-877), p. 17.
22. Lehmann, *I.SS-Panzer-Korps (15 Oct–16 Dec 1944)*, p. 12.
23. Lehmann, *I.SS-Panzer-Korps during the Ardennes Offensive*, p. 16.
24. Meyer, op cit, p. 236.
25. See, for example, the divisional map plan "Skizze IV: Ardennen-Offensive Bewegüngsstreifen der 12.SS-Pz.Div. ünd geplanter Vorstoss," in Kraas, *Die 12.SS-Panzerdivision "Hitlerjugend."*
26. Lehmann, *I.SS-Panzer-Korps during the Ardennes Offensive*, p. 5.
27. A Class 3 road is a secondary road with a metalled (hard) surface and an average 4-meter width. Details of the road network in this area can be found on contemporary maps, and those used in the preparation of this book included the 1:25,000 maps prepared by the 652nd Engineers in January 1945 as AMS M841/GSGS 4414 "Sheet 5504 Hellenthal" and "Sheet 5503 Elsenborn."
28. Priess, (FMS A-877), p. 14.

METAL STORM

1. Parker, *Fatal Crossroads*, p. 287.
2. Reichhelm, *Report of Col. Reichhelm*, p. 2.
3. The reconstructed division was originally called the *574.Volksgrenadier-Division*, but later in September 1944, the division was allowed to revert back to its original *277.Division* designation.
4. Scherer and Broch, *Untergang*, pp. 104–5.
5. Viebig, *Operations of the 277.Volksgrenadier Division*, p. 2.
6. von Wangenheim, *277.Infanterie-Division*, p. 30.
7. Rusiecki, *Key to the Bulge*, p. 16.
8. Viebig, *Operations of the 277.Volksgrenadier Division*, pp. 6–7. Viebig was an Oberst (Colonel) through the end of December 1944 and promoted to Generalmajor on 1 January 1945.
9. These Polish recruits were usually identified as *Volksliste 3 Eingedeutschte* (Ethnic Identity List 3 voluntarily Germanized).
10. A recent study addresses the problems of the *Volksdeutsche* in the *Waffen-SS*, but it deals mainly with the units on the Russian Front rather than the West: Sanders Marble, ed., *Scraping the Barrel: The Military Use of Substandard Manpower 1860–1960* (New York: Fordham University Press, 2012), chapters 9 and 10.
11. *PW Interrogation Report No. 73, Inclosure #1, G-2 Report, 2nd Infantry Division, 20 November 1944*, NARA, RG 407, Entry 427.
12. Viebig, *277th Volksgrenadier Division*, p. 5.
13. The authorized strength for a *Volksgrenadier* division at the time was 10,072 men.
14. The *Organisationsabteilung* of the OKH released two documents on this, on April 25, 1944, and June 15, 1944.

15. Viebig, op cit. (B-754), p. 6.
16. Viebig, op cit., (B-754), p. 8.
17. Engel's diaries were later published as *At the Heart of the Reich: The Secret Diary of Hitler's Army Adjutant*, but they do not cover his combat actions after 1943.
18. Engel at the time was commander of *Grenadier-Regiment.197*. Byers, "Fight for Losheimergraben," p. 6.
19. Engel, *12.Volksgrenadier-Division: 3–29 December 1944*, p. 1.
20. Engel, *12.Volksgrenadier-Division in the Third Battle of Aachen*, pp. 34–35.
21. Engel, *12.Volksgrenadier-Division: 3–29 December 1944*, p.3.

FIRE WALTZ

1. Engel, *12.Volksgrenadier-Division in the Third Battle of Aachen*, p. 36 (p. 33 in German version)
2. Thoholte, "A German Reflects," p. 709.
3. The basic lFH 18 was designed for horse towing. The lFH 18/40 was essentially the same cannon, but with the carriage redesigned for motorized towing.
4. *Nebelwerfer* literally means "smoke launcher" but in fact these weapons were primarily used as substitutes for conventional field guns, firing high-explosive projectiles.
5. Bryja, "Artyleria niemiecka," pp. 34–36.
6. Staudinger, *Artillery Leadership*, p. 18.
7. Preiss, *Commitment of the I.SS-Panzer-Korps*, p. 11.
8. OB West KTB, Anlage 50, *Heerestruppenübersicht: Artillerie*, NARA, RG 242, T311, R18, F7020716-0717.
9. OB West KTB, Anlage 50, *Artillerie, Pz.AOK.6*, NARA, RG 242, T311, R18, F7021052.
10. OB West KTB, Anlage 50, *Artillerie, Pz.AOK.6*, NARA, RG 242, T311, R18, F7021041.
11. Staudinger, *Artillery Command*, p. 11.
12. KStN, or *Kriegsstärkenachweisungen*, was the German equivalent of the US Army's TO&E (Tables of Organization and Equipment), which is a detailed list of the standard equipment authorized for each type of unit. In the German army in 1944, many units did not receive their full allotment of equipment.
13. Divisional records for the *277.Volksgrenadier-Division* were lost during the war, so details of their radio supplies are lacking.
14. German tactical communications are not well covered in the existing literature. The technical aspects are better documented in, for example, Fritz Trenkle, *Die deutschen Funknachrichtenanlagen bis 1945, Band 2: Der Zweite Weltkrieg* (Heidelberg: Telefunker System Technik, 1990).
15. Thoholte, "A German Reflects," p. 712.
16. Staudinger, *Artillery Command*, pp. 7–8.

17. The HARKO (*Heeres Artillerie Kommandeur*) for the *6.Panzer-Armee* prepared a report after the war for the US Army Foreign Military Studies series. Staudinger, *Artillery Leadership*, p. 2.
18. *Ausstattung* is a contraction of the term *Erstausstatung*.
19. This was 8,100 rounds of 105mm and 1,800 rounds of 150mm. The total was somewhat different in a *Volksgrenadier* artillery regiment due to the substitution of the smaller 75mm gun in one battalion. Although the overall tonnage was about the same as in a normal artillery regiment, the number of rounds was higher due to the larger number of 75mm guns.
20. Lehmann, *I.SS-Panzer-Korps during the Ardennes Offensive*, p. 15.
21. Preiss, *Commitment of the I.SS-Panzer-Korps*, p. 17. Staudinger, *Artillery Command*, p. 12.
22. Staudinger, *6.Panzer Army Artillery*, p. 2.
23. This is based on the interrogation of a major from *Werfer-Regiment.54*, captured in mid-January 1945. First Army PWI Report, No. 15, 14/15 January 1945, NARA, RG 407, Entry 427.
24. VII Corps was one of the most battle-hardened US formations in the ETO. Commanded by Lt. Gen. "Lightning Joe" Collins, it fought in the ETO from Utah Beach, through the Cherbourg campaign, the Battle of the Hedgerows, and the Aachen campaign on the Siegfried line as well as in the Ardennes. *German Artillery*, VII Corps Artillery: 1945, p. 22.
25. Staudinger, *Artillery Leadership*, pp. 25–30.

THE BATTLEGROUND: WINTER MUD

1. Kays, *Weather Effects*, p. 9.
2. Parker, *To Win the Winter Sky*.
3. Weather data from the US Army weather station at Maredessous, the closest station to the Elsenborn area, from Appendix 1.3, "Weather Reports During the Battle," in Guillemot, *Battle of the Bulge*, pp. 164–65.
4. The World Bank Climate Change Knowledge Portal, http://sdwebx.worldbank.org/climateportal/index.cfm?page=downscaled_data_download&menu=historical, accessed November 2017.
5. Zaloga, *Siegfried Line*, pp. 76–89.
6. Zaloga, *Metz 1944*, pp. 59–66.

BATTLE BABES: THE DEFENDERS

1. TO&E is the standard army template for military units indicating the organization of and its allotment of troops and equipment.
2. n.a., *Organization, Equipment and Tactical Employment of the Infantry Divisions*, (General Board, USFET: 1945), p. 2.
3. Ratliff, "The Field Artillery Battalion," pp. 116–19.

4. Comparato, *Age of the Great Guns*, pp. 254–56.

5. Baldwin, *Deadly Fuze*.

6. The after-action reports of the 1st Infantry Division artillery does mention the use of VT fuzes (also called POZT fuzes) in its December reports. The 38th Field Artillery Battalion, supporting the 38th Infantry in Krinkelt-Rocherath, mentions employing them "late in the period," the period referring to December 1944.

7. For an overview of the role of field artillery in the Ardennes, see Reeves, "Artillery in the Ardennes," pp. 138–42, 173–84.

8. S-3 Journal, V Corps Artillery, December 1944, NARA II, RG 407, Entry 427, Box 3042.

9. Zaloga, *US Tank*.

10. Daily Tank Status Reports, Headquarters ETO AFV & Weapons Section, NARA, RG 338.

11. *99th Infantry Division, The German Breakthrough (16 Dec 44–16 Jan 45), V Corps Sector, Summary of Action*, NARA II, WWII Operation Reports, Combat Interviews, RG 407, Entry 427A, p. 3.

12. For a more detailed examination of the dams, see Charles MacDonald, *The Siegfried Line Campaign* (Washington, DC: US Army Chief of Military History, 1963), p. 324 *et passim*.

ROLLBAHN A: KRINKELTERWALD ON X-DAY

1. Scherer and Broch, *Untergang*, p. 129.

2. Rader, "Rader, Dutcher, Langford," p. 1.

3. Staudinger, *Artillery Leadership*, p. 5.

4. Viebig, *Operations of the 277. Volksgrenadier Division*, p. 10.

5. The Hollerath Knee (*Hollerather Knie*) was a sharp bend in the International Highway from Hollerath, abruptly heading south along the edge of the Krinkelterwald. It was later called "Purple Heart Corner" by veterans of the 99th Division.

6. Interview with Capt. William Fox, S-3, 3/393rd Infantry, in 99th Infantry Division Combat Interviews, NARA, RG 407, Entry 427A, Box 19066, p. 2.

7. Fieger, *Grenadier Regiment.989*, p. 5.

8. Dettor, "Memorable Bulge Incidents," pp. 19–20.

9. Fieger, *Grenadier Regiment.989*, pp. 6–7.

10. Wijers, *Battle of the Bulge; Volume One*, p. 102.

11. Ibid., p. 102.

12. Plume was captured later in the day and after the war was awarded the Bronze Star for his actions on December 16, 1944. No details of this counterattack are known except for a cryptic reference in the 393rd Infantry Regiment Combat Interviews, NARA, RG 407, Entry 427A, Box 19066.

13. Wijers, *Battle of the Bulge; Volume One*, p. 103.

14. *393rd Infantry Regiment, After Action Report, December 1944, Section VI-Annexes-Battle Experience*, NARA, RG 407, Entry 427, Box 11655.

15. 3/393rd Infantry Regiment Combat Interviews, NARA, RG 407, Entry 427A, Box 19066, p. 5.
16. Ibid.
17. Dettor, "Memorable Bulge Incidents," p. 19.
18. Lehmann, *I.SS-Panzer-Korps: Special Questions*, p. 20.
19. Meyer, *History of 12.SS-Panzerdivision Hitlerjugend*, p. 244.
20. Reynolds, *Men of Steel*, p. 55.
21. 3/393rd Infantry Regiment Combat Interviews, NARA RG 407, Entry 427A, Box 19066.

ROLLBAHN B ON X-DAY

1. *393rd Infantry Regiment After-Action Report for December 1944*, NARA, RG 407, Entry 427, Box 11654.
2. Interview with Capt. Lawrence Duffin, S-3, 1/393rd Infantry, in 99th Division, NARA, RG 407, Entry 427A, Box 19066, pp. 1–2.
3. Duffin interview, p. 2.
4. Duffin interview, p. 2.
5. Duffin interview, pp. 2–3.
6. Scherer and Broch, *Untergang*, pp. 132–33.
7. Viebig, *Operations of the 277.Volksgrenadier Division*, p. 12.
8. Wijers, *Battle of the Bulge; Volume One*, p. 97. After less than a week of fighting, *GR.990* was down to about 200 to 300 men and pulled out of the line. First Army IPW Report No. 8, 24 December 1944, Interrogation of Pfc. Nelles, 6 Co., 990 Regt. 277 VG Div.
9. First Army PWI Report, No. 8, from 0800 23 Dec to 0800 24 December 1944, NARA, RG 407, Entry 427.
10. Viebig, *Operations of the 277.Volksgrenadier Division*, p. 17.
11. Manteuffel quoted in B.H. Liddell Hart, *The Other Side of the Hill*, Cedric Chivers, Bath: 1948, p. 459.

ROLLBAHN C: LOSHEIMERGRABEN ON X-DAY

1. Class 2 roads had hard surfaces and generally had a width of 5.5 meters or more. On reaching Losheimergraben, the International Highway made a sharp turn to the southeast back into Germany, but another road, the contemporary N632, headed northwest into Belgium.
2. This first bridge was at 003977 and the second at 015973 on the 1:25,000 map 5603 of the GSGS 4414 series. Interview with Lt. Col. Robert Douglas, 1st Battalion, 394th Infantry, in 99th Infantry Division Combat Interviews, NARA, RG 407, Entry 427A, Box 19066, p. 2.
3. *Recommendation for the Distinguished Unit Citation of the First Battalion, 394th Infantry Regiment*, 394th Infantry Regiment HQ Records, NARA, RG 407, Entry 427, Box 11661, p. 11.

4. Engel, *12.Volksgrenadier-Division: 3–29 December 1944*, p. 5.
5. Simmons, *Operations of Company K*, p. 11.
6. A recent US Army study concluded that the most important consequence of the German preparatory barrage was the disruption in US Army front-line communication networks. Stephenson et al., "The Impact of Massive Artillery Fires," pp. 58–61.
7. Byers, "Fight for Losheimergraben," p. 8.
8. The 0745 time comes from combat interviews with multiple battalion officers conducted by army historians in the field in late January 1945; the 0930 time comes from the Infantry School report of the battalion executive officer, Major George Clayton, in Clayton, *Operations of the 3rd Battalion*.
9. Some of the prisoners indicated that they were from the *12.SS-Panzer-Division*, but US soldiers may have mistaken this for *12.Volksgrenadier-Division*. There is no evidence that any *Hitlerjugend* troops took part in the initial action at Bucholz Station.
10. Engel, *12.Volksgrenadier-Division: 3–29 December 1944*, p. 6.
11. Cavanagh, *Dauntless*, p. 100.
12. The most detailed account of *Panzer-Brigade.150*, Michael Schadewitz's *The Meuse First and then Antwerp*, does not mention any support of *12.Volksgrenadier-Division* at this point, though there were several jeep teams that had independent missions and are not well documented.
13. Douglas interview, p. 3.
14. There was a *Tiger II* (King Tiger) battalion in *1.SS-Panzer-Division "Leibstandarte Adolf Hitler,"* but it was attached to *Kampfgruppe Peiper* and fought farther west around Stavelot–La Gleize. Gregory Walden, *Tigers in the Ardennes: The 501st Heavy SS Tank Battalion in the Battle of the Bulge* (Atglen, PA: Schiffer, 2014).
15. The later time is contained in the *Recommendation for Distinguished Unit Citation of the First Battalion, 394th Infantry Regiment*, p. 16.
16. Douglas interview, pp. 4–5.
17. Byers, "Fight for Losheimergraben," p. 9.
18. Douglas interview, pp. 5–6.
19. Dolenc was first declared missing in action, but on December 18 it was learned that he had been captured. *Recommendation for Distinguished Unit Citation of the First Battalion, 394th Infantry Regiment*, p. 16.
20. Douglas interview, p. 6.
21. Clayton, *Operations of the 3rd Battalion*, p. 17.
22. The *F* indicated *Forstgebietes* (forest settlement), which identified a few homes near the railway station.
23. Nance, *Sabers through the Reich*, pp. 144–50.
24. *After Action Report of the 14th Cavalry Group (Mecz): Ardennes, 16 Dec–24 Dec 1944*, US Army Military History Institute, AHEC, Carlisle Barracks, PA.
25. Schadewitz, *Meuse First*, p. 93.

26. Interview with Maj. William Kempton, Regimental S-3 (Operations), 394th Infantry, in 99th Infantry Division Combat Interviews, NARA, RG 407, Entry 427A, Box 19066, p. 4.
27. Priess, *Commitment of the I. SS-Panzer Corps*, p. 24.
28. Schadewitz, *Meuse First*, p. 85.
29. *Abwehr* means "defense" in German, a deceptive code name specifically chosen to camouflage the offensive intention of the movement. Krämer, *Commitment of the 6th Panzer Army*, p. 22. Divisional artillery was brought forward by December 10, heavy corps artillery by December 13, infantry divisions by December 14, and the panzer divisions last due to their mobility.
30. Krämer, *Commitment of the 6th Panzer Army*, p. 15.
31. This is based on the December 15, 1944, *Kraftfahrzeug Ausstatung* report, reprinted in Verwicht, "Wacht am Rhein," p. 30.
32. Dietrich, *Interview with Obstgrf. "Sepp" Dietrich*, p. 3.
33. Kraas, *Die 12. SS-Panzerdivision "Hitlerjugend,"* p. 14.

NIGHTFALL, X-DAY: COMMAND PERSPECTIVES

1. Some accounts suggest that the records had been provided, but that the clearing operation had been neglected. Tiemann, *The Leibstandarte*, p. 33.
2. There is some dispute whether the northern *Hitlerjugend Kampfgruppe* was placed under *277. Volksgrenadier-Division* control or vice versa. This is discussed in Meyer's *History of 12. SS-Panzerdivision Hitlerjugend*, p. 245, and also in Lehmann, *I. SS-Panzer-Korps during the Ardennes Offensive*, p. 22.
3. Morris, *Death Spiral*, p. 33.
4. Hogan, *Command Post at War*, p. 209.
5. Sylvan and Smith, *Normandy to Victory*, pp. 213–15.
6. Votaw, *Blue Spaders*, p. 99.
7. Rundstedt's order-of-the-day was a widely distributed flier exhorting the German troops that the hour of destiny had arrived and that victory was in reach. Such missives were not common and strongly suggested that a major offensive was under way.
8. Winton, *Corps Commanders*, pp. 120–21.
9. Wilkerson et al., *V Corps Operations*, p. 344.

X+1: OPENING ROLLBAHN C

1. 254th Engineer Combat Battalion after-action report, reprinted in *The Bulge Bugle*, August 2010, p. 15.
2. After-Action Report, 644th Tank Destroyer Battalion, December 1944, NARA, RG 407, Entry 427.
3. "Memorandum: Destruction of German Armor by 644th Tank Destroyer Battalion (Company B) in Operation 17, 18, and 19 December 1944. In and near Rocherath, Krinkelt, and Wirtfeld, Belgium—Effect of Fire," NARA, RG 407, Entry 427, Box 18573.

4. *Recommendation for Distinguished Unit Citation of the First Battalion, 394th Infantry Regiment*, p. 20.
5. Kempton interview, p. 8.
6. Engel, *12.Volksgrenadier-Division: 3–29 December 1944*, p. 7.

X+1: BREAK-IN ON ROLLBAHN A

1. Meyer, *History of 12.SS-Panzerdivision Hitlerjugend*, p. 246.
2. Interview with Capt. Raymond McElroy, S-3, 3/393rd Infantry, in 99th Infantry Division Combat Interviews, NARA, RG 407, Entry 427A, Box 19066.
3. McElroy interview, p. 13.
4. MacDonald, *Company Commander*, p. 90. MacDonald later went on to become a US Army historian; his book *Company Commander*, in which this particular skirmish is described, is one of the classic accounts of WWII infantry combat.
5. MacDonald, *Company Commander*, pp. 91–92.
6. MacDonald, *Company Commander*, p. 101.

COMMAND PERSPECTIVES: EVENING X+1

1. Interview with Maj. Gen. Walter Robinson, in 2nd Infantry Division Combat Interviews, NARA, RG 407, Entry 427A, Box 19026.
2. Robertson interview.
3. Lehman, *I.SS-Panzer-Korps during the Ardennes Offensive*, p. 25.

THE 2ND DIVISION STANDS FAST

1. 9th Infantry History, December 1944, NARA, RG 407, Entry 427, Box 5360, p. 21.
2. Hancock, *Operations of the 1st Battalion*.
3. 9th Infantry History, December 1944, p. 11.
4. 9th Infantry History, December 1944, p. 24.
5. Interview with Maj. William Hancock, 1st Battalion, 9th Infantry, in 2nd Infantry Division Combat Interviews, NARA, RG 407, Entry 427A, Box 19026.
6. 1st Battalion, 9th Infantry Regiment, 2nd Infantry Division Combat Interviews, NARA, RG 407, Entry 427A, Box 19026.
7. Ibid.
8. Warnock, "Heroic Stand at Lausdell," p. 61.
9. *After Action Report for 1–31 December 1944, 15th Field Artillery Battalion, 2nd Infantry Division*, NARA, RG 407, Entry 427, Box 5346.
10. Hancock, *Operations of the 1st Battalion*, pp. 19–20.
11. *Story of Vitamin Baker*, p. 63.
12. Meyer, *History of 12.SS-Panzerdivision Hitlerjugend*, p. 246.
13. Interview with Capt. Fred Rumsey, Battalion S-3, et al., 1st Battalion, 38th Infantry, in 2nd Infantry Division Combat Interviews, NARA, RG 407, Entry 427A, Box 19027.

X+2: D<small>AWN</small> A<small>TTACK ON</small> L<small>AUSDELL</small> C<small>ROSSROADS</small>

1. *Die 3.Kompanie*, pp. 83–84.
2. Scherer and Broch, *Untergang*, p. 145.
3. 1st Battalion, 9th Infantry Regiment, 2nd Infantry Division Combat Interviews, NARA, RG 407, Entry 427A, Box 19026.
4. Hancock, *Observations of the 1st Battalion*, p. 15.
5. Hancock, *Observations of the 1st Battalion*.
6. Truppner was captured and was sent to the Stalag 13D (Oflag 73) internment camp.
7. Barcellona already had been decorated with the Distinguished Service Cross for his heroic actions on D-Day, when he commanded one of the few tanks of the 741st Tank Battalion to have reached shore in support of the 16th Infantry, 1st Division in the initial wave of the attack.
8. *December 1944 After Action Report, HQ 741st Tank Battalion*, NARA, RG 407, Entry 427, Box 13503.
9. MacDonald, *Time for Trumpets*, pp. 397–98.
10. 9th Infantry History, December 1944, NARA, RG 407, Entry 427, Box 5360, p. 19.

K<small>RINKELT</small>-R<small>OCHERATH</small>: P<small>ANZER</small> G<small>RAVEYARD</small>

1. 38th Infantry Regiment, 2nd Infantry Division Combat Interviews, NARA, RG 407, Entry 427A, Box 19027.
2. The 644th Tank Destroyer Battalion had taken control of elements of two towed anti-tank gun units, Company C, 612th Tank Destroyer Battalion, and three guns of 801st Tank Destroyer Battalion. Major William F. Jackson, et al., *Employment of Four Tank Destroyer Battalions in the ETO* (Fort Knox, KY: Armored School, 1950), p. 55.
3. Col. Franklin Boos, *Addendum to the After Action Report, 38th Infantry Regiment*, 4 January 1945, in 2nd Infantry Division Combat Interviews, NARA, RG 407, Entry 427A, Box 19027.
4. *December 1944 After Action Report, 644th Tank Destroyer Battalion*, NARA, RG 407, Entry 427, Box 1853.
5. For more details on the technical issues of the bazooka, see Zaloga, *Bazooka vs. Panzer*.
6. *December 1944 After Action Report, HQ 741st Tank Battalion*, p. 3.
7. *Die 3.Kompanie*, pp. 87–88.
8. Rumsey interview, pp. 10–11.
9. There are conflicting accounts about the death of the cows. Some troops recalled that it was American troops who shot the cows, thinking that the German tanks would not run them over, while most other accounts indicate it was the *Panther* tank that mowed them down with machine-gun fire.
10. *Die 3.Kompanie*, pp. 90–91.
11. Interview with Lt. Col. Olinto Barsanti, 3rd Battalion, 38th Infantry, in 2nd Infantry Division Combat Interviews, NARA, RG 407, Entry 427A, Box 19027.

12. Field Manual FM 101-10 (October 10, 1943), p. 321, defines a unit of fire as "a tactical unit of measure for ammunition supply within a theater, based upon experience in the theater. It represents a specified number of rounds per weapon, which number varies with the type and caliber of the weapons, and is intended to approximate the average daily expenditure by that weapon in combat." The unit of fire for the 105mm howitzer was 130 rounds per cannon, or 1,560 rounds per battalion. To put the high expenditure rate in the Ardennes in some perspective, the VIII Corps during the siege of Brest in September 1944 expended only about a half-unit of fire per day during the battle.
13. The average daily 105mm howitzer expenditure in the ETO was 86.6 rounds, and 241.6 rounds in offensive operations where usage was generally higher. Lawrence, *War by Numbers*, p. 283.
14. Report of Operations from December 17–19, HQ, 38th Field Artillery Battalion, NARA, RG 407, Entry 427, Box 5356.
15. Thompson, *Tank Fight*, pp. 1–7 (artillery section).
16. *Vitamin Dukei*, p. 67.
17. *Die 3.Kompanie*, pp. 91–92.

X+3: T<small>HE</small> B<small>ATTLE FOR</small> K<small>RINKELT</small>-R<small>OCHERATH</small> R<small>ESUMES</small>

1. 38th Infantry Regiment, 2nd Infantry Division Combat Interviews, NARA, RG 407, Entry 427A, Box 19027, p. 8.
2. Meyer, *History of 12.SS-Panzerdivision Hitlerjugend*, p. 254.
3. 2nd Infantry Division Combat Interviews, NARA, Record Group 407, Entry 427A, Box 19027.
4. Interview with Capt. James Love, Commanding Officer, 38th Infantry Anti-Tank Company, in 2nd Infantry Division Combat Interviews, 2nd Infantry Division, NARA, RG 407, Entry 427A, Box 19026, pp. 8–9.
5. Love interview, p. 9.
6. The 38th Infantry after-action report indicates the attack consisted of fifteen tanks with three knocked out, while the 1/38th Infantry report indicates eleven tanks in the attack, of which eight were knocked out.
7. Hankel, *Operations of Company M*, p. 26.
8. Regarding typical killed-wound ratios in WWII, see Lawrence, *War by Numbers*, p. 194.
9. *Ardennes Campaign Simulation Data Base*, vol. 1, p. II-G-1-9
10. Thompson, *Tank Fight*, p. 7.
11. Dupuy et al., *Hitler's Last Gamble*, p. 469.
12. Wilkerson et al., *V Corps Operations*, p. 363.

W<small>E</small> F<small>IGHT AND</small> D<small>IE</small> H<small>ERE</small>: D<small>OM</small> B<small>ÜTGENBACH</small>

1. Cole, *The Ardennes*, p. 129.
2. Votaw, *Blue Spaders*, p. 99.

3. The identity of the unit of this scout patrol has been questioned in some accounts. One study suggests it was from the *Hitlerjugend* reconnaissance battalion. Vannoy and Karamales, *Against the Panzers*, pp. 282–83.
4. Interview with Lt. Col. Derrill Daniel, et al., 26th Infantry, in 1st Infantry Division Combat Interviews, NARA, RG 407, Entry 427A, Box 19023, pp. 4–5.
5. Engel, *12. Volksgrenadier-Division: 3–29 December 1944*, p. 9.
6. Daniel interview, p. 5.
7. Meyer, *History of 12. SS-Panzerdivision Hitlerjugend*, p. 257.
8. 1st Infantry Division Combat Interviews, NARA, RG 407, Entry 427A, Box 19023.
9. Ibid., p. 258.
10. *26th Infantry After-Action Report, December 1944*, NARA, RG 407, Entry 427, Box 5268, p. 4.
11. Votaw, *Blue Spaders*, p. 106.
12. *26th Infantry After-Action Report, December 1944*, pp. 4–5.
13. Warner displayed similar bravery in repulsing the attacks on December 21 but was killed in the later action. He was awarded the Medal of Honor posthumously.
14. After-Action Report, 745th Tank Battalion. Howenstine, *History of the 745th Tank Battalion*, p. 66.
15. Votaw, *Blue Spaders*, p. 106.
16. Votaw, *Blue Spaders*, pp.106–7.
17. Meyer, *History of 12. SS-Panzerdivision Hitlerjugend*, p. 259.
18. The 1st Infantry Division captured a report by *III./SS-Panzer-Regiment.12* when a courier on a *Kettenkrad* ran over a mine near 16th Infantry positions on December 24. A translated version of the report was reprinted in Selected Intelligence Reports December 1944–May 1945, Assistant Chief of Staff, G-2, 1st Infantry Division, 6 June 1945, in the G-2 files of 1st Infantry Division, NARA, RG 407, Entry 427.
19. *26th Infantry After-Action Report, December 1944*, p. 5.

COMMAND PERSPECTIVES: THE FIRST TURNING POINT

1. Bauer, *Key Dates: Part 1*, p. 20.
2. Warlimont, *Inside Hitler's Headquarters*, p. 490.
3. Bauer, *Key Dates: Part 1*, p. 16.
4. This was noted by Model's operations officer. Reichhelm, *Report of Col. Reichhelm*, pp. 23–24.
5. von Luettichau, *Key Dates: Part 2*, p. 111.
6. Bauer, *Key Dates: Part 1*, p. 16a.
7. Ibid., p 17.
8. von Luettichau, *Key Dates: Part 2*, p. 103.
9. Ibid., p. 101.
10. Krämer, *Interview with Genmaj (W-SS) Fritz Kraemer*, p. 12.

11. Dietrich, *Interview with Obstgrf. "Sepp" Dietrich*, p. 22.
12. von Luettichau, *Key Dates: Part 2*, p. 111.

X+5: ANOTHER ATTACK ON DOM BÜTGENBACH

1. Daniel interview, p. 9.
2. *Die 3.Kompanie*, pp. 97–99.
3. Daniel interview, pp. 6–7.
4. Activities of the 26th Infantry for December 1944, in 1st Infantry Division Combat Interviews, NARA, RG 406, Entry 427A, Box 19023.
5. Meyer, *History of 12.SS-Panzerdivision Hitlerjugend*, pp. 260–61.
6. Ibid., p. 261.
7. Daniel interview, p. 8.
8. Meyer, *History of 12.SS-Panzerdivision Hitlerjugend*, p. 261.
9. Votaw, *Blue Spaders*, p. 108.
10. Daniel interview, p. 8.
11. Howenstine, *History of the 745th Tank Battalion*, p. 66. After-Action Report, 745th Tank Battalion.

X+6: THE FINAL BATTLE FOR DOM BÜTGENBACH

1. Engel, *12.Volksgrenadier-Division: 3–29 December 1944*, pp. 13–14.
2. Recollections of *Unterscharführer* Gunther Burdack of *9.Kompanie, III./SS-Panzergrenadier-Regiment.26* in Wijers, *Battle of the Bulge: Hell at Bütgenbach*, pp. 144–45.
3. *26th Infantry After-Action Report, December 1944*, p. 6.
4. Votaw, *Blue Spaders*, p. 109.
5. Ibid., p. 109.
6. *After Action Report, 745th Tank Battalion, 220001 Dec–230001 Dec 44*.
7. Meyer, *History of 12.SS-Panzerdivision Hitlerjugend*, pp. 262–63.
8. "Excerpts from 26th Infantry Report After Action 16–31 December 1944," in 1st Infantry Division Combat Interviews, NARA, RG 407, Entry 427A, Box 19023, p. 18.
9. The 26th Infantry believed that more than forty-four had been knocked out or abandoned since this figure included only the vehicles that had been found, with others likely to have been missed. Selected Intelligence Reports December 1944–May 1945, p. 15.

THE DEFEAT OF AUTUMN MIST

1. Some details of the US Army historical effort in the ETO can be found in F. D. G. Williams, *SLAM: The Influence of S. L. A. Marshall on the United States Army* (Fort Monroe, VA: Office of the Command Historian, TRADOC, 1999).
2. Wagener, *Main Reasons*, p. 11.
3. Ibid., p. 12.

NOTES

4. Ibid., p. 12.
5. Ibid., p. 4.
6. Krämer, *Commitment of the 6th Panzer Army*, p. 11.

APPENDIX: *HITLERJUGEND* TANK CASUALTIES IN THE ARDENNES

1. A variety of German strength/losses compilations can be found in several appendices in OKH files located at NARA in RG 242, T-78, R-145, F76029 *et. passim*. A more convenient compilation can be found in the Norbert Baczyk article "Goracy rok Panzerwaffe," *Poligon*, May–June 2009, pp. 22–32.
2. I discussed this issue in more detail in Steven Zaloga, *Armored Champion: The Top Tanks of World War II* (Mechanicsburg, PA: Stackpole Books, 2015), pp. 250–51.
3. Meyer, *History of 12.SS-Panzerdivision Hitlerjugend*, p. 254.
4. Reynolds, *Men of Steel*, p. 87.
5. Email to author from Timm Haasler. This consists of eleven *Panther*s, four *PzKpfw IV*s, and two *Panzer IV lg.(V)*s.
6. These consist of four *PzKpfw IV*s, three *Panther*s, four *Jagdpanther*s, and one *Panzer IV lg.(V)*.
7. DMSI was a think tank descended from earlier organizations formed by the noted military historian Trevor Dupuy. Its predecessor was the Historical Evaluation and Research Organization (HERO, 1962–1983). In 1983, T. N. Dupuy Associates Inc. (TNDA) sold its HERO to a new Dupuy corporation called Data Memory Systems Inc. (DMSI). Dupuy's think tanks were at the forefront of the collection of military data to support analytic assessments of combat.
8. A two-volume overview of this project was internally published as the *Ardennes Campaign Simulation Data Base (ACSDB)*. Copies were found at the US Army Military History Institute at Carlisle Barracks, Pennsylvania. The actual database was prepared in dBase III software, and the author obtained a copy from the Defense Technical Information Center (DTIC).
9. This is presumably due to the fact that the OB West war diary *Anlage 50* entry for tank strength of the *12.SS-Panzer-Division* for December 10, 1944, lists a *StuG* category. These vehicles, belonging to *SS-Pz.Jg.Abt.12*, were in fact *Panzer IV lg.(V)*s, as is clear from many other documents.
10. Boos interview, op cit.
11. The most exhaustive examination of US claims was prepared as a special report for the Office of the Chief of Military History in 1952 as part of the effort to support the official US Army history of the Battle of the Bulge: Royce Thompson, *Tank Fight of Rocherath-Krinkelt (Belgium 17–19 December 1944)*.
12. Dugdale's *Panzer Divisions* includes the December 8, 1944, data from the files at the German Bundesarchiv-Militärarchiv in Freiberg. Essentially the same data is also contained in the tables in Nevenkin's *Fire Brigades*, along with the December 31, 1944, and February 1, 1945, reports: pp. 904–22.

13. For example, there is a strength report for December 10, 1944, in the OB West KTB: *Meldung über stand der schw. Waffen der Pz.Divisionen: Stand 10.12.44*, NARA, RG 242, T311, R18 F7021020-1025.

14. This appears to be the source for the figures reported in Dugdale, *Panzer Divisions*, p. 83, for *Hitlerjugend* tank strength.

15. The author has found these numbers to be very unreliable in past studies. It would appear that the staff compiling the maps filled in numbers from previous days' reports when new data was unavailable. This creates a false impression of numerical precision. So, for example, the *Hitlerjugend* figures for December 18, 19, and 20 all list thirty-eight *Panthers* as total strength. The lack of change in these numbers in the midst of major fighting suggests that the map compilers simply had no recent reports and reused older data from several days prior.

16. For example, some reports for December 8, 1944, total thirty-seven *PzKpfw IV*s, while others total forty-two since they include the five *PzBeob. IV* artillery observer tanks attached to the divisional artillery. Likewise, some December 8 reports include only thirty-seven *Panther* tanks; others count forty-two since they include the five radio-equipped *Bef.Pz. V* command tanks.

17. This data can be found in Verwicht, "Wacht am Rhein," p. 30

18. *Sfl.* is usually the abbreviation for self-propelled mount (*Selbstfahrlafette*), which generally covers self-propelled guns.

19. Stärkung 6.Pz-Armee, Generalinspekteur der Panzertruppe, NARA, RG 242, T-78, Roll 622, Frame 1131.

BIBLIOGRAPHY
1. Wood, "Captive Historians," pp. 123 47.

GLOSSARY

1Lt. First lieutenant

2Lt. Second lieutenant

12th Army Group Gen. Omar Bradley's command in northwest Europe

21st Army Group Field Marshal Bernard Montgomery's command in northwest Europe

Abteilung German unit between battalion and regiment in size; abbreviated as *Abt.*

AFV Armored fighting vehicle

AOK *Armee Oberkommando* (Army High Command); German field army headquarters

Armee German field army

Army Formation of several corps

Army Group Formation consisting of several field armies; *Heeresgruppe* in German

Battalion Formation of several companies

Bazooka 2.36-inch anti-tank rocket launcher

Co. Company; unit consisting of several platoons

Corps Formation consisting of several divisions

CP Command post

Division Formation of several regiments or battalions

Ersatzheer Replacement Army; German organization for raising and rebuilding army units inside Germany

ETO European Theater of Operations

FJR *Fallschirmjäger-Regiment*; paratrooper regiment

FK *Feldkanone*; field gun

flak *Flugabwehrkanone*; anti-aircraft gun

Füsilier   German light infantry

G-2   US Army intelligence at divisional or higher level

Generalfeldmarschall   Field marshal

Generalleutnant   Lieutenant general

Generalmajor   Major general

GMC   Gun motor carriage; typically a self-propelled tank destroyer

GR   Grenadier Regiment

Hauptmann   Captain

Hauptsturmführer   *Waffen-SS* captain; abbreviated as *Hstuf.*

Heer   German Army

Heeresgruppe   Army group consisting of several field armies

Kampfgruppe   Battle group; extemporized formation a few companies to a regiment or more in size; abbreviated as *KG*

Kompanie   German army company

Korps   Corps; formation consisting of several divisions and supporting units

KTB   *Kriegstagebuch*; war diary

lFH   *leichte Feld Haubitze*; light field howitzer

LAH   *Leibstandarte Adolf Hitler*; Adolf Hitler Bodyguard

Mecz.   US Army abbreviation for "mechanized"

MG   Machine gun

Mrs   *Mörser*; mortar

OB West   *Oberbefehlshaber* West; High Command West

Oberführer   *Waffen-SS* brigadier; abbreviated as *Oberf.*

Oberst   Colonel

Oberstleutnant   Lieutenant colonel

Obersturmbannführer   *Waffen-SS* lieutenant colonel; abbreviated as *Ostubaf.*

Obersturmführer   *Waffen-SS* first lieutenant; abbreviated as *Ostuf.*

OKH   *Oberkommando der Heeres* (Army High Command); primarily responsible for Russian Front

OKW *Oberkommando der Wehrmacht* (Armed Forces High Command); in charge of Western Front

PaK *Panzerabwehr Kanone*; anti-tank gun

Panzerfaust German anti-tank rocket launcher

Panzergrenadier German equivalent of US armored infantry

Panzerjäger Tank destroyer

Pionier German engineer unit

PzKpfw *Panzerkampfwagen*; tank

Regiment Formation of several battalions

s.Pz.Abt. *schwere Panzer Abteilung*; heavy tank battalion, usually a *Tiger* battalion

s.Pz.Jg.Abt. *schwere Panzerjäger Abteilung*; heavy tank destroyer battalion

Sd.Kfz. *Sonderkraftfahrzeug* (special vehicle); designation for a specialized German military vehicle

sFH *schwere Feld Haubitze*; heavy field howitzer

SHAEF Supreme Headquarters Allied Expeditionary Force; Eisenhower's headquarters

SS *Schutzstaffel*; paramilitary wing of the Nazi Party

Standartenführer *Waffen-SS* colonel; abbreviated as *Staf.*

StuG *Sturmgeschütz*; German assault gun, typically the *StuG III* on a *PzKpfw III* chassis with a 75mm gun

Sturmbannführer *Waffen-SS* major; abbreviated as *Stubaf.*

VAK *Volks-Artillerie-Korps* (Peoples Artillery Corps)

VGD *Volksgrenadier-Division*

Volksgrenadier People's Grenadier; typical a reduced-scale 1944 army division for defensive missions

Waffen-SS Military arm of the SS

Wehrmacht German armed forces

Werfer Multiple rocket launcher

Zug German army platoon

347

BIBLIOGRAPHY

THIS BOOK WAS PREPARED USING ARCHIVAL RECORDS, UNPUBLISHED US ARMY studies, and published books and articles.

The primary repository for US Army records is the National Archives and Records Administration II (NARA II) in College Park, Maryland. The principal records group for World War II units is RG 407. Divisional records generally start with division-wide records such as unit histories, then the constituent units' records starting with the divisional headquarters and its constituents, and then the regiments and battalions; within each subheading, the material is arranged chronologically. There is a finding aid for the records in the NARA II Research Room that breaks down the divisional records by sub-unit.

The extent of the records varies from unit to unit depending on unit size; for example, the 1st Infantry Division records total eighty-four archival boxes, while the 741st Tank Battalion totals three boxes. I primarily used the divisional history files; the divisional and regimental G-3/S-3 (Operations), G-2/S-2 (Intelligence), and combat arms AAR (After-Action Reports); General Orders; and Unit Journals. Each of these different sets of records have specific value in crafting a narrative of the unit in combat.

Some of the divisions have unit histories written during the war. The G-3/S-3 records generally contained useful surveys of the conduct of the campaign and sometimes include map overlays that help explain the combat actions. G-2/S-2 records sometimes include useful information on German units based on prisoner-of-war interrogations. The actual content of division records vary enormously, and sometimes entire files are lost or missing.

The unit after-action reports tend to be very terse, and a far more useful source for narrative accounts of the major battles is the separate Combat Interviews collection. The US Army attached small teams of historians to most divisions in the European Theater of Operations with the task of conducting interviews with the principal officers after all major battles. The Ardennes reports are generally contained in a group called "The German Breakthrough (16 Dec 44–16 Jan 45)" and found in each division collection.

Aside from excellent interview accounts of the fighting, the historians attempted to reconstruct maps of the battle by doing overlays on tracing paper over standard 1:25,000-scale maps. US Army G-3/S-3 staffs tended to do daily reporting on acetate map overlays that were often wiped clean from day to day or not preserved, so the Combat Interview collection provides a unique carto-graphical resource for reconstructing the battle. These overlays are not easy to use, since the associated maps are often missing from the files. However, the Cartographic Division at NARA II has most of these editions in their collection. Some care must be exercised in using the maps since the various printed editions differ in grid references; there was a change in US Army grid references in the 1950s. While the 1950s maps are very similar to the wartime maps, the grid references do not correspond. I also consulted a wide range of contemporary maps and some World War I–era maps to clarify certain features.

To prepare the tactical maps in this book, I obtained copies of the original US Army maps and created digital copies of the Combat Interview overlays. I then combined these using digital graphics software, Adobe Photoshop. For this book, I primarily used the 1944–45 editions of the 1:25,000 Army Mapping Service AMS M841/GSGS 4414: Sheet 5504 Hellenthal and Sheet 5503 Elsenborn, which were the principal maps used by the divisions themselves during the war.

The US Army Military History Institute, part of the US Army Heritage and Education Center (USAHEC) at Carlisle Barracks, Pennsylvania, also has an extensive library of US Army unit histories and other resources such as the Foreign Military Studies mentioned below.

Among the useful sources on US Army units in the Ardennes are two veterans' newspapers, *The Checkerboard* of the 99th Infantry Division Association and *The Bulge Bugle* of the Battle of the Bulge Association.

German military records captured at the end of the war by American and British forces were returned to Germany in the 1950s and reside at Bundesarchiv Freiburg and other facilities. Microfilm copies of most of these records were made by the United States and are located at NARA II, primarily in Record Group 242. From the German perspective, one of the most useful set of records for the Ardennes campaign from the higher level of command is the *Heeresgruppe D Kriegstagebuch* (KTB: War Diary), Anlage (Appendix) 50. *Heeresgruppe D* was the forerunner of OB West and was absorbed into the new theater command in 1941. The records remain under the *Heeresgruppe D* name, though they are in fact the OB West records. This particular appendix contains many planning documents for *Wacht am Rhein*, Plan Martin, and *Herbstnebel*. A microfilm version is available at NARA II in Record Group 242, T311, Roll R18. An interesting set of OKW *Feindlage* (Enemy Situation) maps for the autumn of 1944 are located in the Cartographic Division of NARA II in RG242-GERSITWF.

Other German unit records at lower levels of command are generally lacking for the Ardennes campaign. There are very few records remaining from the *6.Panzer-Armee, I.SS-Panzer-Korps,* or *12.SS-Panzer-Division "Hitlerjugend."* A small number of *Hitlerjugend* documents exist at NARA II in the Record Group 242 microfilm collection (T-354, Roll 155), but these are mainly personnel records and not very useful for a campaign narrative.

The most extensive source of documents dealing with the German units in the Ardennes was collected immediately after the war by the US Army Center of Military History under their Foreign Military Studies (FMS) program.[1] This originally started as a series of interviews conducted by US Army historians of key German officers and was later transcribed into the ETHINT (European Theater Historical Interviews) series. These are generally very short reports dealing with specific questions of interest to army historians.

The program later evolved to collect the recollections of senior German commanders. German officers still in postwar prisoner-of-war camps took part in an effort to write reports on the conduct of their operations against the US Army. Many of the early reports were written without the benefit of German unit records or war diaries and so often lack detail. They have to be used with caution since dates and times are sometimes incorrect. In spite of their many shortcomings, they constitute some of the only surviving records for many of these units in the Ardennes campaign. They are especially useful in gaining an appreciation of the viewpoints of these commanders of the plans and intentions of their combat formations.

Collections of these reports can be found at NARA II as well as at the US Military History Institute, US Army Heritage and Education Center, Carlisle Barracks. They generally exist in both the original German and translated English versions. The German versions are useful, as they usually contain the situation maps lacking in the English versions. Also, the English translations are sometimes rough, and odd translations of German military terms can be rectified by consulting the German version.

Separate from the A series and B series of FMS reports is a lesser-known collection in the R series. These reports were prepared by US Army historians Charles von Luettichau and Magna Bauer as a resource for the preparation of the official US Army World War II histories, better known as the "Green Books" series. The Ardennes volume was written by Hugh Cole, the army historian who started the ETO Combat Interview program. Several R series studies on the Ardennes campaign were prepared based on captured German records to provide a better appreciation for the German side of the story. In the case of the Ardennes reports, these generally deal with high command decision-making rather than campaign narratives.

In the area of specialist military history, *Kampfgruppe Peiper* and the Malmedy massacre controversy have far overshadowed the battles in the northern sector. There is no comprehensive history of the *12.SS-Panzer-Division* in the Ardennes, though the *Hitlerjugend* is covered in broader treatments such as Reynolds's *Men of Steel* and Meyer's divisional history of the *Hitlerjugend*. There is far more extensive coverage of the *12.SS-Panzer-Division* in Normandy than in the Ardennes. Needless to say, the German infantry divisions involved in the Ardennes battle have seen even less attention.

Unless otherwise noted, the photos in this book come from official US sources including NARA II; the US Army Military History Institute, Carlisle Barracks; the Patton Museum, formerly at Fort Knox; and the Library of Congress. Photos on pages 229, 261, 285, and 295 are reprinted by permission of the Colonel Robert R. McCormick Research Center, First Division Museum at Cantigny Park, Wheaton, Illinois.

ARCHIVAL MATERIAL

Unit WWII Operations Records, NARA II, Record Group (RG) 407, Entry 427

1st Infantry Division	Boxes 05001–05284
2nd Infantry Division	Boxes 05285–05387
99th Infantry Division	Boxes 11606–11671
V Corps Artillery	Boxes 3042–3050
644th Tank Destroyer Battalion	Boxes 18572–18574
741st Tank Battalion	Boxes 13502–13504

Combat Interviews, WWII Operations Records, NARA II, Record Group (RG) 407, Entry 427A

1st Infantry Division	Box 19023
2nd Infantry Division	Boxes 19026–19027
99th Infantry Division	Box 19066

US ARMY FOREIGN MILITARY STUDIES (FMS)

Foreign Military Studies

Bauer, Magna. *The Cost of the Ardennes Offensive*. FMS R-60 (1955).
———. *The Idea for the German Ardennes Offensive in 1944: An Attempt to Determine the Authorship of the Idea and its Historical Development*. FMS R-9 (1952).
———. *Key Dates during the Ardennes Offensive 1944: An Attempt to Show When Hitler and the German Commanders Realized the Failure of Their Offensive 16 December 1944–28 January 1945: Part 1*. FMS R-15 (1952).

Denkert, Gen. Maj. Walter. *Commitment of the 3rd Panzergrenadier Division in the Ardennes Offensive.* FMS B-465 (1947).

Dietrich, Oberst Gruppenführer Sepp. *An Interview with Obstgrf. "Sepp" Dietrich: Sixth Panzer Army in the Ardennes Offensive.* ETHINT 15, August 8–9, 1945.

———. *An Interview with Obstgrf "Sepp" Dietrich: Sixth Panzer Army Planning for the Ardennes Offensive.* ETHINT 16, July 10, 1945.

Engel, Generalleutnant Gerhard. *The 12. Volksgrenadier-Division in the Third Battle of Aachen: 16 Nov–3 Dec 1944.* FMS B-764 (1946).

———. *The 12. Volksgrenadier-Division: 3–29 December 1944.* FMS B-733 (1946).

Fieger, Oberst Georg. *Grenadier Regiment.989: 14–17 December 1944.* FMS B-025 (1946).

Kraas, Hugo. *Die 12. SS-Panzerdivision "Hitlerjugend" in der Ardennen Offensive.* FMS B-522 (1951).

Krämer, Generalmajor Fritz. *Commitment of the 6th Panzer Army in the Ardennes 1944–45.* FMS A-924 (1945).

———. *An Interview with Genmaj (W-SS) Fritz Kraemer, Sixth Pz Army (16 Nov 44–4 Jan 45).* ETHINT 21, August 14–15, 1945.

Lehmann, Oberst Rudolf. *The I. SS-Panzer-Korps during the Ardennes Offensive.* MS B-779 (1954).

———. *I. SS-Panzer-Korps (15 Oct–16 Dec 1944).* FMS B-577 (1947).

——— . *I. SS-Panzer-Korps: Special Questions.* FMS A-926 (1946).

Preiss, General der Waffen-SS Hermann. *Commitment of the I. SS-Panzer-Korps during the Ardennes Offensive (16 Dec 1944–25 Jan 1945).* FMS A-877 (1946).

Reichhelm, Oberst Günther. *Commentary on Kraemer's Report of Oct 1945 "Commitment of the Sixth Pz Army in the Ardennes 1944/45."* FMS B-676 (1947).

———. *Report of Col. Reichhelm of the General Staff Concerning His Activity as Operations Officer of Army Group B during Operations in the West from Fall 1944 to Spring 1945.* FMS A-925 (1950).

Staudinger, Gen. Lt. Walter. *The Artillery Command of the 6 Panzer Army during the Ardennes Offensive 1944–45.* FMS B-347 (1946).

———. *Artillery Leadership and Artillery Assignment during the Course of the Ardennes Campaign.* FMS B-759 (1948).

———. *6. Panzer Army Artillery in the Ardennes Offensive.* ETHINT 62, August 11, 1945.

Stumpff, Gen. Horst. *Tank Maintenance in the Ardennes Offensive.* ETHINT 61, August 11, 1945.

Viebig, Generalmajor Wilhelm. *Operations of the 277. Volksgrenadier Division, November–December 1944 during the Ardennes Offensive.* FMS B-273 (1946).

———. *The 277th Volksgrenadier Division 26 January–9 March 1945.* FMS B-754 (1946).

von der Heydte, Oberst Friedrich Freiherr. *Battle-Group von der Heydte: 25 Oct–22 Dec 1944.* FMS B-823 (1948).

von Luettichau, Charles. *The Ardennes Offensive, Planning and Preparation; Chapter II: The Framework for Operation Wacht am Rhein.* FMS R-13 (1953).

———. *The Ardennes Offensive, Planning and Preparation; Chapter III: Strategic Concentration.* FMS R-14 (1953).

———. *The Ardennes Offensive, Progressive Build-Up and Operations 11–19 December 1944.* FMS R-8 (1952).

———. *Armor in the Ardennes Offensive: A Comparative Study of the Potential, Authorized, and On-Hand Strength of Panzer Units in the West, November 1944–February 1945.* FMS R-16 (1952).

———. *Key Dates during the Ardennes Offensive 1944: An Attempt to Show When Hitler and the German Commanders Realized the Failure of Their Offensive 16 December 1944–28 January 1945: Part 2.* FMS R-11 (1952).

———. *Report on the Interview with Thiusko von Wetzsch on Operations of Army Group B and Its Role in the German Ardennes Offensive.* FMS R-10 (1952).

von Wangenheim, Oberstleutnant Horst. *The 277.Infanterie-Division 25 Jul–26 Aug 1944.* FMS B-679 (1946).

Wagener, Generalmajor Carl. *Main Reasons for the Failure of the Ardennes Offensive.* FMS A-963 (1945).

Zimmermann, Generalleutnant Bodo, et al. *OB West, Part 2.* FMS T-123 (1954).

US ARMY REPORTS

The Ardennes Campaign Simulation Data Base (ACSDB), 2 vols. Fairfax, VA: DMSI, 1990.

Buckhout, Maj. Laurie Moe. *Signal Security in the Ardennes Offensive 1944–45.* Fort Leavenworth, KS: Command and General Staff College, 1997.

Callaway, Maj. George. *38th Regimental Combat Team: Battle of the Bulge.* Fort Leavenworth, KS: Command and General Staff College, 1947.

Clayton, Major George. *The Operations of the 3rd Battalion, 394th Infantry (99th Division) in the German Ardennes Counter-Offensive, 16 December–1 January 1945.* Fort Benning, GA: Infantry School, 1948.

German Artillery, VII Corps Artillery, 1945.

Hancock, Maj. William. *The Operations of the 1st Battalion, 9th Infantry (2nd Infantry Division) in the Hasty Defense against an Armored Attack North of Rocherath, Germany, 17–18 December 1944: Personal Experiences of a Battalion Executive Officer.* Fort Benning, GA: Infantry School, 1950.

Harley, Maj. Jeffrey. *Reading the Enemy's Mail: Origins and Development of US Army Tactical Radio Intelligence in World War II: European Theater of Operations.* Fort Leavenworth, KS: Command and General Staff College, 1980.

Jarkowsky, Maj. Jeffrey. *German Special Operations in the 1944 Ardennes Offensive.* Fort Leavenworth, KS: Command and General Staff Colege, 1994.

Kays, Marvin. *Weather Effects during the Battle of the Bulge and the Normandy Invasion.* US Army Atmospheric Sciences Laboratory, White Sands Missile Range, August 1982.

Kennedy, Maj. James L., Jr. *The Failure of German Logistics during the Ardennes Offensive of 1944.* Fort Leavenworth, KS: Command and General Staff College, 2000.

McMillin, Lt. Col. C. D. *Manchus at the Crossroads: Defending the Northern Shoulder of the Bulge.* Carlisle, PA: Army War College, 1987.

Morris, Maj. Alan, Jr. *Death Spiral: Luftwaffe Airlift Training, Operation Stösser, and Lessons for the Modern US Air Force.* Ft. Leavenworth, KS: Command and General Staff College, 2015.

Simmons, Capt. Wesley. *Operations of Company K, 394th Infantry (99th Division) in Defensive Action near Elsenborn, Belgium, 16–21 December 1944.* Fort Benning, GA: Infantry School, 1950.

Stephenson, Lt. Col. Roy, et al. "The Impact of Massive Artillery Fires on Command, Control, and Communications in the European and North African Theaters During World War II." In *CSI Report No. 13: Tactical Responses to Concentrated Artillery.* Fort Leavenworth, KS: Combat Studies Institute, 1990.

Thompson, Royce. *Dom Butgenbach Action, 26th Infantry (1st Division), 19–22 December 1944.* Office of the Chief of Military History (OCMH), January 10, 1952.

———. *Tank Fight of Rocherath-Krinkelt (Belgium 17–19 December 1944).* Office of the Chief of Military History (OCMH), February 13, 1952.

Wilkerson, Lt. Col. Edgar, et al. *V Corps Operations in the ETO: 6 Jan 1942–9 May 1945, V Corps,* 1945.

BOOKS

Baldwin, Ralph. *The Deadly Fuze: The Secret Weapon of World War II.* Novato, CA: Presidio, 1980.

Baschin, Joachim, and Martin Block. *Jagdpanzer IV: Part 2—L/70 (Sd.Kfz. 162/1) (Vomag & Alkett).* Nuts & Bolts, vol. 38. Neumünster, Germany: Nuts & Bolts Press, 2016.

Beevor, Antony. *Ardennes 1944: Hitler's Last Gamble.* New York: Viking, 2015.

Bernage, George, and Hubert Meyer. *12.SS-Panzer-Division "Hitlerjugend."* Bayeux, France: Editions Heimdal, 1991.

Caddick-Adams, Peter. *Snow & Steel: The Battle of the Bulge 1944–45.* Oxford: Oxford University Press, 2015.

Cavanagh, William C. C. *The Battle East of Elsenborn & the Twin Villages.* Barnsley, UK: Pen & Sword, 2004.

———. *Dauntless: A History of the 99th Infantry Division.* Dallas, TX: Taylor Publishing, 1994.

———. *Krinkelt-Rocherath: The Battle for the Twin Villages.* Norwell, MA: Christopher Publishing, 1986.

Cole, Hugh. *The Ardennes: Battle of the Bulge.* Washington, DC: Office of the Chief of Military History, 1965.

Comparato, Frank. *The Age of the Great Guns.* Harrisburg, PA: Stackpole, 1965.

Cooke, David, and Wayne Evans. *Kampfgruppe Peiper: The Race for the Meuse.* Barnsley, UK: Pen & Sword, 2005.

Die 3.Kompanie: SS-Panzer-Regiment 12, 12.SS-Panzer-Division "Hitlerjugend." Oldendorf, Germany: Kompanie-Kameradschaft, 1978.

Doherty, J. C. *The Shock of War: Unknown Battles That Ruined Hitler's Plan for a Second Blitzkrieg in the West, December–January 1944-1945.* Alexandria, VA: Vert Milon Press, 1994.

Dugdale, J. *Panzer Divisions, Panzergrenadier Divisions, Panzer Brigades of the Army and Waffen SS in the West, Autumn 1944–February 1945; Ardennes and Nordwind; Their Detailed and Precise Strengths and Organizations.* Vol. 1, Part 4C, *December 1944, Refitting and Re-Equipment.* Milton Keynes, UK: Military Press, 2005.

Dupuy, Trevor N., et al. *Hitler's Last Gamble: The Battle of the Bulge, December 1944– January 1945.* New York: HarperCollins, 1994.

Eisenhower, John S. D. *The Bitter Woods.* New York: G. P. Putnam, 1969.

Engel, Gerhard. *At the Heart of the Reich: The Secret Diary of Hitler's Army Adjutant.* New York: Skyhorse Publishing, 2005.

First United States Army: Report of Operations 1 August 1944–22 February 1945. Washington, DC: FUSA, 1945.

Guillemot, Philippe. *The Battle of the Bulge: The Failure of the Final Blitzkrieg.* Vol. 1, *Towards a New Dunkirk?* Paris: Histoire & Collections, 2015.

Haasler, Timm, et al. *Duel in the Mist: The Leibstandarte during the Ardennes Offensive.* Vol. 1, Morpeth, UK: AFV Modeler Publications, 2007. Vol. 2, Old Heathfield, UK: Panzerwrecks, 2012. Vol. 3, Old Heathfield, UK: Panzerwrecks, 2014.

Hankel, Captain Halland. *Operations of Company M, 38th Infantry (2nd Infantry Division) in the Vicinity of Krinkelt, Belgium, 17–20 December 1944: The Personal Experience of a Company Commander.* Fort Benning, GA: Infantry School, 1949.

Hart, B. H. Liddell. *The Other Side of the Hill.* Bath, UK: Cedric Chivers, 1948.

Hogan, David W., Jr. *A Command Post at War: First Army Headquarters in Europe 1943–45.* Washington, DC: Center of Military History, 2000.

Howenstine, Harold D. *History of the 745th Tank Battalion: August 1942–June 1945.* Nuremberg, Germany: 1945.

Humphrey, Robert. *Once upon a Time in War: The 99th Division in World War II.* Norman: University of Oklahoma Press, 2008.

Jung, Hermann. *Die Ardennen Offensive 1944/45: Ein Beispiel für die Kriegsführung Hitlers.* Göttingen, Germany: Muster-Schmidt Verlag, 1992.

Knickerbocker, H., et al. *Danger Forward: The Story of the First Division in World War II.* Nashville, TN: Battery Press, 2002.

Lauer, Walter. *Battle Babies: The Story of the 99th Infantry Division in World War II.* Nashville, TN: Battery Press, 1985.

Lawrence, Christopher. *War by Numbers: Understanding Conventional Combat.* Lincoln, NE: Potomac Books, 2017.

MacDonald, Charles. *Company Commander.* Washington, DC: Infantry Journal Press, 1947. Reprint, Ithaca, NY: Burford Books, 1999.

———. *The Siegfried Line Campaign.* Washington, DC: US Army Chief of Military History, 1963.

———. *A Time for Trumpets: The Untold Story of the Battle of the Bulge.* New York: William Morrow, 1985.

Merriam, Robert E. *Dark December: The Full Account of the Battle of the Bulge.* New York: Ziff-Davis, 1947.

Meyer, Hubert. *The History of 12.SS-Panzerdivision Hitlerjugend.* Winnipeg: Federowicz Publishing, 1994.

Milner, Marc. *Stopping the Panzers: The Untold Story of D-Day.* Lawrence: University Press of Kansas, 2014.

Morelock, J. D. *General of the Ardennes: American Leadership in the Battle of the Bulge.* Washington, DC: National Defense University Press, 1994.

Nance, William. *Sabers through the Reich: World War II Corps Cavalry from Normandy to the Elbe.* Lexington: University Press of Kentucky, 2017.

Nevenkin, Kamen. *Fire Brigades: The Panzer Divisions 1943–1945.* Winnipeg: Federowicz, 2008.

Parker, Danny S. *Battle of the Bulge.* Conshohocken, PA: Combined Books, 1991.

———. *Battle of the Bulge, The German View: Perspectives from Hitler's High Command.* Mechanicsburg, PA: Stackpole Books, 1999.

———. *Fatal Crossroads: The Untold Story of the Malmedy Massacre at the Battle of the Bulge.* New York: Da Capo Press, 2012.

———. *Hitler's Ardennes Offensive: The German View of the Battle of the Bulge.* Mechanicsburg, PA: Stackpole Books, 1997.

———. *To Win the Winter Sky: Air War over the Ardennes 1944–45.* Conshohocken, PA: Combined Publishing, 1999.

Pogue, Forrest. *Pogue's War: Diaries of a WWII Combat Historian.* Lexington: University Press of Kentucky, 2001.

Reynolds, Michael. *Men of Steel: I.SS-Panzer Corps, The Ardennes and Eastern Front 1944–45.* New York: Sarpedon, 1999.

Rusiecki, Stephen. *The Key to the Bulge: The Battle for Losheimergraben.* Westport, CT: Praeger, 1996.

Schadewitz, Michael. *The Meuse First and then Antwerp: Some Aspects of Hitler's Offensive in the Ardennes.* Winnipeg: Federowicz Publishing, 1999.

Scherer, Wingolf, and Ernst-Detlef Broch. *Untergang: Kampf und Vernichtung der 277. Division in der Normandie und in der Eifel.* Aachen, Germany: Helios, 2005.

Scherer, Wingolf. *Wiederkehr: Fotos und Aufzeichnungen von Infanteristen der 277.ID/ VGD aus den Kämpfen in Frankreich (Normandie) und in der Eifel.* Aachen, Germany: Helios, 2008.

The Story of Vitamin Baker (741st Tank Battalion): We'll Never Go Overseas. Pilsen, Czechoslovakia: Grafik, 1945.

Sylvan, William, and Francis Smith, Jr. *Normandy to Victory: The War Diary of Courtney Hodges and the First US Army.* Lexington: University Press of Kentucky, 2008.

Tiemann, Ralf. *The Leibstandarte.* Vol. 4/2. Winnipeg: Federowicz, 1998.

US Army. *Combat History of the Second Infantry Division in World War II.* Nashville, TN: Battery Press, 2001.

Warlimont, Gen. Walter. *Inside Hitler's Headquarters 1939–45.* Novato, CA: Presidio, 1990.

Wheeler, James. *The Big Red One: America's Legendary 1st Infantry Division from World War I to Desert Storm.* Lawrence: University Press of Kansas, 2007.

Wijers, Hans. *The Battle of the Bulge: Hell at Bütgenbach.* Self-published, 2004. Republished as *Battle of the Bulge; Volume Two: Hell at Bütgenbach / Seize the Bridges,* Mechanicsburg, PA: Stackpole Books, 2010.

———. *Battle of the Bulge; Volume One: The Losheim Gap / Holding the Line.* Mechanicsburg, PA: Stackpole Books, 2009.

Winton, Harold. *Corps Commanders of the Bulge: Six American Generals and Victory in the Ardennes.* Lawrence: University Press of Kansas, 2007.

Vannoy, Allyn, and Jay Karamales. *Against the Panzers: United States Infantry versus German Tanks 1944–45.* Jefferson, NC: McFarland, 1996.

Votaw, John, et al. *Blue Spaders: The 26th Infantry Regiment 1917–1967.* Wheaton, IL: Cantigny First Division Foundation, 1997.

Zaloga, Steven. *Battle of the Bulge.* Oxford: Osprey, 2010.

———. *Battle of the Bulge (1): St. Vith and the Northern Shoulder.* Oxford: Osprey, 2003.

———. *Battle of the Bulge (2): Bastogne.* Oxford: Osprey, 2004.

———. *Bazooka vs. Panzer: Battle of the Bulge 1944.* Oxford: Osprey Duel 77, Osprey Publishing, 2016.

———. *Metz 1944: Patton's Fortified Nemesis.* Oxford: Oxford Publishing, 2012.

———. *Panther vs. Sherman: Battle of the Bulge 1944.* Oxford: Osprey Duel 13, Osprey Publishing, 2008.

———. *The Siegfried Line 1944–45: Battles on the German Frontier.* Oxford: Osprey Publishing, 2007.

———. *US Tank and Tank Destroyer Battalions in the ETO 1944–45.* Oxford: Osprey Publishing, 2005.

ARTICLES

Bryja, Marcin. "Artyleria niemiecka w ofensywie w Ardenach." *Poligon,* no. 2 (2012).

Byers, Dick. "Fight for Losheimergraben." *The Checkerboard,* March 1991.

Dettor, Robert W. "Memorable Bulge Incidents." *The Bulge Bugle,* vol. 13, no. 4 (November 1994).

Rader, Don W. "Rader, Dutcher, Langford Escape the Net." *The Checkerboard*, July 1999.

Ratliff, Lt. Col. Frank. "The Field Artillery Battalion Fire-Direction Center—Its Past, Present, and Future. *Field Artillery Journal*, May–June 1950.

Reeves, Lt. Col. Joseph. "Artillery in the Ardennes." *Field Artillery Journal*, March 1946.

Rivette, Capt. Donald. "The Hot Corner at Dom Butgenbach." *Field Artillery Journal*, October 1945.

Sullivan, Michael. "Combat Motivation and the Roots of Fanaticism: The 12th SS Panzer Division in Normandy." *Canadian Military History*, vol. 10, no. 3 (2001).

Thoholte, General der Artillerie Karl. "A German Reflects upon Artillery." *Field Artillery Journal*, December 1945.

Warnock, Bill. "Heroic Stand at Lausdell." *WWII History*, July 2007.

Wood, James. "Captive Historians, Captivated Audience: The German Military History Program 1945–1961." *Journal of Military History*, January 2005.

Verwicht, Alain. "Wacht am Rhein, Décembre 1944: la 12.SS-Panzer-Division Hit lerjugend." *Panzer Voran!*, no. 3 (July–September 1999).

INDEX

Aachen, *113*, 276; artillery importance at, 67; defense of, 61
A Company, 26th Infantry, 301–2, 304
A Company, 394th Infantry, 157–58
Adams, George, 248
aerial reconnaissance, counter-battery missions and, 108
airborne mission, 171; failure of, 275
Allen, Jack, 127, 129, 132, 134–35, 138, 185–87
anti-aircraft guns, 264
anti-tank barriers, *128*, 129
anti-tank guns, 151, 156, *169*, 230, 268–69, 272–73, 291–92; anti-aircraft guns as, 264; on half-tracks, *44*; *Panther* tanks and, 224; 75mm PaK 40 anti-tank gun, 68; towed, 111–12, *112*, 178. *See also* 57mm anti-tank gun
anti-tank half-tracks, *44*
anti-tank mines, 204, 205, 272
anti-tank rocket launchers, 268, 270. *See also* bazookas; *Panzerfaust*; *Panzerschreck*
anti-tank weapons, 29, 187, 203–4, 205, 224–25, 227, 228
Antwerp, 18, 19, 24, 276
Ardennes offensive: artillery innovations in, 71; German historical literature on, 309; intelligence picture, December 7, 1944, *13*; Model and planning, 11–12; planning, 6–16; Rundstedt, G., and, 10–12; *Schwerpunkt* of, 17–31, 279–82, 307; Staudinger on artillery in, 79–80; strategic setting, 3–5; weather condition during, 90–96
Ardennes region, early winter weather in, 90–92
Arenberg, 117
ARKO. *See Artilleriekommandeur*

Armed Forces High Command (OKW), 6, 275, 277; Ardennes map, *13*
armored cars, 42
armored fire support, 81–83; for US infantry divisions, 109–13
armored infantry support, 29
Army Group A, 86
Army Group B, 3, 53, 276, 277; assessment of offensive, 279; Autumn Mist planning and, *11*; Watch on the Rhine planning and, 11–12
Army Group Center, 3, 11
Army Group G, 3
Army Group North Ukraine, 11
Army Group South, 10
Army Group Student, 11, 24
Army Specialized Training Program (ASTP), 98–99
Artilleriekommandeur (ARKO), 70
artillery: at Aachen, 67; ammunition supplies, 77–78, 104, 190; armored fire support, 81–83; Autumn Mist plans for, 25–28; at Büllingen, 263, 283, 284; captured Soviet guns, 71; centralization of, 70; corps, 70–80, *107*, 108, *109*, 207, 255; divisional, 67, 73–74, 106–7, 207, 255, 304; at Dom Bütgenbach, 266, 268, 286–87, 289–95, 298, 304; field, 66, *66*, 76, 102, 290; forests and, 27; GHQ, 67, 73; importance of, 66–69, 102; initial attack preparation with, 123–24, 126–27, 130, 152–53; intelligence, 76; Krinkelterwald forest density and effectiveness of, 127; in Krinkel-Rocherath defense, 239–40, 254–55; in Lausdell crossroads battle, 205–7, 216–18; mobility, 76–77, 104; motorized, 104; officer training and, 73; Staudinger on, in Ardennes campaign,

361

INDEX

roads, 311–12; in Belgium, 86, 88, 90; beyond
Bütgenbach, 274, 279, 283; Krinkelt,
141; in Krinkelterwald, 95; Rollbahn
A, *123*, 127, 143; Rollbahn C, 148;
Wahlerscheid-Rocherath, 200
Robertson, Walter, *119*, *315*, 316; Krinkelt-
Rocherath withdrawal planning, 245;
Lausdell crossroads and, 200, 207; 99th
Division command post visit, 173–74,
200; preparations for defense by, 174–77,
194–96; Rocherath reinforcement and,
238; Wahlerscheid withdrawal planning,
176–77, 194–95
rocket launchers, 69, 71, *82*
Roer river, 61; offensive to take dams on,
115–17, 120, 172, 174, 176, 194
Rollbahn A, 25, 120, 137, 139, 168, 171, 185,
189, 212, 315; battle plans for, 48–49;
forest road through, *123*, 127, 143;
memorial at, *311*; Rollbahn C failures
and, 167; Westwall fortifications and, *87*,
128. *See also* Krinkelterwald
Rollbahn B, 128, 140, 199; battle plans for,
49; initial attack, 141–42; suitability for
mechanized traffic, 143
Rollbahn C, 63, 167, 170, 199, 315; battle
plans for, 49–50; crowding of approaches
to, 256; road quality, 148; X-Day attack,
152–60. *See also* Losheimergraben
Rollbahn D, 148, 178
Rollbahn E, 161, 168, 178, 181
Rollbanh routes, 24–25, *30*
Rollings, Edward, 209
Romanian oil fields, 3, 4
Russian Front, 3, 4, 59, 308, *313*, 314

Salazar, Isabel, 228–29
Scherer, Wingolg, on initial artillery barrage,
124
Schittenhelm (*Untersturmführer*), 288–89
Schnee Eifel sector, 29, 116, 161
Schulze, Richard, 185–88, 204
Schwarzenbüchel hill, 269, 270
Scott, Jean, 124, *126*, 138
Sd.Kfz.251/9 half-track, *42*, 181, 301
Sd.Kfz.251/22 half-track, 301
Sd.Kfz.251 half-track, 303

searchlights, 123–24
2nd Armored Division, 307
2nd Battalion, 394th Infantry, 150
2nd Infantry Division, 29, *116*, 116–17,
117, 161, 195; casualties, December
16-23, 253–54; at Dom Bütgenbach,
302; field artillery battalions, 290;
Heartbreak Crossroads and, *118*, 120; in
Krinkelterwald, *186*; Krinkelt-Rocherath
as tactical victory for, 254; Krinkelt-
Rocherath forward defense by, 184; Roer
river dams offensive by, 172, 174, 176;
withdrawal from Wahlerscheid, 176–77
2.Panzer-Division, 307
secrecy, artillery usage and, 26
Seitz, John, 257, 298
745th Tank Battalion, 269, 296, 302
745th Tank Destroyer Battalion, 262
741st Tank Battalion, 218, 224, 226, 229,
241, 252, 323; in Krinkelt-Rocherath,
208–9, 255; vehicle losses in Krinkelt-
Rocherath, 253
703rd Tank Destroyer Battalion, 262
734th Tank Destroyer Battalion, 262
7.Armee, 12, 61
75mm *Feldkanone 40*, 68
75mm PaK 40 anti-tank gun, 68
644th Tank Destroyer Battalion, 225, 234,
249, 252, *296*, 323; vehicle losses in
Krinkelt-Rocherath, 253
635th Tank Destroyer Battalion, 294
6.Panzer-Armee, 12, 14, 274; armored
support units, 81–83, *83*; artillery
commands, 71; artillery composition,
71–73, *72*, *73*; artillery usage, 25; attack
plan problems, 312; Autumn Mist
plan, 17–18, *19*; casualties, December
1944-January 1945, 253; commander,
19–22; end of X-Day and, 168; at
evening of X+1, 197–99; front assigned
to, 23, 86, 88; organization of, 22–23;
poor performance of, 277; recognition of
failure of attack, 279
6.SS-Panzer-Armee, 308, *313*
6th Army Group, 15
67.Armee-Korps, 274
Skorzeny, Otto, 31, 156, 165, 171, 275